Inside the Great House

Inside the Great House

Planter Family Life in Eighteenth-Century Chesapeake Society

DANIEL BLAKE SMITH

Cornell University Press

ITHACA AND LONDON

First published 1980 by Cornell University Press.
Published in the United Kingdom by Cornell University Press Ltd., 2–4 Brook Street, London W1Y 1AA.

International Standard Book Number 0-8014-1313-3
Library of Congress Catalog Card Number 80-14557
Printed in the United States of America
Librarians: Library of Congress cataloging information appears on the last page of the book.

For Linda and all my family

Illustrations follow page 125.

Contents

Acknowledgments

In trying to turn four years of research and writing on planter families into a book, I have profited from the wise counsel and valuable criticisms of a number of scholars both within and outside the growing field of American family history. At the University of Virginia, W. W. Abbot, Joseph F. Kett, and David Little provided helpful commentaries on the work and constantly urged me to write for an audience larger than that of fellow family historians. Later, Lois Green Carr and Lorena Walsh made useful suggestions on a portion of the manuscript. Daniel Scott Smith and Philip Greven read the entire work, and their criticisms were extremely helpful in the making of final revisions. None of these people will be entirely happy with what I have done with their suggestions—my stubbornness won out in many questionable areas—but I am thankful to all for their efforts. I am also grateful to Mary Jo Wheatley, who typed the manuscript, and to Betty Gatewood, who did a superb job of copy editing the work.

Several organizations made the research for this book much easier. A grant-in-aid from the Colonial Williamsburg Foundation, a fellowship at the Newberry Library (Colonial Wars in the State of Illinois Fellowship), and a summer grant from the University of Kentucky Research Foundation provided both financial aid and encouragement for the project when they were needed. I would also like to thank the editor of the *Psychohistory Review* for allowing me to reprint in Chapter 1 portions of an article originally published in that journal as "Autonomy and Affection: Parents and Children in 18th Century Chesapeake Families," VI (1977–78), 32–51.

This book is dedicated to my wife, Linda, and to my own family, who have had nothing to do with the writing of the book except that along the way—by word and deed and all the mysteries in between—they have taught me something important about life inside a loving family.

D.B.S.

Lexington, Kentucky

Abbreviations and Sources

Manuscripts

Quotations from the personal papers, diaries, and other documents listed below have been used in this book by the kind permission of several repositories. These documents are cited in abbreviated form in the notes that follow.

AFP — Ambler Family Papers (Accession No. 1998), University of Virginia Library.

BFP — Baylor Family Papers (#2257), Manuscripts Department, University of Virginia Library.

BP — Bland Papers (MSS.1 B6108a), Virginia Historical Society.

CALP — Callister Papers, from the Maryland Diocesan Archives, on deposit in The Maryland Historical Society.

CARP — Carroll Family Papers (MS. 1873), The Maryland Historical Society.

CTFP — Carr-Terrell Family Papers (#4757-d), Manuscripts Department, University of Virginia Library.

CP — Custis Papers (MSS. 1C9698a), Virginia Historical Society.

DP — Dulaney Papers (MS. 1265), The Maryland Historical Society.

FD — William Faris Diary (MS. 1104), The Maryland Historical Society.

FTD   Francis Taylor Diary Acc[ession]. 18710, Personal Papers Collection, Archives Branch, Virginia State Library.

GL   Gilpin Letterbook, Maury Family Papers Collection, University of Virginia Library.

HFP   Hollyday Family Papers (MS. 1317), The Maryland Historical Society.

IDP   Isaac Davis Papers, Manuscripts Department, University of Virginia Library.

JFP   Thomas Jones Family Papers, Library of Congress.

MFP   Mallory Family Papers (Accession No. 1932), University of Virginia Library.

NFP   Nourse Family Papers (#3490), Manuscripts Department, University of Virginia Library.

NTP   Nicholas Philip Trist Papers (#2104), Southern Historical Collection, Library of the University of North Carolina at Chapel Hill.

PFP   Parker Family Papers, City Library of Liverpool, microfilm in Colonial Williamsburg Foundation—Research Center.

RCL   Robert Carter Letterbook, 1727–28 (MSS. 1C2468a3—4), Virginia Historical Society.

RRD   Robert Rose Diary, typescript in the Colonial Williamsburg Foundation—Research Center. Published in Ralph Emmett Hall, ed., *The Diary of Robert Rose: A View of Virginia by a Scottish Colonial Parson, 1746–1751* (Verona, Va., McClure Press, 1977).

SBL   Stephen Bordley Letterbooks (MS. 81), The Maryland Historical Society.

TCP   Tucker-Coleman Papers, Swem Library, College of William and Mary.

TFP   Tazewell Family Papers, Acc[ession]. 24194, Personal Papers Collection, Archives Branch, Virginia State Library.

WP   Wallace Family Papers (Accession No. 38-150), Manuscripts Department, University of Virginia Library.

WPC   Webb-Prentis Collection (Accession No. 1932), Manuscripts Department, University of Virginia Library.

Published Works

Byrd Correspondence   Marian Tinling, ed., *The Correspondence of the Three William Byrds of Westover, Virginia, 1684–1776* (2 vols., Charlottesville, Va., 1977).

Byrd Diary, 1709–12   Louis B. Wright and Marian Tinling, eds., *The Secret Diaries of William Byrd of Westover, 1709–1712* (Richmond, 1941).

Byrd Diary, 1739–41   Marian Tinling and Maude H. Woodfin, eds., *Another Secret Diary of William Byrd of Westover, 1739–1741* (Richmond, 1942).

Carter Diary   Jack P. Greene, ed., *The Diary of Colonel Landon Carter of Sabine Hall, 1752–1776* (2 vols., Charlottesville, Va., 1965).

MHM   *Maryland Historical Magazine.*

VMHB   *Virginia Magazine of History and Biography.*

WMQ   *William and Mary Quarterly.*

Inside the Great House

Introduction

Family and kinship hold a special place in the minds and hearts of southerners; for many they assume an almost mystical quality, as if the South's pride in the past and strong sense of place were embedded in the customs and values of a particular kind of family psychology and structure. Moreover, an enduring attachment to the land and a long history of slave labor—both in the "great house" and in the fields—seem to set southerners off from other Americans, especially in terms of family and social experiences. Regional novelists and social scientists alike have often looked to household and kin for the essence of a presumably distinctive southern identity.[1]

Historical interest in the southern family has been much less visible, especially among students of early America. Colonial historians have contributed some of the most provocative research to the "new" social history of family and community life, but thus far their work has dealt mainly with demographic patterns in early New England and Quaker settlements in the middle

[1] I am thinking here of the work of prominent southern writers such as Faulkner and Eudora Welty. Social science research on the southern family can be followed in such journals as *Rural Sociology*.

colonies.[2] Despite a recent revival of interest in the social history of the colonial South, very little has been written on family life in the South before 1800.[3]

What this book attempts to do is to explore the character of family experience in the preindustrial South, focusing on the Chesapeake region (Virginia and Maryland) in the eighteenth century. By family experience I refer to the personal values, beliefs, and emotions given expression in the daily life of the family, the "emotional texture" of the household. In assessing Chesapeake family life in this qualitative perspective, a wide range of valuable questions can be raised: What, for instance, was the quality of relationships between members of a family in the preindustrial era? How did parents raise and discipline their children? Did other relatives or friends help in child-rearing? To what extent did children appear to adopt their parents' values? In what ways were daughters treated differently in the home from

[2]The leading studies of family life in early America are Philip J. Greven, Jr., *Four Generations: Population, Land and Family in Colonial Andover, Massachusetts* (Ithaca, N.Y., 1970), and John Demos, *A Little Commonwealth: Family Life in Plymouth Colony* (New York, 1970). More recently, Greven has completed a provocative study, *The Protestant Temperament: Patterns of Child-Rearing, Religious Experience, and the Self in Early America* (New York, 1977).

[3]The demographic studies of Darrett and Anita Rutman, Russell Menard, and Lorena Walsh have been most effective in stimulating research on the social history of the colonial South. Two important essays by the Rutmans include "Of Agues and Fevers: Malaria in the Early Chesapeake," *WMQ*, 3d ser., XXXIII (1976), 31–60, and "'Now-Wives and Sons-in-Law': Parental Death in a Seventeenth-Century Virginia County," in Thad W. Tate and David Ammerman, eds., *The Chesapeake in the Seventeenth Century: Essays on Anglo-American Society and Politics* (Chapel Hill, N.C., 1979), 153–82. See also in this volume the essay by Lorena Walsh, "'Til Death Us Do Part': Marriage and Family in Seventeenth-Century Maryland," 126–52. Other recent articles on Chesapeake family life include the following: Lorena S. Walsh and Lois G. Carr, "The Planter's Wife: The Experience of White Women in Seventeenth-Century Maryland," *WMQ*, 3d ser., XXXIV (1977), 542–71; Walsh and Russell Menard, "Death and the Chesapeake: Two Life Tables for Men in Colonial Maryland," *MHM*, LXIX (1974), 211–27; Daniel Blake Smith, "Autonomy and Affection: Parents and Children in 18th Century Chesapeake Families," *Psychohistory Review*, VI (1977–78), 32–51; *idem.*, "Mortality and Family in the Colonial Chesapeake," *Journal of Interdisciplinary History*, VIII (Winter 1978), 403–27. Edmund S. Morgan's brief, impressionistic study, *Virginians at Home: Family Life in Eighteenth-Century Virginia* (Williamsburg, 1952), is the only published volume on the early southern family. The most

sons? Were marriages controlled by parents for economic reasons or by the participants themselves out of feelings of companionship? What do inheritance patterns reveal about kinship bonds, lines of authority in the household, and economic concern for the family? How did family members respond to sickness and death within and outside the family?

Given the fragmentary source materials for early America, one may regard these and similar questions as interesting but unanswerable. A high rate of illiteracy (especially among women and in the early South) and the general disinclination of people in the colonial era to reveal their personal feelings and family affairs—either in correspondence or even private journals—make a study of preindustrial American family life difficult.

Moreover, the daily experience and impact of slaves in white planter households is particularly hard to assess. Slavery, which stands as perhaps the most visible, distinctive institution of southern family and social life, remains almost impervious to study—at least in the seventeenth and eighteenth centuries—simply because of the paucity of surviving sources. Barely a handful of reliable documents (a fragment of a letter or diary here and there) exists to help shed light on the personal relationship between slaves and their masters inside the "great house." The silence of the documents on the slave experience in planter households is overwhelming and is one of the biggest disappointments for historians of the family in the colonial South.

Despite these limitations, a good deal can still be learned about the nature of early American families. Indeed, if the history of the family in this era is to be fully uncovered, it is most accurately revealed, albeit still indirectly, in the evidence specific families have created in their own daily lives: letters, diaries, reminiscences, wills, and deeds, as well as the vital records analyzed by historical demographers. It is mainly through these personal documents, in conjunction with the insights of demography,

---

informative volume on domestic life in the colonial South remains Julia C. Spruill, *Women's Life and Work in the Southern Colonies* (Chapel Hill, N.C., 1938).

anthropology, and psychology, that we can begin to glimpse the nature of interpersonal relationships and social values within the family.[4]

The problem with documents of this kind, of course, is that they mostly concern families whose economic standing gave them the time, the capability, and perhaps the motivation to leave behind written evidence of their activities and feelings. Any intimate portrait of the early American family, then (as opposed to demographic studies of family structure and household composition) will probably focus on families in the upper social and economic ranks. But if we hope to begin answering some of the most intriguing questions about colonial domestic life, then ultimately we must depend on the surviving personal sources that speak, often quite eloquently, about the inner life of the family.

At first glance the least promising area in which to study the early American family is in the Chesapeake. Here illiteracy and mortality were high; southern planters, unlike New England Puritans, were often more concerned with survival than with introspective diary-keeping or letter-writing. This is certainly true for the seventeenth century. There are very few materials, other than probate records and demographic data, for studying the Chesapeake family before 1700. But a surprisingly rich vein of family papers, diaries, and memoirs has survived for much of the eighteenth century. Some of this material has been published, but most of it has to be ferreted out in various manuscript depositories.[5] It is from these personal documents of planter families that the following portrait of Chesapeake family life has been drawn.

---

[4]The phrase "personal documents" is from Alan Macfarlane, *The Family Life of Ralph Josselin: A Seventeenth-Century Clergyman* (Cambridge, 1970). Macfarlane's work, along with David Hunt's *Parents and Children in History: The Psychology of Family Life in Early Modern France* (New York, 1970), with their imaginative use of limited, but revealing, documents on the preindustrial family, have profoundly shaped my thinking on the study of early American family life.

[5]The early issues of the *William and Mary Quarterly, Virginia Magazine of History and Biography,* and the *Maryland Historical Magazine* contain a large number of letters and diary entries from the seventeenth- and eighteenth-century Chesapeake.

In the following chapters, which can be read as self-contained essays on planter families and as parts of a larger mosaic of a changing plantation society, I have attempted to place family and kinship both in the context of new interpretations of the history of the family in the West, and less grandly, as part of an emerging synthesis of studies on the Chesapeake in preindustrial times. I trust that these two purposes are not incompatible.

Both concerns have led me to organize many of my questions about these planter families around the theme of growing privatism in eighteenth-century Virginia and Maryland. While much continuity is evident in Chesapeake family patterns throughout the eighteenth century, the personal documents of these families reveal a significant shift in attitudes and behavior during the latter half of the century. This gradual but unmistakable reorientation in family and kin life suggests a collapse of what might be called the "well-ordered" patriarchal family that prevailed in most well-to-do households since the late seventeenth century, and the emergence after mid-century of a more intimate private family and kin experience.

In the "golden age" of Chesapeake plantation society, which lasted roughly from the late seventeenth century through the first half of the eighteenth century, planter family life was characterized by a strong sense of order, authority, and self-restraint. These households were often open, inclusive affairs with much kin contact and visitation from outside the family. Such prominent planters as William Byrd of Westover presided over the family with unchallenged authority, especially in marital and career decisions. Indeed, matters of paternal preference, economic class, and social status, rather than companionship or romantic love, frequently dominated marriage choices. In these rather authoritarian, patriarchal families, moderation and restraint governed family relationships. Strong emotional attachments between family members were muted in the overriding concern for order and clear lines of authority and obedience within the household.

During the second half of the eighteenth century, planter family life changed significantly. The key features of this transformation were the development of a strikingly affectionate family environment (one in which children became the centerpiece of family attention); the growing belief in the autonomy of sons and daughters, especially regarding the selection of marriage partners and careers; and the increasingly private nature of the planter family, as reflected in the weakening ties of kinship outside the nuclear family. By the early 1800s Chesapeake families, like a growing number of families throughout early America, had turned their emotional energies inward to focus on an intimate, sentimental family unit that stood apart from the larger society as a private enclave for mutual support and sociability.

I have tried to trace this transformation in family and personal values in a number of ways. The first three chapters explore the character of parent-child relationships in the eighteenth-century Chesapeake, stressing the growth of affection and independence-training in planter child-rearing styles. As I explain in Chapter 2, however, sex roles grew more rigid in the eighteenth century, making it difficult for women to experience the freedom of movement and sense of independence that young men enjoyed. Chapter 4 examines the rise of autonomy and companionship in late-eighteenth-century marriages. Planter kin networks also took a remarkably "modern" cast toward the end of the century. Chapters 5 and 6, which contain a reconstruction of the kin and friend "universe" of a few planters, based on a detailed study of their diaries, and an analysis of bequethal patterns in selected Chesapeake counties, together suggest the increasingly exclusive, privatistic nature of Chesapeake kin ties. In Chapter 7, dramatic shifts in personal values and family relationships are glimpsed through a study of attitudes toward illness and death within and outside the home. Finally, the concluding chapter interprets the experience of these planter families in the larger context of social change and regional variation in early American family life.

Although the evidence clearly suggests a reorientation in family experience after mid-century, it is only fair to point out that none of the changes I see developing in eighteenth-century planter family life was so clear-cut in time or space as to be measurable in any systematic way. As I have noted earlier, only the well-to-do planters can be spoken of with any confidence in the following pages. While it is certainly plausible, indeed even likely in my view, that the middling and lower ranks fashioned their families in similar ways or at least sought to do so, the evidence simply does not take us into these far more numerous households. Moreover, there are doubtless regional variations within the Chesapeake that are obscured in the generalizations I have made about Virginia and Maryland families. Although some of these differences can be detected in the quantitative analysis of inheritance patterns, most of my research dwells in the more subjective domain of feelings and values, and the evidence here is so uneven that the difference between settled and frontier regions, and Anglican and dissenter families, for example, can only be guessed at. It may be safely assumed, though, that unless noted otherwise, when I refer to Chesapeake planter families, I am dealing primarily with well-to-do Anglican men and women living in the more densely settled regions of Tidewater Virginia and Maryland.

Finally, the shifts in family and kin life I have identified in Chesapeake society cannot be dated with precision. Historians have found that the basic structures and social values of the family change gradually, often almost imperceptibly, over several generations. Thus, one must observe family experience over long periods, which perhaps is another way of saying that the family is essentially a conservative unit, resisting change or adapting slowly to it so that sometimes past family values persist even in times of profound social change.[6] For example, part of the "deep change" in family and personal life in the late eighteenth-century Chesapeake, especially the emergence of the child-centered household, can be observed in some instances as early as the 1720s. Other trends, such as the development of a narrowly based, selective kin "universe," did not become apparent until

---

[6]The theoretical literature on the nature of the family and social change is vast, but for a similar view of the family as an essentially passive agent in change, see Jonathan Prude, "The Family in Context," *Labor History*, XVII (1976), 422–36.

the 1780s or 1790s. The bulk of the evidence, however, points to near the middle of the century as the critical era in which families began to organize and perceive themselves in new ways.

Chapter One

Autonomy and Affection

Parents and Children
in Chesapeake Families

In the spring of 1765, Margaret Parker scribbled a brief letter to her husband, James. She was preoccupied, as she often tended to be, with their young son Charles, for whom she felt so much concern and affection that the prospect of spoiling him constantly preyed on her mind. "I endeavour as much as possible to gaurd against it," Margaret contended, "but find it requires more resolution than I am mistress of to help doting on him." In later correspondence we can glimpse James's similar attachment to his children—in this case his infant daughter, Susan, born in the winter of 1777. "God bless the Dear [one] how I long to hold it to my heart," he wrote to Margaret.[1]

Such undisguised parental fondness for young children seems common enough today, perhaps even natural, but it actually has a relatively short history. For as historians of childhood have discovered, until the very recent past—essentially the last two centuries—children played a distinctly secondary role in the family; they were valued chiefly as potential laborers and as continuing "representatives" of the family in the community, embodiments of the "family arrow in time."[2]

[1]Margaret Parker to James Parker, March 31, 1765, and James Parker to Margaret Parker, March 24, 1777, PFP.

[2]Much of this new work on the history of childhood can be found in the pages of the *Journal of Psychohistory* (previously titled *The History of Childhood Quar-*

Like most parents, past and present, James and Margaret Parker expected their children to be useful and loyal to family and kin. But they also found the presence of infants and small children an important source of pleasure and diversion, a central emotional focus in the life of the family. Indeed, what the personal documents of the Parker family and those of numerous other Chesapeake households suggest is that the affectionate, sentimental family which would become commonplace in antebellum America was clearly emerging in these planter households in the eighteenth century, especially after 1750. That parents treated children as inherently good and pleasurable creatures was a new and significant development in the history of the family. It is the texture of this child-centered family life in eighteenth-century Virginia and Maryland that this chapter will explore.

Fertility and the "Terrors of Childbirth"

Colonial Chesapeake families grew to only modest proportions, especially in the seventeenth century. The withering death rates stunted family size, limiting most parents to four or five children, only two or three of whom usually survived to maturity.[3] The increasing life expectancies of the eighteenth century

---

terly). Its editor, Lloyd deMause, however, appears to be primarily interested in discovering child abuse or neglect in times past. For a statement of his position, see deMause, ed., *The History of Childhood* (New York, 1974), 1–73. See also Edward Shorter, *The Making of the Modern Family* (New York, 1975), chap. 5. The phrase "family arrow in time" comes from the very perceptive essay by Natalie Z. Davis, "Ghosts, Kin and Progeny: Some Features of Family Life in Early Modern France," *Daedalus,* 106 (1977), 87–114.

[3]Darrett B. and Anita H. Rutman, "'Now-Wives and Sons-in-Law': Parental Death in a Seventeenth-Century Virginia County," in Thad W. Tate and David Ammerman, eds., *The Chesapeake in the Seventeenth Century: Essays on Anglo-American Society and Politics* (Chapel Hill, N.C., 1979), 153–92; Daniel Blake Smith, "Mortality and Family in the Colonial Chesapeake," *Journal of Interdisciplinary History,* VIII (1978), 403–27. Russell R. Menard reports somewhat larger families in seventeenth-century Somerset County, Maryland; see Menard, "The Demography of Somerset County, Maryland: A Preliminary Report," paper

and the relatively early age at marriage—about twenty-four for men and a year or two younger for women by the mid-eighteenth century—allowed families to expand to seven or eight children per marriage with five or six of these children normally reaching adulthood.[4] Family size was likely to be greatest when the parents were in their late thirties or early forties, for by that time most of the children would have been born, but few, if any, would have reached their majorities (eighteen for women, twenty-one for men) and left the household.

Families might have become larger but for the prevailing nursing practices. Most women breastfed their children for about eighteen months. Maternal lactation seems to have served as a contraceptive, whether intentional or not. That some primitive form of birth control was at work is suggested by the relatively long birth interval among women in colonial Virginia and Maryland: usually between twenty-four and thirty months, with a slightly longer interval between the last few children.[5]

Childbirth was an important event in the life of the family, but it was often marred by sickness and death. Medical knowledge about pregnancy, delivery, and infant care was slight, even by eighteenth-century standards. Until late in the century, obstetrics and pediatrics remained particularly weak and unexplored

presented to the Stony Brook Conference on Social History, Stony Brook, New York, June 1975.

[4]Allan Kulikoff, "Tobacco and Slaves: Population, Economy, and Society in Eighteenth-Century Prince George's County, Maryland" (unpub. Ph.D. diss., Brandeis University, 1975), 44; Philip J. Greven, Jr., "The Average Size of Families and Households in the Province of Massachusetts in 1764 and in the United States in 1790: An Overview," in Peter Laslett and Richard Wall, eds., *Household and Family in Past Time* (Cambridge, England, 1972), 551.

[5]Smith, "Mortality and Family"; Menard, "The Demography of Somerset County." For similar nursing patterns elsewhere in the colonies, see Robert V. Wells, "Quaker Marriage Patterns in Colonial Perspective," *WMQ*, 3d ser., XXIX (1972), 440–41; John Demos, *A Little Commonwealth: Family Life in Plymouth Colony* (New York, 1970), 133. For a discussion of the effect of lactation on delaying conception, see A. R. Perez, "First Ovulation after Childbirth: The Effects of Breastfeeding," *American Journal of Obstetrics and Gynecology*, CXIV (1972), 1141–47; J. K. Vanginneken, "Prolonged Breast Feeding as a Birth Spacing Method," *Studies in Family Planning*, XI (1974), 201–6.

27

branches of medicine.[6] Some planters followed the advice of "experts" in midwifery—usually English authors—but the information obtained from these sources often proved unreliable. Pregnancy, for example, was usually considered a sickness; thus expectant mothers were often bled near the end of their term, precisely when a reservoir of strength was most needed. Some believed that bleeding prevented miscarriage.[7] But on the whole, planters depended more on past experience than on medical literature. Experienced midwives helped men decipher the mysteries of pregnancy and birth. Even someone as learned as William Byrd carefully took down a local midwife's theory that twenty weeks would elapse "from the time a woman is quick when she will seldom fail to be brought to bed."[8]

Childbirth at home could be chaotic and full of danger for mother and child. When Becky Hansen of Maryland gave birth to a son in September of 1783, "confusion & distraction" reigned throughout the house.[9] Another woman described the delivery of her sister-in-law as a "Scene of Sickness" with two children "dangerously ill" and the mother "so much complaining, and so low spirited in her lying-inn." Mrs. John Taylor's delivery of twins in 1771 ended in the death of one who "hanged himself in the navelstring."[10] On July 7, 1766, Landon Carter was called

---

[6]John Rendle-Short, "Infant Management in the Eighteenth Century with Special Reference to the Work of William Cadogan," *Bulletin of the History of Medicine,* XXXIV (1960), 97–122.

[7]Louis B. Wright and Marian Tinling, eds., *The Secret Diary of William Byrd of Westover, 1709–1712* (Richmond, 1941), 141–42, 344, 364; Jack B. Greene, ed., *The Diary of Colonel Landon Carter of Sabine Hall, 1752–1776* (2 vols., Charlottesville, Va., 1965), II, 620. Eighteenth-century Englishmen considered pregnancy as a "nine-month sickness." See Randolph E. Trumbach, "The Aristocratic Family in England, 1690–1780: Studies in Childhood and Kinship" (unpub. Ph.D. diss., The Johns Hopkins University, 1972), 24–25.

[8]*Byrd Diary, 1709–12,* 77; Catherine M. Scholten, "'On the Importance of the Obstetrick Art': Changing Customs of Childbirth in America, 1760 to 1825," *WMQ,* 3d ser., XXXIV (1977), 426–45.

[9]Horatio Belt to Catherine Belt, Sept. 30, 1783, DP. An unusually high adult female mortality rate prevailed in the colonial Chesapeake because of deaths "associated with childbirth and childbirth-related septicemia." Rutman and Rutman, "'Now-Wives and Sons-in-Law.'"

[10]Eliza Tucker to St. George Tucker, May 29, 1783, TCP.

back to his house when his daughter-in-law went into labor. He arrived to find the house in an uproar: "I found every body about her in a great fright and she almost in dispair. The child was dead and the womb was fallen down and what not." Eventually a "large dead child much squeezed and indeed putrified was delivered." His daughter-in-law's unusually quick recovery ran counter to what Carter had read by experts in midwifery and convinced him of the complexity and unpredictability of the childbirth process. "If she should continue so [well] books and experience have not yet amounted to all the particular cases in Midwifery."[11]

Carter's close involvement in the delivery (probably because he was a widower) was extraordinary, for childbirth was normally managed by a midwife and an assortment of female kin and servants. Although a doctor was sometimes present, women controlled the entire delivery and recovery process.[12] Occasionally a husband did help to arrange for the midwife and other women to aid his wife's "lying-in." Three weeks before his wife delivered a daughter, James Gordon of Lancaster County, Virginia, brought in a local midwife, Mrs. Miller, "to wait on my wife."[13] It was not uncommon for fathers to remain completely away from the delivery scene. The Reverend Robert Rose rode to the home of his mother-in-law in Stafford County, Virginia, in August of 1747, where he found his wife "safely delivered of a Boy."[14] Richard Lloyd learned of the birth of his daughter from

---

[11]*Carter Diary,* II, 621. See also William Byrd II to Jane Pratt Taylor, July 28, 1728, in Marion Tinling, ed., *The Correspondence of the Three William Byrds of Westover, Virginia, 1684–1776* (2 vols., Charlottesville, 1977), I, 385.

[12]*Carter Diary,* II, 859; Francis Taylor Diary, Feb. 2, 1792, July 25, 1786; Henry Hollyday to James Hollyday, Aug. 5, 1782, HFP. Landon Carter had an "old midwife" who alerted him to slave girls in labor, *Carter Diary,* I, 514. Women dominated the childbirth process throughout the preindustrial West. See Scholten, "Changing Customs of Childbirth," 429–33; Joseph E. Illick, "Child-Rearing in Seventeenth-Century England and America," in deMause, ed., *The History of Childhood,* 305–6; and David Hunt, *Parents and Children in History: The Psychology of Family Life in Early Modern France* (New York, 1970), 84.

[13]"The Journal of James Gordon of Lancaster County, Virginia," *WMQ,* 1st ser., XI (1903), 228.

[14]RRD, Aug. 19, 1747.

his house mistress, who had supervised the delivery from a friend's home.[15] Even though his wife was "very big with child," Landon Carter's son Robert left on an extended trip to Fredericksburg on the first day of October in 1774. "Wild Bob," according to his father, was foolishly "sure of his wife's Punctuality in reackoning" and thus assumed that she would not need a midwife for another month. The same day that Carter left, his wife went into labor and produced a dead child.[16]

A mother, sister, aunt, or some other female relative usually helped a woman in childbirth. Women often developed close emotional attachments through the care they provided each other during childbirth and recovery.[17] Molly Tilghman was kept busy in the frequent lyings-in of her sisters during the late 1780s. She spent all of the winter of 1785 and 1786 in the home of her sister and brother-in-law nursing their child and supervising her sister's recovery. When her brother's wife had a child in January 1788, Molly was there to help and did not leave the house until three weeks after the delivery.[18] Martha Jefferson Carr also recognized that women had to care for one another in childbirth. Her niece Patsy Randolph had a child in 1794 "to increase her family" and Martha stayed with her to "assist in nursing her." Martha lived too far from her daughter Lucy Terrell to help her when she was brought to bed in the summer of 1794, but Mrs. Carr wrote Lucy frequently and insisted that she get "some good female friend that will act the Mother and sooth you with her compassion when the painful hour arrives and soften by her Tenderness the necessary time of retirement."[19]

Recovery often came slow to mothers and infants after the trauma of childbirth. Women were usually confined to bed for a

[15]Richard Lloyd to James Hollyday, March 4, 1780, HFP.

[16]*Carter Diary*, II, 859. See also William Byrd to Mr. Robinson, and same to Thomas Byrd, March 8, 1686, *Byrd Correspondence*, I, 52–53.

[17]For a discussion of female friendship networks, see Chapter 3.

[18]Molly Tilghman to Polly Tilghman, April 13, 1786, January 29, 1788, "Molly and Hetty Tilghman Letters," *MHM*, xxi (1926), 138, 232.

[19]Martha Jefferson Carr to Lucy Terrell, Aug. 9, 1794, CFP. See also Mary Dulaney to Walter Dulaney, Aug. 7, 1783, DP; Edwards M. Riley, ed., *The Journal of John Harrower* (New York, 1963), 124; and "Diary of Mrs. William Thornton, 1800," *Columbia Historical Society Records*, x (1907), 100.

week or more after delivery and did not become fully active again for a month.[20] Two weeks after giving birth to a son in the fall of 1749, Henry Callister's wife still had not recovered her strength. He noted that "she is now but ill able to sit to a Table to write."[21] The journal of James Gordon in 1761 records the suffering and precarious health of his wife and their infant daughter. After the delivery, Gordon noted, his wife and child were "both as well as can be expected." Five days later his wife was improving very slowly, and soon her recovery was complicated by an attack of the "ague & fever." She was not able to sit up for a week. Both parents had little hope that their new daughter Sally would survive more than a short while. She began to have "fits" and high fevers within three months. A few weeks later she died. "Oh, happy change!" Gordon exclaimed on that day while insisting that one should be prepared for such a loss. He buried his daughter the next day.[22]

When childbirth ended in the death of the infant, nearby friends and close relatives provided emotional comfort to the distressed mother. The day after William Byrd's wife miscarried in February of 1710, her cousin, Elizabeth Harrison, and the minister's wife came to see Mrs. Byrd "to comfort her in her affliction." Cousin Harrison, the nurse, and several other women made frequent visits to see Mrs. Byrd after another miscarriage a year later.[23]

The Joys of Parenthood

The world of family and kin that surrounded a newborn child usually offered a warm, affectionate environment for its de-

---

[20]The wife of John Pendleton, an Orange County, Virginia, planter, was confined to her room for nine days, "mending," after the premature birth ("born before its time") of her daughter. FTD, Dec. 26, 1794, January 4, 1795. Alan Macfarlane found approximately the same recovery time for women in the Josselin family of seventeenth-century England. See his *The Family Life of Ralph Josselin: A Seventeenth-Century Clergyman* (Cambridge, 1970), 86.

[21]Henry Callister to Ewan Callister, Nov. 13, 1749, CALP.

[22]"Journal of James Gordon," 229–30, 232.

[23]*Byrd Diary, 1709–12*, 142, 364–67.

velopment.[24] Indeed an "increase in the family" brought considerable pride and elation to parents and kin. The paternal self-pride engendered at childbirth is suggested in the praise Thomas Davis gave St. George Tucker at the birth of Tucker's daughter in 1779. Davis was excited "at learning my much-esteemed, Thy amiable Fanny had escaped the Danger of Child-Birth & had presented to my Friend such a lovely Image of himself."[25] John Galloway of Maryland was delighted when he saw his infant daughter in 1787. His wife's nurse commented on the "admiring Papa, and his graceful fondness."[26]

Grandparents—something of a rarity in the seventeenth-century Chesapeake due to short life expectancies—and other relatives played an increasingly important role in eighteenth-century families. Their fondness for young children provided another source of affection for children growing up in the eighteenth century. Some grandparents took an active interest even in prospective children. Charles Carroll of Annapolis, for example, was distressed that his pregnant daughter-in-law, Molly Carroll, had neglected to tell him that "she felt the little one 4 weeks past, Tell her I think Her a perverse Girl for not letting me know it sooner."[27] Another grandfather, Robert Carter Nicholas, proudly announced that his daughter-in-law had "presented us with a Jolly Girl."[28] Relatives often celebrated childbirth in the

[24]This should be contrasted with the comparative indifference with which infants were received in much of the seventeenth-century West. See Shorter, chap. 5.

[25]Thomas Davis to St. George Tucker, Oct. 3, 1779, TCP.

[26]Molly Tilghman to Polly Tilghman, Oct. 6, 1787, HFP. See also Robert Innes to St. George Tucker, March 25, 1783, Eliza Tucker to Frances Tucker, May 29, 1783, TCP; Richard Tilghman to Abraham Tilghman, March 15, 1750, in "Letters of the Tilghman Family, 1697–1764," *MHM*, XXXIII (1938), 167; and James Parker to Margaret Parker, March 24, 1777, PFP.

[27]Charles Carroll of Annapolis (hereafter Charles Carroll of A) to Charles Carroll of Carrollton (hereafter Charles Carroll of C), May 4, 1770, CARP.

[28]Robert C. Nicholas to John Norton, Oct. 15, 1773, in Frances Norton Mason, ed., *John Norton and Sons Merchants of London and Virginia (Being the Papers from their Counting House for the Years 1750 to 1795)* (Richmond, 1937), 356. In 1728, Robert Carter wrote "I have the blessing of seeing my children's children before me and as far as matrimony everyone has the comforts of descendants." Robert Carter to John Pratt, Aug. 8, 1728, RCL.

family with gifts. In 1774, Frances Norton sent her niece "a set of small China for her amusement," while the child's grandmother gave her a cap.[29] Mrs. Henry Callister received from her brother-in-law Ewan Callister a half-dozen silver tablespoons in honor of the birth of her son.[30]

Parents arranged christenings and baptisms—usually within a few weeks after birth—to bring kin and friends together in celebration of parenthood.[31] These ceremonies, held in private homes in most cases, were often quite festive affairs with dinner and dancing. Relatively small groups of perhaps a dozen or so kin and close friends usually attended.[32] William Byrd went to the christening of the Reverend Charles Anderson's son in 1709 where, according to Byrd, everyone dined and danced well into the evening. Anderson, Byrd noted, "was beyond measure pleased with the blessing God had sent him."[33] Philip Fithian, plantation tutor for Robert Carter of Nomini Hall, reported in 1773 that christenings were "one of the chief times for Diversion here."[34] Godparents were announced on these occasions; parents frequently chose a brother or sister or close family friend as symbolic guardian of the child. For some men, such as the Presbyterian James Gordon of Orange County, Virginia, a child's baptism carried a significant religious meaning. Gordon named his son Nathaniel at the baptismal ceremony in September of 1762 and later recorded in his diary a solemn wish for his son's spiritual fate: "O, may the Lord grant that he be a Nathaniel, indeed: the gift of God, & his name written in the Book of Life."[35]

---

[29]Frances Norton to John Hatley Norton, Sept. 6, 1774, in Mason, ed., *John Norton and Sons*, 374.

[30]Henry Callister to Ewan Callister, Nov. 12, 1749, CALP. See also *Byrd Diary, 1709–12*, 60.

[31]RRD, Oct. 8, 1749; *Byrd Diary 1709–12*, 249.

[32]FTD, June 16, 1799, Nov. 2, 1796; RRD, Oct. 8, 1749; *Carter Diary*, I, 376–77; *Byrd Diary, 1709–12*, 2; "Journal of James Gordon," 9, 232.

[33]*Byrd Diary, 1709–12*, 2.

[34]Hunter Dickinson Farish, ed., *Journal and Letters of Philip Vickers Fithian, 1773–1774* (Williamsburg, 1943), 47.

[35]"Journal of James Gordon," 9.

"Getting and Taking": Feeding and Caring for Infants

A child's first important experience in the world comes in his relationship with his mother or nurse, especially in the feeding process.[36] In this earliest stage of development, until about the age of two, a child is mainly concerned with the simple but essential task of "getting" and "taking," as Erik Erikson has suggested. His success in this incorporative mode of behavior depends in part on the willingness and ability of the parents to provide the nourishment a child needs and demands. And most important, the nursing bond significantly influences a child's earliest perceptions of the trustworthiness of the people around him.[37]

Studies of childhood suggest that children in the preindustrial West often failed in their crucial efforts at "getting" and "taking." Many remained underfed and were left in the hands of mothers and nurses who distrusted their "primitive" demands for survival. Seventeenth-century European parents were ambivalent about children, whom they felt obligated to protect, but who were also, they sometimes believed, "demanding and dangerous little animals."[38]

As a result of these tensions, the relationship between nurse or mother and child in early modern Europe resembled a struggle more than a cooperative effort. Mothers, especially after a difficult delivery, viewed breastfeeding as a debilitating experience, one in which an infant drained a mother of her vital substances. Some mothers feared that breastfed children might transmit to them some dread disease.[39] Consequently, most women who could afford it put their children out to nurse, despite the advice

[36]According to Peter L. Giovacchini, "the early mothering experience is the most important single relationship in the child's life." See Giovacchini, "The Submerged Ego," *Journal of the American Academy of Child Psychiatry,* III (1964), 439.

[37]Erik Erikson, *Identity, Youth and Crisis* (New York, 1968), 96–99.

[38]See Hunt, *Parents and Children in History: The Psychology of Family Life in Early Modern France* (New York, 1970), 123.

[39]Ibid., 105.

of physicians that an infant would thrive best when nourished by its own mother. Moreover, poorly prepared solid food was often fed to children before they were fully able to digest it. High infant mortality rates of between 20 and 30 percent for seventeenth-century Europe reflect in part this low level of maternal care of children.[40] It was not until the mid-eighteenth century that critics of child care in England and France became effective in encouraging maternal nursing.[41]

In the colonial Chesapeake, maternal nursing was probably the most common form of infant feeding. Little is known about parent-child relations in Virginia and Maryland during the seventeenth century due to the scarcity of personal documents such as family papers and diaries. The fragmentary evidence that does exist, however, indicates that mothers probably breastfed their children. Nonetheless, infant and childhood mortality rates remained extremely high, perhaps as high as 40 percent, because of the endemic malarial environment that prevailed in the early Chesapeake. Infants frequently received from diseased mothers a short-term immunity to malaria which allowed many of them to survive infancy, only later to succumb to the disease as small children when their immunity had worn off.[42]

In the eighteenth century, even though a larger number of families could afford to hire wet nurses, most women, except when ill, seem to have continued to nurse their own children. One woman in 1780, for example, was reported to be "too weakly

[40]Elizabeth Wirth Marvick, "Nature Versus Nuture: Patterns and Trends in Seventeenth-Century French Child-Rearing," in deMause, 263–66, 282–83; Hunt, 122. See Edward Shorter's compilation of infant and childhood mortality rates for early modern Europe, *The Making of the Modern Family,* Appendix 5.

[41]Bogna W. Lorence, "Parents and Children in Eighteenth-Century Europe," *Journal of Psychohistory,* II (1974), 1–30; *The Works of Dr. John Tillotson* (3 vols., London, 1728), I, 488–89. By 1780 a substantial proportion of aristocratic women in England were breastfeeding or dry nursing their own children. See Trumbach, "The Aristocratic Family in England, 1690–1780," 90.

[42]See Darrett B. and Anita H. Rutman, "Of Agues and Fevers: Malaria in the Colonial Chesapeake," *WMQ,* 3d ser., XXXIII (1976), 31–60; Smith, "Mortality and Family," 411–13; and Lorena S. Walsh, "'Till Death Us Do Part': Marriage and Family in Seventeenth-Century Maryland," 126–52, in Tate and Ammerman.

to Suckel her little Girl & is Obliged to put it out to nurse."[43] Another woman was seen "nursing her little girl, to whom she is quite devoted."[44] In sharp contrast to parents in early modern Europe who feared that infants might communicate disease to those who nursed them, parents in the eighteenth-century Chesapeake worried more about children becoming ill from contact with sick mothers. For instance, Margaret Parker of Norfolk, Virginia, wrote to her husband in 1771 that their infant boy had "Sucked the fever from me I believe. I was obliged to get a woman to Suckle him a while till I get my milk again which the fever dryed up."[45] Other women nursed their infants despite the pain and inconvenience.[46] Breastfeeding, many women believed, ruined the shape of the breasts and doubtless some women hesitated to nurse their children for this reason.[47] The experience of Mary Dulaney of Maryland, however, suggests that a mother's affection for a child could outweigh such concerns. A friend noted that Mary breastfed her infant boy despite her fear that "her good looks may be injured by nursing her fine son."[48]

Maternal love, though, was not always the central motivation for mothers who decided to nurse their own children. Given the discomfort of frequent pregnancies and the danger and violent pain associated with childbirth in the eighteenth century, some mothers chose to nurse their offspring because the lactation period tended to delay conception. Landon Carter certainly felt that this was the strategy of his daughter-in-law in 1770 when, according to him, she continued to breastfeed her baby girl despite being sick herself. Carter complained that "the poor little baby Fanny is every time to share her Mamma's disorder by sucking her, and this because she should not breed too fast. Poor children! Are you to be sacrificed for a parent's pleasure? I have

[43]Anne Tucker to St. George Tucker, April 13, 1780, TCP. See also Frances Tucker to Frances Bland Tucker, June 16, 1783, ibid.; *Carter Diary,* I, 345, II, 765.
[44]"Diary of Mrs. William Thornton," 174.
[45]Margaret Parker to James Parker, 1771, PFP.
[46]FTD, April 23, 1790; Molly to Polly Tilghman, Jan. 29, 1789, "Molly and Hetty Tilghman Letters," 232–33.
[47]Trumbach, 57–59; Rendle-Short, 114.
[48]Catherine Belt to Mary Dulaney, May 2, 1802, DP.

been a Parent and I thought it murder and therefore hired nurses or put them out." Despite Carter's protest, his granddaughter, "little Fanny," continued "to suck the poizon" from her mother's "morbid breast."[49]

In exceptionally wealthy and large families (of perhaps ten or more children) mothers sometimes relied on nurses—both black and white—to breastfeed some of their children.[50] Fithian noted this practice in 1773. "I find it is common here for people of Fortune to have their young children suckled by the Negroes!" Mrs. Carter, who had given birth to thirteen children, told Fithian that "wenches have suckled several" of her infants.[51]

Fithian, however, was speaking of a very small minority of women—only those with great wealth and burdened by huge families, like Mrs. Carter. Most mothers, except when seriously weakened by childbirth or sickness, nursed their own infants— often out of strong maternal sentiment. As a result of this natural maternal nursing bond, deep emotional attachments were established between mothers and children. As a child gained confidence in the accessibility of its mother as an attachment figure, the anxiety and fear about the world around it declined. It was perhaps from such an early atmosphere of maternal warmth that planters' children developed a strong measure of self-confidence and independence.[52]

The weaning process, however, threatened to disrupt the close ties between a child and its nurse or mother. Sometime in their

[49]*Carter Diary*, II, 511–12, 515. For a discussion of the effect of lactation on delaying conception, see Perez, 1141–47; Vanginneken, 201–6. Some men may have opposed maternal breastfeeding because of medical objections to nursing women engaging in sexual intercourse. See Illick, 310; Hunt, 106–7; Trumbach, 89.

[50]The decision to put infants out to nurse could probably be correlated—if enough evidence were available—with growing family size and high economic status. See Marvick, 266.

[51]Farish, ed., *Journal and Letters of Fithian*, 52. Jonathan Boucher considered the practice among Maryland's elite of giving their children to slaves to nurse "a monstrous Fault." Boucher to Rev. John James, Aug. 7, 1759, in "Letters of Jonathan Boucher," *MHM*, VII (1912), 6.

[52]See John Bowlby, *Attachment and Loss* (2 vols., New York, 1973), I, 308, II, 335, 362.

37

second year, children were removed from their secure source of nourishment. Weaning was critical in the child's first moves toward autonomy, which normally characterize the second year of life.[53] It proved to be a difficult time for parents, too, for they worried incessantly that their children might become ill during this uncertain stage in their development.

Parents separated children from the breast at different times in early modern Europe and America. In the seventeenth and eighteenth centuries, children in England and France were weaned at around twenty-four months, often abruptly among wealthy families.[54] Parents in colonial America appear to have allowed a more gradual weaning, but began the process earlier, which suggests in part that they encouraged an earlier sense of autonomy in the child than their European counterparts. In seventeenth-century Plymouth and the colonial Chesapeake, the scattered evidence indicates that weaning began between twelve and eighteen months.[55] A starchy mixture of flour and milk, such as gruel or pap, was introduced into the child's diet sometime in the first year to begin to accustom him to eating solid food. Mothers often dabbed mustard, pepper, or some bitter substance on their breasts to discourage the child from nursing.[56]

Weaning was particularly trying to parents since many probably felt ambivalent about separating the child from its mother's breast. Parents were clearly relieved when weaning was accomplished without pain or illness. In September of 1728, Dolly Jones was reported to have "weaned herself" at age one. As her nurse explained to Dolly's mother, she "won't touch the breast when offered her, which I think you'll have no reason to be sorry for, but it was first occasioned by her being kept from it when she took the bark, but she never seemed to desire it."[57] Mothers,

[53]Demos, 136; Macfarlane, 87–88.
[54]Illick, 309; Trumbach, 95–96; Marvick, 275–76.
[55]Demos, 136. Middle-class families in modern America wean their children at around six months. See John W. M. Whiting and Irving L. Child, *Child Training and Personality* (New Haven, 1953), 70–71.
[56]Illick, 309.
[57]Rachel Cocke to Elizabeth Jones, Sept. 17, 1728, JFP.

nurses, and occasionally grandmothers seemed to have controlled the weaning process. Frances Tucker, her husband noted, had gone to Port Royal, Virginia, in the spring of 1784, where she was "weaning our last little Brat."[58]

Parents also found teething a difficult period in the child's early development. It was an event that usually signaled the beginning of weaning, for mothers stopped breastfeeding near the time that children began cutting teeth—at the end of the first year.[59] Teething brought on a period of pain and sickness that left parents and kin fearful and anxious. William Prentis, for example, worried that his one-year-old son John had the same "disease" that all of his children had developed the year they were weaned: "a disorder in the bowels, and cutting of Teeth."[60] In 1725 Elizabeth Pratt empathized with her suffering two-year-old son: "poor Billy has been pulled down by his hard breeding of teeth."[61] And Martha Jefferson Carr was anxious to hear whether her fourteen-month-old granddaughter Martha Terrell had "got safely through the worst of her teething."[62]

Teething concerned parents and kin mainly because of the physical discomfort children experienced during this period. The biting stage also represented an important test of the child's basic trust in the nurturant and protective attitudes of its parents. For teething compelled the child to bite to ease the pain at the same time that the mother was intent upon weaning the child.[63] But as we have seen, parents showed considerable sensitivity to the difficulties children faced during weaning and teething.

[58]Thomas Tudor Tucker to St. George Tucker, April 14, 1784, TCP.
[59]See Macfarlane, 87–88.
[60]William Prentis to Joseph Prentis, July 28, 1801, WPC.
[61]Elizabeth Pratt to William Pratt, Sept. 7, 1725, JFP.
[62]Martha Jefferson Carr to Richard Terrell, Oct. 11, 1794, CFP. For other examples of parental concern over the teething problems of children, see Theodorick Bland, Jr. to John Randolph, Sept. 14, 1770, BP; Elizabeth Holloway to Elizabeth Jones, June 27, 1751, JFP; *Byrd Diary, 1709–12*, 125; John Marshall to Polly Marshall, Aug. 18, 1798, in Frances Norton Mason, ed., *My Dearest Polly: Letters of Chief Justice John Marshall to His Wife, 1779–1831* (Richmond, 1961), 121–22.
[63]Erik H. Erikson, *Childhood and Society*, 2d ed. (New York, 1963), 248.

Child-Centered Families

Anyone who reads through the family letters and diaries from the eighteenth-century Chesapeake will discover an abundance of evidence of parental tenderness and affection toward young children.[64] These sources clearly suggest that children were not treated as sinful beings whose willfulness and sense of autonomy had to be controlled, if not quashed, by age two or three—as children were apparently seen in much of Puritan New England.[65] Rather, parents in Virginia and Maryland during the eighteenth century seemed to delight in the distinctively innocent and playful childhood years of their offspring. Parents and an assortment of kin—grandparents, uncles, aunts, and cousins—who frequently helped in child-rearing were usually quite fond of children and considered their activities pleasant diversions. Indeed, as we shall see, family and kin often indulged young children and granted them considerable freedom.

It is not likely that during the seventeenth century children had enjoyed such a prominent emotional place in Chesapeake households. Because of oppressive infant and child mortality rates and a short life expectancy in early Virginia and Maryland, parents may have invested less of their emotional life in their children than did eighteenth-century parents. When infants or

[64]One historian of eighteenth-century American childhood, however, maintains that children appeared as little more than afterthoughts in the letters of their parents. See John F. Walzer, "A Period of Ambivalence: Eighteenth-Century American Childhood," in deMause, 359. The evidence from the eighteenth-century Chesapeake suggests a different conclusion.

[65]Demos, 136–38; Philip Greven, The Protestant Temperament: Patterns of Child-Rearing, Religious Experience and The Self in Early America (New York, 1977), 32–61. Greven's evidence also shows that more moderate child-rearing practices prevailed in some households in New England and the middle colonies, particularly during the latter half of the eighteenth century. In these households a combination of affection and duty characterized parent-child ties, and parental authority grew more flexible and less absolute as it emphasized carefully molding the child's habits to develop strong character rather than breaking the will—a pattern common to most evangelical homes (ibid., 151–91). For a discussion of New England sermons and prescriptive literature on child-rearing, see Peter Gregg Slater, Children in the New England Mind (Hamden, Conn., 1977) and Ross W. Beales, "In Search of the Historical Child: Miniature Adulthood in Colonial New England," American Quarterly, XXVII (1975), 379–98.

children died, parents—especially fathers—showed little emotion or deep concern.[66] Moreover, Protestant religious thought, which stressed the inherently sinful and inferior condition of children, shaped the character of family life in the seventeenth century. Fathers remained emotionally detached from infants and small children, insisting on the child's acceptance of self-control and obedience to paternal authority.[67]

In eighteenth-century Virginia and Maryland, however, where the increasingly secular culture was committed to an expanding tobacco economy based largely on slave labor, religious values rarely intruded into family life and child-rearing, especially in Anglican households. Churchgoing became more of a social activity than a spiritual concern in gentry families; Sundays were occasions more for visiting and conviviality than for piety and prayer.[68]

[66]Familial attitudes toward death are discussed at length in Chapter 7 below.
[67]Illick, 323, 325. Greven, *The Protestant Temperament*, 28–55. A good example of seventeenth- and early eighteenth-century religious opinion on childhood comes from the widely read essays of Benjamin Wadsworth. See especially "The Nature of Early Piety" in his *A Course of Sermons on Early Piety* (Boston, 1721).
[68]Rhys Isaac, "Evangelical Revolt: The Nature of the Baptists' Challenge to the Traditional Order in Virginia, 1765 to 1775," *WMQ*, 3d ser., xxxi (1974), 345–68. For this casual view of religion, see the comments of one teen-aged girl in Virginia: "The Frances Baylor Hill Diary of 'Hillsborough' King and Queen County, Virginia (1797)," in *Early American Literature Newsletter*, ii (1967), 15–17, 22, 36, 38. In my reading of letters and diaries of Chesapeake families, I have rarely seen any mention of religious instruction for children. The Reverend Devereux Jarratt noted an irreligious tone in most planter households, though pointing out his own parents' interest in family religion. "The Autobiography of the Reverend Devereux Jarratt, 1732–1793," *WMQ*, 3d ser., ix (1952), 356, 363–64. Only three other instances of family religious instruction could be found in extant letters and diaries. The Reverend Robert Rose occasionally read prayers to his family "& a few others." RRD, Sept. 29, 1749. In the 1770s Robert Carter Nicholas apparently taught his daughter Elizabeth the principles of the established church "with strictness, if not bigotry." Quoted in Victor Golladay, "The Nicholas Family in Virginia" (unpub. Ph.D. diss., University of Virginia, 1973), 172. See also "An Exhortation to Family Prayer," 1778, Robert Carter Papers, 1760–1815, Virginia Historical Society. A systematic sampling of wills in York County and Albemarle County, Virginia, in the eighteenth century revealed that less than 5 percent of all testators made reference to, or provision for, religious instruction in the family. Dissenter families doubtless showed more concern for religion in the home than Anglican parents. See, for example, the discussion of sermons and family prayers in the Presbyterian household of James Gordon, "Journal of James Gordon," 4, 218. Almost all sermons to planter audiences and Anglo-American advice litera-

In the absence of overriding spiritual influences, Chesapeake parents tended to stress the positive, pleasurable capacities of children. Indeed, the personal documents of planter families, especially after mid-century, reveal a familial and social environment in which children were often the centerpiece of family affection. Mothers and fathers and kin, at least in well-to-do families, lavished attention on their children. One father from Queen Anne's County, Maryland, for example, was reported to be "Excessively fond of his Daughter a fine sprightly girl."[69] Richard Tilghman confided to a friend in 1763 that his three-year-old daughter Anna Maria was "the plaything of the family."[70] And Thomas Jefferson told his daughter Mary Jefferson Randolph that he hoped his granddaughter "will make us all, and long, happy as the center of our common love."[71]

When away from their families, fathers who wrote home almost always asked to be remembered to their children. While staying in Williamsburg in the fall of 1755, George Braxton told his wife to "Give little Molly a thousand kisses for me."[72] St. George Tucker was particularly fond of his children and step-children. His letters to his wife Frances ("Fanny") during his service in the Revolution suggest the pleasure he derived from parenthood. "Remember me with a Tenderness Truly Parental to my Boys," he wrote Fanny, "and let Patty and Maria be assured I am neither unmindful nor indifferent in regard to them." Tucker, like many parents, used affectionate nicknames for his children.

---

ture emphasized the need for religious child-rearing. See, for example, Benjamin Wadsworth, *The Well-Ordered Family,* 2d ed. (Boston, 1719); Samuel Davies, *Little Children Invited to Jesus Christ* (Hartford, 1766), a sermon preached in Hanover County, Virginia, May 8, 1758; John Witherspoon, *A Sermon on the Religious Education of Children* (Princeton, 1789).

[69]Richard Lloyd to James Hollyday, June 14, 1756, HFP.

[70]Richard Tilghman II to the Rev. P. Crump (after June 1763) in "Letters between the English and American Branches of the Tilghman Family, 1697–1764," *MHM,* xxxiii (1938), 173.

[71]Thomas Jefferson to Mary Jefferson Randolph, May 31, 1791, in Sarah N. Randolph, *The Domestic Life of Thomas Jefferson* (New York, 1939), 202.

[72]George Braxton to Mrs. Braxton, Nov. 16, 1755, in Frederick Horner, *The History of the Blair, Banister and Braxton Families: A Collection of Letters* (Philadelphia, 1898), 181. See also Sarah Cary to Betsy Braxton, Oct. 20, 1781, ibid., 58.

"My poor little Monkies are insensible to all that a parent can feel for them."[73]

Parents were diverted by, rather than impatient with, the nonsense language and "childish" behavior of their young offspring. Jane Swann wrote to her uncle of the satisfying moments she and her husband spent with their four-year-old girl. Their daughter, she said, was "very lively & full of Inocent Prattle with which She often pleasantly amuses her Father & my Self. May the Almighty preserve her long with us."[74] Surrounded by the familiar and attentive faces of parents and kin, children provided their families with displays of uninhibited and seemingly irrational behavior unacceptable in the adult world. The experience of Eliza Custis as a child growing up in Virginia in the 1770s demonstrates vividly that children were welcome diversions to their parents.

I can now remember standing on the table when not more than 3 or 4 years old, singing songs which I did not understand—while my father & other gentlemen were often rolling in their chairs with laughter—& I was animated to exert myself to give him delight—The servants in the passage would join their mirth, & I holding my head erect, would strut about the table to receive the praises of the company, my mother remonstrated in vain—& her husband always said his little Bet could not be injured by what she did not understand that he had no Boy & she must make fun for him, until he had—he would then kiss her to make his Peace, & giving me a Nod my voice which was uncommonly powerful for my age resounded through the rooms, & my Mother who could not help laughing, used to retire & leave me to the gentlemen, where my fathers caresses made me think well of myself.[75] ["Self-Portrait, Eliza Custis, 1808," 93–94]

[73]St. George Tucker to Frances Tucker, March ? 1781, TCP. See also in this collection, ibid., March 13, 1781, June 28, 1781, Frances Tucker to St. George Tucker, Feb. 1780, March 24, 1781. See also Richard Terrell to Lucy Terrell, Nov. 26, 1793, CTFP; William Byrd to Mrs. Otway, Oct. 2, 1735, "Byrd Letters," *VMHB*, XXXVI (1928), 119–20.

[74]Jane Swann to Thomas Jones, Oct. 19, 1743, JFP. See also John Marshall to Polly Marshall, Feb. 3, 1796, July 10, 11, Aug. 3, Sept. 9, 1797, Aug. 18, 1798, *My Dearest Polly,* 76, 97–98, 108, 110, 121.

[75]"Self-Portrait, Eliza Custis, 1808," *VMHB*, LXI (1953), 93–94. See also *Carter Diary,* II, 861–62, 1149; Charles Carroll of A to Charles Carroll of C, June 19, 1772, CARP. Children's birthdays were often remembered by their parents who paid special attention to them on these days. See, for example, *Byrd Diary, 1709–12,*

For Thomas Gilpin of Maryland in the 1790s, proper child-rearing involved a close friendship between parents and children. Parental participation in a child's world of play, he believed, encouraged sound character and virtuous conduct in the child as he matured. Gilpin's wife observed that her husband took great pleasure in cultivating "a freedom and sociability with his Tender offspring In order to Unite Filial Obedience with [paternal?] affection in the Closest tyes of Friendship which he often used to say was the surest way for Parents to Secure the affection of their Children." According to his wife, Gilpin spent a lot of time with the two children, often giving them "little Inocent amusements to keep them in from the street and out of others [pernicious?] Company and would often be one of their party himself thereby discovering the great pleasure that their little Inocent Company and Diverting Actions Afforded him." This kind of intimate relationship, Gilpin assumed, helped a child choose proper "Friends and Confidents and none was so proper as their Parents."[76]

Childhood had clearly become a distinctive period in the minds of Chesapeake parents and kin during the eighteenth century. The presence of grandparents was extremely influential in shaping these child-centered families. The short life expectancy in the seventeenth century—to about the mid-forties among adult men and women—precluded the development of an elderly generation and a large body of supporting kin. Indeed, family life in the early Chesapeake was often limited to contact between two generations—and with such high death rates, these relationships usually proved to be rather short-lived, as the profusion of stepparents and orphans in this period suggests.[77] With the improvement in life expectancy during the eighteenth century—to

---

60, 483. Parents sometimes entertained their children. Thomas Bolling, while visiting Byrd's house in 1740 "entertained the children with his tricks." M. Tinling and Maude H. Woodfin, eds., *Another Secret Diary of William Byrd of Westover, 1739–1741* (Richmond, 1942), 79.

[76]Mrs. Gilpin to Joshua Gilpin, 1796? GL.

[77]On the near absence of grandparents in the seventeenth-century Chesapeake, see Smith, "Mortality and Family in the Colonial Chesapeake," 421; Rutman and Rutman, "'Now-Wives and Sons-in-law'"; and Walsh, "Marriage

about the mid-fifties for adult men—family relationships among three generations became commonplace.[78] As a result, by mid-century planters frequently sent their children to stay with grandparents and other relatives, where they were often indulged and fondly cared for.

Family letters from this period allow us to glimpse the quality of kin attachments to children. Six-year-old Betty Pratt spent much of the fall of 1728 with her aunt, who admitted to Betty's mother that the girl was receiving too much attention. "She is exceedingly fondled at [the] other House, more than I think, is necessary tho she manages herself with it better than one could expect from a Child of her age."[79] Charles Carroll of Annapolis was particularly attached to his granddaughter Molly Carroll, the daughter of Charles Carroll of Carrollton. He ended almost every letter to his son or daughter-in-law with affectionate expressions for Molly, such as: "I long to kiss my little Granddaughter."[80] Charles sent her gifts—once a pocketbook, purse and money— and when she received them, Carroll instructed his son to "tell her I sent it." Molly's frequent and lengthy visits to her grandfather's plantation strengthened his commitment to her, sometimes at the expense of Carroll's concern for his son. He once confided to his son, "it is no Compliment to you & Molly [Carroll's daughter-in-law] when I tell you that it seems to me I long more to see my Dear little Granddaughter than either of you."[81] Children and their grandparents sometimes exchanged pictures—or "miniatures," which were usually placed in a locket—or other personal items as a permanent expression of

---

and Family in Seventeenth-Century Maryland." That grandparenthood had become a widespread phenomenon by the last quarter of the eighteenth century is reflected in the calculations Alan Kulikoff has made from the census for Prince George's County, Maryland, in 1776. In that year 49 percent of all children under four, 44 percent between five and nine, and 40 percent between ten and fourteen, had at least one living grandparent. See Kulikoff, 58.

[78]Kulikoff, 439.

[79]Rachel Cocke to Elizabeth Pratt, Sept. 17, 1728, JFP.

[80]Charles Carroll of A to Charles Carroll of C, Dec. 5, 1770. See also same to same, April 2, June 3, Aug. 8, 1771, June 12, Sept. 2, 1772, CARP.

[81]Charles Carroll of A to Charles Carroll of C, April 8, 1773, ibid.

their affection.[82] In 1784, Henry Tucker, Sr. sent his granddaughter Nancy Tucker a locket of his hair, which, as he told his son, he hoped would please her—"the device is paternal affection."[83]

"Lusty and Willful" Children

Despite the pleasure parents and kin clearly derived from young children, they approached child-rearing with serious purposefulness. They expected to develop in their offspring powers of self-discipline which, parents believed, would produce self-reliant, independent adults. And it was the warm, nurturant attitudes of Chesapeake parents that have been described above that allowed them to shape children into dutiful sons and daughters.

Parents were especially mindful of developing powers of self-sufficiency and strength in their children. They applauded but rarely demanded precocity in their children, unlike seventeenth-century Anglo-American parents, who sought to hurry children out of their childhood dependency.[84] Still, initial signs of mobility and autonomy, suggested in early efforts at walking and talking, attracted close attention from observant parents. Lucy Terrell, according to her grandmother, Martha Jefferson Carr, "prattles everything she hears," and was "very spiritly." Years later, Mrs. Carr expressed the same interest in another granddaughter, one-year-old Martha Terrell. She was anxious to see "little Martha's attempts to prattle & to see her shuffling across the room."[85] Frances Randolph was equally proud of her daughter, "Mopsey," who "talks *prodigiously.* She

[82]Richard Henry Lee to Thomas Lee Shippen, Jan. 17, 1785, in James C. Ballagh, ed., *The Letters of Richard Henry Lee* (New York, 1970), 322. See also John Marshall to Polly Marshall, Aug. 18, 1798, *My Dearest Polly*, 121–22.

[83]Henry Tucker, Sr., to St. George Tucker, Aug. 21, 1784, TCP. Horatio Belt confessed to the same kind of affection toward his granddaughter. He told his wife in 1783 to "give my love" to his grandsons "for in spite of my reason I can't help loving them." Horatio Belt to Catherine Belt, Sept. 30, 1783, DP.

[84]Illick, 312.

[85]Martha Jefferson Carr to Richard Terrell, May 18, 1793, Oct. 11, 1794; Martha Jefferson Carr to Lucy Terrell, Aug. 9, 1794, March 28, 1796, CTFP.

will walk in a fortnight."[86] In 1779 Charles Carroll of Annapolis reported to his son and daughter-in-law that their daughter Kitty, who was visiting Carroll, "has a language of her own and Endeavours to talk."[87]

Parents took a close interest in the early muscle control and coordination of their sons, who were especially encouraged to move about on their own. The observations of Thomas and Elizabeth Jones in the 1720s are revealing in this connection. In July of 1728, Thomas Jones reported at length to his wife, then visiting relatives in England, on the growth and character of their three children. Lusty, exuberant children clearly appealed to Jones. His youngest son, two-year-old Tom, particularly pleased him, for as Jones noted, "he runs about the house, hollows & makes a noise all day long and as often as he can, gets out of Doors." Tom's father was keenly aware of the boy's progress in walking. After returning from a trip, Jones noticed the "great alteration in the use of his Feet in so short a time, and I believe [he] is as forward in that as most children of two years old." Taking his first tentative steps became a lesson in self-sufficiency for young Tom: "when he falls I order him not to be taken up by which means he takes it patiently, unless he hurts himself pretty much." Young Tom was a less remarkable talker, however, which seemed to bother his father somewhat: "he is very backward with his tongue, I use him to pa-pa; & Ma-ma, and in a morning he will say (not Tea) but Tee, and sometimes mo' which is all the improvement he has made that way; he grows Tall and is a fine Boy."[88]

To encourage a hardy constitution in children, parents followed the advice of John Locke by dressing them in loose-fitting

[86]Frances Randolph to St. George Tucker, March 22, 1781, TCP.

[87]Charles Carroll of A to Charles Carroll of C, July 21, 1779, CARP. See also Thomas Jefferson to Mary Jefferson Randolph, May 8, 31, 1791, Randolph, *The Domestic Life of Thomas Jefferson*, 200, 202.

[88]Thomas Jones to Elizabeth Jones, July 8, 1728, JFP. See also Henry Tucker, Jr., to St. George Tucker, Nov. 4, 1782, TCP; William Byrd II to Charles Boyle, Feb. 5, 1728, *Byrd Correspondence*, I, 370; John Marshall to Polly Marshall, July 11, Aug. 3, 1797, *My Dearest Polly*, 98, 108.

clothes and allowing them plenty of time in the open air. [89] Locke's prescriptions for early child care seem to have been in the mind of one father who, while away from home on business, inquired about his son's upbringing: "How goes the dear little thing. Do you permitt Charles to run half-naked as he should do, feed him on Mush Milk &c, do you sufficiently correct his little [Fancy?] faults, keep him in due Subjection toward his little [servant?] . . . ?"[90] During early childhood, boys and girls were dressed alike in distinctive children's clothing—a kind of long robe that opened down the front to provide unrestricted movement. A pair of ribbons hanging from the back of the gown, which had been used in the seventeenth century to support children in their early attempts to walk, became simply ornamental by the eighteenth century. By the age of six or seven, boys were put into breeches and shirts, perhaps symbolizing their first step toward manhood.[91]

The goal of most eighteenth-century Anglo-American parents was to develop the honest, republican virtues of self-reliance and self-control in their children. Child-rearing literature since the late seventeenth century had advised parents to inculcate these values as early as possible in their offspring, preferably in infancy or early childhood when a child's character and temperament were most pliable and susceptible to parental guidance.[92] Parental authority, Locke argued, should be a strategic combination of indulgence—to gain a child's lasting affection and gratitude—and firm discipline—to ensure obedience and a continuing sense of

---

[89]James Axtell, ed., *The Educational Writings of John Locke* (Cambridge, 1968), 123–24.

[90]James Parker to Margaret Parker, March 8, 1776, PFP.

[91]Alice Morse Earle, *Childlife in Colonial America* (New York, 1899), 41–44, 55–58; William Nelson to John Norton, Aug. 14, 1767, Mason, ed., *John Norton and Sons*, 32; Philippe Ariès, *Centuries of Childhood: A Social History of Family Life*, trans. Robert Baldick (New York, 1962), 51–58.

[92]A firm show of parental authority, Locke suggested, should begin early in the child's life but diminish as he matures: "If you would have him stand in Awe of you, imprint it *in his Infancy;* and as he approaches more to a Man, admit him nearer to your Familiarity: So shall you have him your obedient Subject (as is fit) whilst he is a Child, and your affectionate Friend, when he is a Man." Axtell, ed., *Educational Writings of Locke*, 145.

duty to parents. Punishment was most effective when administered through shame, rather than through whippings, which, at best, produced only a temporary remedy. Only by inducing fear of parental displeasure early in a child's life could parents instill habits of obedience and self-control.[93]

While Chesapeake parents in general seem to have adopted elements of this child-rearing style—especially its emphasis on developing hardy, self-reliant children—parent-child relationships in this eighteenth-century agrarian society took on a form different from what Locke and other critics would have advised. The wide-open and uncrowded plantation environment, with land abundant and vices scarce, allowed planters to raise their children under more optimistic and permissive assumptions about childhood and parental conduct. Obedience and respect for parental authority remained important for the development of strong character and stable family life, but parents placed considerably more emphasis on developing a child's, and especially a son's, freedom of movement and sense of personal autonomy.

Chesapeake households were often complex units with servants and kin living on the plantation, making constant parental supervision of children unnecessary. Indeed, one senses from the letters and diaries of the period that children were allowed, and perhaps encouraged, to explore their immediate environment with little parental supervision. While visiting his friend Colonel Eppes in February of 1711, William Byrd was asked to help locate a small child who had just learned to walk and had wandered off from his little friends. "All the people on the plantation were looking for it," Byrd explained, "& I went likewise to look [for] it

---

[93]Ibid., 154–55; Richard Allestree, *The Ladies Calling* (London, 1673), 48, 50. The most provocative study of Anglo-American child-rearing literature is in Daniel Calhoun, *The Intelligence of a People* (Princeton, 1973), 134–205. See also Edwin G. Burrows and Michael Wallace, "The American Revolution: The Ideology and Psychology of National Liberation," *Perspectives in American History,* VI (1972), 169–89. There are, however, serious difficulties in trying to understand child-rearing practices from a reading of advice literature. For a perceptive analysis of these problems, see Jay Mechling, "Advice to Historians on Advice to Mothers," *Journal of Social History,* IX (1975), 44–63.

& at last found it, for which the women gave me abundance of blessings."[94] Parents clearly admired rambunctious, energetic children, whom they seem to have given the run of the plantation. Margaret Parker reported to her husband that their young son was doing well, as he had been "employed all day making bonfirs."[95] Landon Carter's grandson, despite being ill, was permitted to go hunting all day, and his younger brother George had to be "fetched" at the stables that evening "after candlelight."[96] One woman who went to see her cousin noted that her cousin's two children, a two- and three-year-old, "were fighting on the carpet, during the whole visit."[97]

Children thrived on companionship and vigorous play with other children, parents believed; confining them at home weakened their important instinct for sociability. White and black children often mingled freely on the plantation, relatively unsupervised by parents.[98] Parents and kin became concerned when children missed opportunities for companionship in their early years. One man, fretting over the limited social contacts his eight-year-old nephew had with other boys, complained that it "is not so proper for a boy to be under so much Confinement; and to live so remote without any Company."[99]

Not only did young children experience considerable freedom of movement on the plantation, but they also lived under few parental restraints to their conduct. Parents and kin, at least in middle- and upper-class families, apparently made little effort to stifle childhood willfulness and self-assertion. To be sure, overt disobedience was not countenanced, but parents did not attempt

[94]*Byrd Diary, 1709–12,* 307. Byrd's young son William attended church by himself and frequently left the plantation with his playmates. See *Byrd Diary, 1739–41,* 122–23, 130, 148.

[95]Margaret Parker to James Parker, c. 1770, PFP.

[96]*Carter Diary,* II, 661–62.

[97]Molly Tilghman to Polly Tilghman, 1783 or 1784, "Letters of Molly and Hetty Tilghman," 33. See also Henry Hollyday to James Hollyday, Sept. 22, 1754, HFP; Frances Tucker to St. George Tucker, April 1787, TCP.

[98]Farish, ed., *Journal and Letters of Fithian,* 82, 94; Henry Hollyday to James Hollyday, May 17, 1777, HFP; Karen Dawley, "Childhood in Eighteenth-Century Virginia" (unpub. M.A. thesis, University of Virginia, 1972), 25.

[99]Henry Pratt to Elizabeth Jones, Dec. 27, 1731, JFP.

as a matter of principle to root out autonomous behavior in young children—in sharp contrast to most English and American parents in the seventeenth century. Paternal indulgence—anathema to Locke and other child-care advisors—appears far more frequently in the records than concern for strong discipline.[100] William Byrd, for example, stood up for his three-year-old daughter Evie when his wife forced the child "to eat against her will."[101] Thomas Jones seemed almost pleased that his young nephew Frederick "Strutts around the House and is as Noisy as a Bully." Jones's sister-in-law commented on his excessive fondness for his two-year-old son Tom. Tom's boisterous behavior, she noted "is enough to distract all about him except his pappa & to him I believe all his noys is musick if he can't have & do everything he has a mind to he is ready to tare the house down, but if Nanny has opportunitys, she will bring him to better order before you return."[102]

The presence of uncles and aunts, grandparents, and other kin, who sometimes stayed with a family for weeks or months at a time, probably helped lend a permissive tone to Chesapeake family life. Disciplining a child was largely the father's responsibility, and relatives who helped care for children tried to avoid applying punishment. Instilling a sense of shame or guilt in disobedient children came hard for Rachel Cocke, an aunt of the Jones children. Mrs. Cocke had grown so close to one of her nieces, who often visited her, that she could not bring herself to chastise the girl for telling lies, "for all I can do I can't make her think there is any harm in a ly if she is not found out in it, nor can I be angry with her if she does it so innocently." Despite her

[100]To counter the tendency of mothers and servants to become excessively fond of children, Locke emphasized the need for firm paternal discipline. Otherwise children would never learn the essential lesson of self-control. Calhoun, 141.
[101]*Byrd Diary, 1709–12*, 180–81.
[102]Rachel Cocke to Elizabeth Jones, Sept. 17, 1728, JFP. See also Thomas Jones to Elizabeth Jones, Nov. 10, 1736, ibid. For a similar assessment of indulgent child-rearing practices among the "genteel," see Greven, *The Protestant Temperament*, 269–74. Greven makes no regional or chronological distinctions for this rather permissive child-rearing mode, but in fact his evidence suggests that the "genteel" approach to children developed mainly in the southern and middle colonies in the post-1750 period.

fondness for her niece, Mrs. Cocke eventually succeeded in shaming her into compliance: "if she thinks I'm angry in good earnest she's sadly frightened & falls to begin my pardon & promises never to do so again & I do assure her that she is one of the most orderly, best children that ever was borne."[103]

Committed to the principle of self-sufficiency, Chesapeake parents tried to avoid crushing the assertive instincts of children. Like many modern parents, planters employed reason and parental affection to control unruly behavior in their offspring. As a result, parental discipline was often accomplished by negotiation and bargaining rather than by a show of authority. Thus one finds a father like Thomas Jones explaining to his wife how he had managed to win an argument with his ten-year-old son. "Saturday after you went, Tom & I had some difference, but I got the better. Since which he has been a very orderly good Boy and is very good Company."[104] Other parents offered rewards as incentives for orderly conduct. Lewis Joynes asked that his daughter Susanna "be a good girl and I will bring her a Book and a Thimble." Susanna's younger brother Jack, age five, was likewise instructed "to be a good Boy and not go near the Steers and I will not forget his great coat."[105]

The relatively permissive and nurturant environment that parents and kin seem to have provided infants and small children in the eighteenth-century Chesapeake shaped children's perceptions of parental authority and the larger society. The evidence from the personal documents of planter families, fragmentary as it is, suggests that fathers, far from remaining indifferent to young children, entered their affective world very early, perhaps as early as fathers do in modern families.[106] Thus children, espe-

[103]Rachel Cocke to Elizabeth Jones, Sept. 17, 1728, JFP. See also Jean Blair to Mary Blair, Oct. 14, 1769, Horner, *The History of the Blair, Banister and Braxton Families*, 137.

[104]Thomas Jones to Elizabeth Jones, Sept. 17, 1736, JFP.

[105]Lewis Joynes to Anne Joynes, Nov. 4, 1788, "Joynes Family Letters," *VMHB*, LVI (1948), 149–50.

[106]Fred Weinstein and Gerald Platt, *The Wish To Be Free: Society, Psyche and Value Change* (Berkeley and Los Angeles, 1969), 191–92, 295–97.

cially sons, may have absorbed paternal values and feelings of affection long before reaching the age when paternal guidance became more explicit—usually after six or so. Recent psychological studies of parent-child relationships demonstrate that children are more likely to adopt the behavior of nurturant models than those who are indifferent to them.[107] The strong ties of affection and filial duty which bound many children to their parents in the eighteenth-century Chesapeake—often until the parents' deaths—were in part rooted in the close emotional regard that fathers, as well as mothers, displayed toward them during childhood. In short, many planters appear to have gained the lifelong gratitude and respect of their children more from fond paternal treatment than from assertions of authority or coerced obedience.

That fathers took such an early, affectionate interest in their offspring probably encouraged a strong sense of emotional security in their children. Parents seem to have offered themselves more as a collective unit for nurturance and discipline than as a sharply differentiated pair in which mothers provided the affection while fathers distanced themselves as stern disciplinarians. In the absence of clashing male and female child-rearing styles, children could form a clearer, more secure self-identity.[108]

Moreover, the nature of child-rearing in planter families encouraged children very early in life to sense the meaning of the world beyond the immediate family. From infancy on, children were introduced to a network of grandparents, uncles and aunts, and in-laws who helped in the child-rearing process. Young children were not confined at home with their parents, but sent out freely to relatives, whom they sometimes visited for weeks or months at a time. Because of this early experience with other families, children could perceive their parents, and especially

[107]See Philip Slater, "Parental Role Differentiation," in Rose L. Coser, ed., *The Family: Its Structures and Functions* (New York, 1794), 270. See also Justin Aronfreed, "The Concept of Internalization," in David A. Goslin, ed., *Handbook of Socialization Theory and Research* (Chicago, 1969), 283, 307.
[108]See Weinstein and Platt, 178–92.

their fathers, as immediate representatives of a "known community of adults" with whom they could easily identify.[109] A supporting web of kin helped ease the transition from childhood to adulthood in this plantation society.

[109]Slater, 266–71.

Chapter Two

Sex Roles and Female Identity

The unqualified affection parents felt for infants and the sense of common purpose they shared in nurturing and training children into self-reliant young adults took on a different character as their offspring passed out of early childhood. By the time children reached the age of six or seven, child-rearing clearly became a sex-related enterprise. Boys were drawn closer to their fathers, who began to shape their lives more actively; girls remained under the influence of their mothers and a circle of female relatives and friends, who by example and instruction suggested the female model most girls willingly accepted. While men played an important part in imposing on women predetermined female sex roles, it was women, and especially mothers, who actively defined and gave substance to female identity.

Chesapeake families, then, created a distinct place for women within the household and the community. The establishment of a strong, secure sense of gender identity in girls was a major preoccupation of parents throughout the eighteenth century, for a well-ordered family, parents believed, depended above all on a clear understanding of sex roles. Only girls who fully grasped their special familial and cultural responsibilities made acceptable marriage partners and mothers, the two ultimate life goals of most women.

Distinguishing Softness from Strength:
Sex-Role Identification on the Plantation

It is difficult to trace the earliest parental efforts to emphasize sex-related differences in their children. Fond as parents were of their infants, adults rarely set down detailed reflections about newborn children in diaries or letters. Fathers did make distinctions between the economic futures of sons and daughters, however, even before they were born. Pregnancy clauses frequently appeared in wills, making provisions for an unborn child depending on its sex. Tucker Woodson, Sr., of Albemarle County, Virginia, for example, stated in his will of 1779 that if the child his wife then carried was a boy, £3000 was to be placed in trust for him; if it was a girl, one-third that amount was to be set aside.[1] With few exceptions, Chesapeake parents decided early on to entrust the bulk of the family estate—especially family land—to their sons.

Family affection, however, was spread among sons and daughters much more evenly than family wealth. Daughters, as infants and small children, received the same fond attention as their brothers. Mothers and fathers eagerly watched and praised their daughters' physical and cognitive growth.[2] Little girls, like their brothers, often served as a pleasant diversion for their parents and kin, who enjoyed their "agreeable prattling." Both parents joined in nurturing and disciplining their infant sons and daughters and appeared to make few sex-related distinctions between them at this early age.[3]

When children reached the age of five or six, however, parents—especially fathers—began a dramatic segregation of the

[1]Albemarle County Wills, 1779, Book III, 374. All citations to wills refer to the microfilm copy available from the Virginia State Library, Richmond. For other examples of paternal favoritism to unborn males, see the following Albemarle County wills: 1788, IV, 46–47, 1766, II, 212; 1776, III, 374–75. One case was found where a father made no distinction between a prospective boy or girl: 1755, I, 17–19.

[2]See, for example, Frances Tucker to St. George Tucker, March 22, 1780, TCP.

[3]Thomas Tudor Tucker to St. George Tucker, March 26, 1781, and John Randolph to St. George Tucker, July 10, 1781, TCP. See also William Byrd II to Charles Boyle, May 26, 1729, in *Byrd Correspondence*, I, 397.

sexes. At this age boys were taken out of the long robes they and their little sisters had worn since infancy and were put into breeches. This "breeching of a boy" was the first symbolic effort of fathers to begin the important process of breaking the symbiotic bond between a son and his mother. For many boys it may have been their first visible step into the masculine world.[4]

Parents now began to "see" in their children masculine or feminine traits. As observers of child play and growth, adults expressed a clear preference for boys who were strong and physically active and girls who appeared passive but "charming." Any discrepancy in these sex-related attributes was worrisome to parents. Henry Tucker, for instance, boasted of one young boy in his household who had "the Limbs and Strength of an Hercules" but complained that his eight-year-old son Jack was "often mistaken for A girl—he is puny & delicate." Tucker later confided that Jack's "Delicacy" and "Softness" would be more properly found in his sister.[5]

Differentiating the masculine from the feminine world became an abiding concern for parents when children, at around the age of six, began to make their first efforts at independence in their

[4]William Nelson to John Norton, Aug. 14, 1767, in Frances Norton Mason, ed., *John Norton and Sons Merchants of London and Virginia (Being the Papers From Their Counting House for the Years 1750 to 1795)* (Richmond, 1932), 32; Alice Morse Earle, *Child Life in Colonial Days* (New York, 1899), 41–42. Distinguishing children by dress occurred at roughly the same age in elite families in eighteenth-century England. See Randolph E. Trumbach, "The Aristocratic Family in England, 1690–1780: Studies in Childhood and Kinship" (unpub. Ph.D. diss., The Johns Hopkins University, 1972), 23. Because of the dramatic distinction in dress for young sons, Philippe Ariès has called boys "the first specialized children." See his *Centuries of Childhood: A Social History of Family Life,* trans. Robert Baldick (New York, 1962), 58. In almost all societies, children develop an irreversible understanding of their sexual identity by the age of three. But the specific masculine or feminine behaviors associated with their identity can vary considerably. See Lawrence A. Kohlberg, "A Cognitive-Developmental Analysis of Children's Sex-Role Concepts and Attitudes," in E. E. Maccoby, ed., *The Development of Sex Differences* (Stanford, 1966), 82–173; Paul H. Mussen, "Early Sex-Role Development," in David A. Goslin, ed., *Handbook of Socialization Theory and Research* (Chicago, 1969), 707–31.

[5]Henry Tucker to St. George Tucker, Feb. 4, 1780, March 3, 1780, TCP. Recent psychological studies suggest that fathers show more interest in differentiating between the sexes than mothers. See E. E. Maccoby and T. Jacklin, *The Psychology of Sex Differences* (New York, 1975), 348.

home environment.[6] Strong believers in the power of emulation and modeling in bringing up children, parents divided child-rearing responsibilities so that boys and girls would have the parent of the same sex to follow. One can glimpse some aspects of this parental sex-role differentiation in family letters and diaries of the period. On his marriage to a Mrs. Richard in 1769, Richard Henry Lee happily noted that she would be "a most tender attentive and fond mother to my dear little girls"; presumably, he himself would supervise the rearing of his ten- and twelve-year-old sons.[7] In the Robert Carter Nicholas household, Nicholas made decisions for his sons on everything from the clothes they wore to the education they needed; his wife handled similar matters for the girls.[8] And preadolescent sons and daughters seem to have spent much of their leisure time with their fathers and mothers, respectively.[9]

For girls the process of sex-role identification in the family proceeded more smoothly and perhaps more completely than for boys, since girls usually felt a less compelling psychological need to differentiate themselves from their mothers.[10] Indeed, throughout their maturing years, girls remained enclosed in a world of females, usually inhabited by mother, aunts, grand-mother, and female servants, who clarified for young women the meaning of female identity in planter households.

The most powerful ways in which girls learned sex-role behavior was through observing and helping in the daily chores on the plantation. Here young girls first perceived the particular duties of women in a planter's world, duties that for most would

[6]Parental efforts to establish appropriate sex-role behavior in children corresponds roughly with stage three of Erik Erikson's psycho-developmental theory of the "eight ages of man." In this stage of "initiative versus guilt" parents seek to control the growing manipulative powers of the child and instill in him a sense of the proper roles he will play in the world beyond the family. See Erikson, *Childhood and Society,* 2d ed. (New York, 1963), 255–58.

[7]Richard Henry Lee to William Lee, Dec. 17, 1769, James Ballagh, ed., *The Letters of Richard Henry Lee* (New York, 1911), I, 40.

[8]Robert Carter Nicholas to John Norton, July 30, 1773, Mason, ed., *John Norton and Sons,* 340. See also James Parker to Margaret Parker, March 24, 1777, Dec. 29, 1778, Margaret Parker to James Parker, March 2, 1788, PFP.

[9]Francis Taylor Diary, March 14, 1786, UVa; *Byrd Diary, 1739–41,* 50; Richard Grafton to Polly Grafton, Sept. 3, 1737, DP.

[10]Maccoby and Jacklin, 287.

never change throughout their lives. Family labor, like so many other aspects of Chesapeake society, was segregated by sex. Men devoted their time to working outside the home—supervising the slaves, inspecting the crops, or laboring in the fields themselves. Women managed domestic affairs inside and around the "great house." Typically, women and their house servants were charged with such tasks as tending the vegetable garden, caring for the dairy and poultry yards, cooking, cleaning, making clothes, spinning, sewing, and knitting. In wealthy households, female servants performed much of this work while the planter's wife supervised and her daughters helped wherever they were needed.[11] Only on the frontier and in the poorest families did women really share any of the hard physical labor, such as drive a plow or work in the fields.[12]

Women's work, then, although varied, was strictly segregated from men's work in well-to-do eighteenth-century Chesapeake families. Girls, surrounded by women who performed this domestic labor, quickly came to understand the role of women in a plantation society. William Byrd II recognized the socialization process by which girls learned to become dutiful women. Boasting of his daughters' work routine to an English friend, Byrd claimed that "they are every Day up to their Elbows in Housewifery, which will qualify them effectually for useful Wives and if they live long enough, for Notable Women."[13] The observations of

---

[11]See, for example, the work activities of women in the Hollyday family of Maryland: Henry Hollyday to James Hollyday, Feb. 27, July 7, Aug. 25, Oct. 9, 1780, Sept. 19, 1781, HFP. See also FTD, Dec. 24, 1795. The best study of the role of women in colonial America is Julia C. Spruill, *Women's Life and Work in the Southern Colonies* (New York, 1938). See her discussion of female work roles, 74–76.

[12]William Byrd II gave the following report of a well-to-do frontier woman he met in 1710 while working on the dividing line: "She is a very civil woman and shews nothing of ruggedness, or Immodesty in her carriage, yett she will carry a gunn in the woods and kill dear, turkeys, &c., shoot down wild cattle, catch and Tye hoggs, knock down beeves with an ax and perform the most manful Exercises as well as most men in those parts." "Boundary Line Proceedings, 1710," *VMHB*, v (1897), 10.

[13]"Letter to John Lord Bayle, Feb. 2, 1726–7," *VMHB*, xxxii (1924), 30. One traveler in Virginia in 1760 noted that Virginia women spent all their time "sewing and taking care of their families." Andrew Burnaby, *Travels through the Middle Settlements of North America*, 3d ed. (New York, 1970), 58.

Philip Fithian, a tutor at Robert Carter's Nomini Hall in 1773 and 1774, also suggest how the behavior of adult women in the household powerfully shaped female identity in young girls: "It is curious to see the Girls imitating what they see in the great House; sometimes tying a string to a chair & then run buzzing back to imitate the Girls spinning; then getting Rags & washing them without water—Very often they are Knitting with Straws, small round stockings, Garters, etc—Sometimes they get sticks & splinter one end of them for *Brushes* or they call them here *Clamps*, & spitting on part of the floor, they scrubb away with great vigor." The play of the Carter girls indicates that they also grasped early in life (at ages ten and six) their central role as child-bearers. Fithian noted that the girls "by stuffing rags & other Lumber under their Gowns just below their Apron-Strings, were prodigiously Charmed at their resemblance to Pregnant Women."[14]

The sex-segregated upbringing of planters' children was vividly described in one traveler's account of plantation work roles in early eighteenth-century North Carolina: "The mothers took the care of the girls, they were train'd up under them, and not only instructed in the family duties necessary to the sex, but in those accomplishments and genteel manners that are still so visible amongst them, and this descended from Mother to daughter. As the father found the labours of his boys necessary to him, he led them therefore to the woods, and taught the sturdy lad to glory in the stroke he could give with his Ax, in the Trees he felled, and the deer he shot; to conjure the wolfe, the bear and the Alligator; and to guard his habitition from Indian inroads was most justly his pride, and he had reason to boast of it."[15]

The close bond between mother and daughter, established in infancy, was expected to persist through childhood and adolescence, providing girls with a constant guide to proper female

[14]Farish, ed., *Journal and Letters of Fithian*, 249, 254, 68. See also Henry Hollyday to James Hollyday, May 28, Oct. 31, 1783, HFP.

[15]Evangeline W. Andrews, ed., *Journal of a Lady of Quality: Being the Narrative of a Journey from Scotland to the West Indies, North Carolina and Portugal, in The Years 1774 to 1776* (New Haven, 1923), 154–55.

conduct. Landon Carter, for example, understood the importance of deep mother-daughter ties. At the death of Mrs. Robert Carter of Corotoman in February of 1770, Landon Carter worried about the care her daughters would receive from their father and future stepmother. Even after their father remarried, Carter believed, the girls would constantly miss "the *Tender and instructive care* of their natural Mother."[16] While Carter was voicing his concern about the inadequacies of stepmotherhood, his comment also implied that the socialization of girls belonged in the hands of the mother. John Hatley Norton was also convinced that girls needed the guiding presence of a maternal figure. After his wife's death, Norton moved his two teen-age daughters Courtnay and Nancy from Virginia to Philadelphia to live with their aunt, but kept his son Hatty with him in Winchester.[17] That mothers were meant as models for their daughters was obvious to Stephen Bordley, as revealed in the advice he gave to his sister Elizabeth in 1729. After praising her for her reading and "cyphering," and "other things fitting your sex," Stephen emphasized the opportunity and obligation she had to become "a discreet woman of which you have a pattern without going out of your own door whom I hope you will always endeavour to oblige & obey according to what she is, that is, a good & Tender Mother."[18]

Educating "the Delicate Sex"

Sex-related differences in the rearing of children were nowhere more clearly evident than in parental and kin attitudes toward educating boys and girls. In an agricultural society offering few career alternatives to farming, the role of women was relatively

[16]*Carter Diary*, I, 352.
[17]John H. Norton to Edmund Randolph, July 5, 1790, Mason, ed., *John Norton and Sons*, 494.
[18]Stephen Bordley to Elizabeth Bordley, Jan. 22, 1728/9, SBL. See also Frances Norton to John H. Norton, June 27, 1771, Mason, ed., *John Norton and Sons*, 162. In evangelical homes of eighteenth-century New England this mother-daughter bond took on a deeply religious character. See Philip Greven, *The Protestant Temperament: Patterns of Child-Rearing, Religious Experience and the Self in Early America* (New York, 1977), 35–38.

easily defined and maintained through the generations. Women were to serve in marriage as man's helpmate and manager of domestic affairs. To perform these tasks required little if any formal education. In fact, most men believed that women who sought the same educational training as men were somehow defying their "natural" feminine nature. In making arrangements for the education of their children, parents fully accepted the dominance of men in political, economic, and religious life. Mothers as well as fathers recognized that sons, rather than daughters, had to be well educated if they were to be successful.[19] The educational provisions in wills also reveal parental assumptions about the different educational needs of sons and daughters. Some men saw no value in devoting part of their estate to educate their daughters. James Garland of Albermarle County, Virginia, for example, asked that his executor use his financial resources to educate only his male heirs.[20] More often, though, fathers tried to provide some schooling for all their children, but usually stipulated that boys receive a longer education than their sisters. One father before his death in 1764 requested that his sons at age twelve be placed in school for two years and then be apprenticed in some respectable calling. His daughters, on the other hand, were simply to attend school for one year.[21] It is not surprising that literacy rates remained low for Virginia women throughout the eighteenth century, hovering around 50 percent, while over two-thirds of adult males were literate.[22]

[19]See for example, Jane Swann to Thomas Jones, March 8,1756, JFP. The discrepancy in education for men and women in eighteenth-century America is discussed in Joan Hoff Wilson, "The Illusion of Change: Women and the American Revolution," in Alfred F. Young, ed., *The American Revolution: Explorations in the History of American Radicalism* (DeKalb, Ill., 1976), 410–14.

[20]Albemarle County Wills, 1781, III, 387.

[21]See the will of John Foster, Albemarle County Wills, 1764, II, 163–64.

[22]Kenneth A. Lockridge, *Literacy in Colonial New England: An Enquiry into the Social Context of Literacy in the Early Modern West* (New York, 1974), 77, 92. Lockridge found that adult female literacy in New England and Pennsylvania also remained around 50 percent throughout the eighteenth century, while for women in England it was 35 percent. This leads Lockridge to the conclusion that until well into the nineteenth century, "nowhere was women's literacy raised enough to erase an ancient legacy of discrimination" (97).

Sex-typed educational plans were more fully developed among prominent and wealthy men who had the time and means to train their children according to appropriate male and female roles. In these families schooling began earlier and continued longer. Between the ages of six and fourteen, boys learned music, math, writing, and languages, either at a neighborhood school, with a family tutor, or in a few cases, at a private academy in England or France. Those girls who received any schooling at all, on the other hand, were given only a brief instruction in math and rudimentary training in reading and writing until around the age of ten.[23]

Some daughters of learned and wealthy parents could expect a more complete education, but even enlightened fathers (and it is noteworthy that *fathers* nearly always attended to their daughters' intellectual life) eventually guided their maturing girls into culturally acceptable female roles. The early life of Eliza Custis (the granddaughter of Martha Washington) illustrates this point. As a young girl growing up in Virginia in the 1780s, Eliza had been taught spelling and reading by her mother and cousin. After her mother remarried, Eliza's new stepfather attempted to broaden her education. He found her a private tutor and pushed Eliza to begin reading more sophisticated material, such as *The Spectator.* But all along her stepfather seemed to recognize that serious intellectual training was useful only for boys, for he told Eliza's instructor that she "was an extraordinary child & would if a *Boy,* make a Brilliant figure." Eliza's relatively advanced education came to an abrupt halt when she insisted on learning Greek and Latin. Both her stepfather and her tutor refused, declaring that "women ought not to know those things," and suggested that she concentrate instead on writing, arithmetic, music and needlework.[24]

---

[23]Farish, ed., *Journal and Letters of Fithian,* 48, 168; Spruill, 206–7; "Journal of James Gordon," *WMQ,* 1st ser., xi (1903), 100. Girls may have lamented the educational advantages their brothers enjoyed. See Betty Pratt to Keith William Pratt, Aug. 10, 1732, JFP.
[24]"Eliza Custis, Self-Portrait, 1808," *VMHB,* lxi (1953), 93–94.

Thomas Jefferson was interested in producing a well-educated daughter, as long as she understood her prime responsibility as a domestic manager. Jefferson constantly admonished his daughter Martha, as he did young men, against idleness and ennui and encouraged her to develop habits of self-discipline in her studies and her work. He even suggested that she try to conquer Livy's works by herself. Despite the inquiring frame of mind he urged Martha to cultivate, Jefferson stressed that she protect herself from apathy mainly through a variety of "feminine" subjects—music, drawing, and dancing. Above all, she needed to learn "the needle and domestic economy," for the mistress of the family, Jefferson pointed out, must be able to sew if she expects to direct the servants' work.[25]

Thomas Mann Randolph argued even more explicitly for the distinct educational needs of women. Randolph firmly believed that there were certain "departments of learning which particularly belong to females," such as drawing. Only a little training in the sciences was acceptable for "an accomplished woman," but "great depth in them is not only unnecessary but even disagreeable." Philosophy or speculation was also an inappropriate female pursuit; rather "the elegant and agreeable occupation of Poetry and the fine arts surely become the delicate sex more." Above all, a woman's education should fit her sensitive emotional structure, Randolph insisted, and "the refined & soft pleasure" of artistic training "seem calculated by nature for them to enjoy." But little of this female education in the more "delicate" subjects was to have any intrinsic value for women, Randolph suggested. Instead, becoming an accomplished lady was important to a woman only to the extent that it helped her win the complete "approbation" of discerning men.[26]

Clearly the real education of girls in well-to-do households came during the development of feminine "accomplishments" outlined by Randolph and others. While boys continued their

[25]Thomas Jefferson to Martha Jefferson, March 28, 1787, April 11, 1790, in Sarah N. Randolph, ed., *The Domestic Life of Thomas Jefferson* (New York, 1939), 115–16, 181.
[26]Thomas Mann Randolph to Ann Cary Randolph, May 7, 1788, NTP.

schooling or served out apprenticeships, girls, beginning around age twelve or thirteen, worked on refining their skills in music or dancing.[27] The point of such training was to endow young women with the charm and grace they would need to attract genteel suitors. Dancing was considered particularly useful for developing elegant qualities. Parents sent their daughters to dancing school and mothers regularly organized dances or "balls" for girls and their friends.[28] Young men were eager to learn dancing too for it was an important form of social contact between the sexes.[29] Maria Tilghman understood the significance of accomplished dancing for women in meeting and impressing young men. Maria was excited about taking dancing lessons from a "Monsieur Le Grave" in the spring of 1780, for he taught dancing "in the utmost perfection" and "promises to bestow the Graces on all that will put themselves under his tuition," which apparently cost six dollars. Nothing, Maria insisted, would prevent her from "acquiring airs and graces enough to make a splendid figure at the Assemblies we are to have this winter."[30]

Underlying these earnest efforts among women to attain grace and charm was the deeply held belief of both sexes that masculine and feminine virtue were fundamentally different, though complementary. Rules for proper conduct were based on the assumption that men and women possessed opposing temperaments, which, like magnets, provided the attractive force between the

---

[27]*Carter Diary,* I, 336. See also ibid., 553. Planters seemed to have viewed the transition from girlhood to womanhood as beginning around the age of twelve or thirteen. See Abraham Tilghman II to Richard Tilghman III, May 1, 1740, "Letters between the English and American Branches of the Tilghman Family, 1697–1764," *MHM,* xxxii (1938), 162.

[28]See John Hanson to Philip Thomas, July 23, 1782, Hanson Papers, Maryland Historical Society; Farish, ed., *Journal and Letters of Fithian,* 47; and Frances Norton to John H. Norton, June 27, 1771, Mason, ed., *John Norton and Sons,* 162. Andrew Buraby observed that dancing was "almost the only amusement [women] partake of." Burnaby, 58.

[29]See Burnaby, ibid.; Farish, ed., *Journal and Letters of Fithian,* 177; and Jane Carson, *Colonial Virginians at Play* (Williamsburg, Va., 1965), 21–35. For a perceptive view of the symbolic importance of leisure activities among the Virginia gentry, see Rhys Isaac, "Evangelical Revolt: The Nature of the Baptists Challenge to the Traditional Order in Virginia, 1765 to 1775," *WMQ,* 3d ser., xxxi (1974), 352.

[30]Maria Tilghman to Anna Maria Tilghman, April 9, 1780, HFP.

sexes. For women this assumption meant that they were always to present themselves through their natural beauty and delicate nature as man's agreeable companion. To a few social critics, this view of female sex roles created problems. In one issue of *The Spectator* in 1711, Richard Steele lamented the typical parental expectations of their daughters. "To make her an agreeable Person is the main Purpose of her Parents... and from this general Folly of Parents we owe our present numerous Race of Coquets."[31] Nevertheless, most parents throughout the eighteenth century, no matter how enlightened, tried to shape their daughters' character in relation to the masculine world. Jefferson, for example, advised his daughter Martha to dress herself meticulously before meeting men. He expected her to wear clothes "neat, whole and properly put on" and always to be clean and fully dressed around the house. "Nothing is so disgusting to our sex as a want of cleanliness and delicacy in yours." For Martha to have been seen by "any gentleman" with "a pin amiss, or any other circumstance of neatness wanting" was revolting to her father.[32]

The notion of the unequal but complementary nature of masculine and feminine virtues was made abundantly clear by Lord Halifax in *The Lady's New Year's Gift or Advice to a Daughter:* "You must first lay it down for a Foundation in general, that there is *Inequality* in the *Sexes,* and that for the better Oeconomy of the World, the Men, who were to be the Law Givers, had the better share of *Reason* bestow'd upon them; by which means your Sex is the better prepar'd for the *Compliance* that is necessary for the better performance of those *Duties* which seem to be most properly assign'd to it. ... We are made of differing *Tempers,* that our Defects may the better be Mutually Supplied: Your *Sex* wanteth our *Reason* for your *Conduct,* and our *Strength* for your *Protection;* Ours wanteth your *Gentleness* to soften and to entertain us."[33]

[31]Daniel McDonald, ed., *Joseph Addison and Richard Steele, selected essays from "The Tattler," "The Spectator" and "The Guardian"* (Indianapolis, 1973), 235–36.
[32]Thomas Jefferson to Martha Jefferson, Dec. 22, 1783, Randolph, *The Domestic Life of Thomas Jefferson,* 71.
[33]Halifax's book, published in London in 1688, went through fifteen editions between 1688 and 1765. See Spruill, 216.

In almost all the female advice literature beginning in the late seventeenth century, women were reminded, largely by condescending men, that God had "drawn a distinction" between masculine and feminine natures, making that "comely for the one Sex, which often is not (at least in the same degree) for the other." Books such as *The Ladies Calling* (1673) and Dr. John Gregory's *A Father's Legacy to his Daughters* (1774), which were popular in literate households of the southern colonies, explicitly outlined the distinct feminine virtues. These authors exhorted women to develop their natural traits of modesty, meekness, compassion, affability, and piety. The central virtue for the accomplished lady was modesty, which one writer claimed was "the most indispensable requisite of a woman; a thing so essential and natural to the sex, that every the least declination from it, is proportionate receding from Womanhood." Meekness was appropriate for women because God had placed them in a subordinate position to men. Women displayed compassion and piety due to their "native Tenderness" and because their absence from public life allowed them to focus their energies on the smaller domestic world. Men, on the other hand, worked in more competitive political and economic arenas, which distracted them from spiritual and altruistic pursuits.[34]

An essential dimension of proper female conduct and personality was what might be termed a becoming passivity—that is, the development of a compliant nature, but always with an "agreeable" disposition. Most married women tried to behave this way around their husbands; communicating this sex-role expectation to their daughters was thus often an expression of personal experience. In 1770 Mary Ambler of Virginia transcribed the following portion of a "Sermon to a Young Woman" for her daughter, whom she hoped would read and "observe it well all her Life": "If to Your natural softness You join that christian

---

[34]Richard Allestree, *The Ladies Calling* (London, 1673); Wilson, 427–29. The reading material of one teenaged girl from Virginia, which included Dr. Gregory's "Legacy to his Daughter," reflected this belief in distinctly "female" traits and virtues. See "The Frances Baylor Hill Diary of 'Hillsborough,' King and Queen County, Virginia (1797)," in *Early American Literature Newsletter*, II (1967), 12, 15, 19, 45.

meekness ... both together will not fail, with the assistance of proper reflection and friendly advice, to accomplish you in the best & truest kind of breeding. You will not be in danger of putting your-selves forward in company, of contradicting bluntly, of asserting positively, of debating obstinately, of affecting a superiority to any present, of engrossing the discourse, of listening to yourselves with apparent satisfaction, of neglecting what is advanced by others, or of interrupting them without necessity."[35]

Male and female sex roles in the eighteenth-century Chesapeake, at least within well-to-do families, developed about as rigidly as Halifax and others suggested they should. Differing concepts of masculine and feminine virtues fused with discrete sex roles in family work to create an emotional and physical segregation of men and women on the plantation. Planters lived an active public life as domineering masters, overseers of the plantation economy, and leaders in religious and political spheres. They stood as the arbiters of culture and centers of authority within the family and the community. Women, on the other hand, served as a counterpoint to man's forceful public character, for their existence was circumscribed by the relatively private world of the "great house," to which their peculiarly soft and delicate nature presumably brought tranquility and charm.[36] It was not an instinct for religious life, then, that gave women special value in the home, as some would suggest by the early nineteenth century; rather, a woman's unique role lay in her lifelong commitment to pleasing the men around her and to ensuring a harmonious, stable family.[37]

[35]"The Diary of M. Ambler, 1770," *VMHB*, XLV (1937), 170.

[36]This polarization of male and female work roles has a psychological dimension as well. Erik Erikson has theorized that male and female personalities reflect differences in anatomy as well as in socialization. Linking genital morphology to personality, Erikson suggests that women emphasize "inner space"—vulnerability to fear, compassion, strong emotions—while men tend toward an "outer space"—a more intrusive, impulsive mode of behavior. "Womanhood and the Inner Space," in Erik Erikson, *Identity, Youth and Crisis* (New York, 1968), 261–94.

[37]Barbara Welter, "The Cult of True Womanhood, 1820–1860," *American Quarterly*, XVIII (1966), 151–74. After 1800 many southern women, as well as men,

The Struggle over Passions:
Women and Sex in the Planter Mind

Although women were considered by nature passive and delicate creatures, they were also perceived as emotionally volatile and given to shifting, unpredictable moods—both of which were worrisome qualities to men devoted to steadiness and sobriety in character and feelings. Women were often chided as "silly creatures," too irrational and impractical to participate in the pragmatic world of men.[38] And to some men it was clear that women made strategic use of their flights of passion in personal relationships. William Byrd II withdrew from an emotional scene with an overseer's wife "for fear of being persuaded by her Tears which women have always ready to command." Believing that his own wife was also prone to emotional excesses, Byrd—always the domineering patriarch—felt obliged to control her outbursts. "Female Passions," he wrote, "require to be managed sometimes, to confine them in Bounds & keep them like a high-Mettled Horse, from running away with their owner."[39] Landon Carter echoed this feeling years later, claiming that "Passi[on] is a [danger]ous Thing in a woman especially, for they have a vast fund of tears to make a gust." Prone to hyperbole and irrational displays of emotion, women, it was thought, occupied one extreme of an emotional continuum, while men silently guarded the other.[40]

The emotional gap separating the sexes in the Chesapeake widened to a chasm in matters of sexual life. Eighteenth-century man prized above all his commitment to sensible, rational affections toward the opposite sex; erotic passions had to be carefully regulated for the stability of society and family. Women, however,

---

became engulfed in what was clearly a more religious world view. See Jan Grimmelmann, "This World and the Next: Religion, Death, Success, and Love in Jefferson's Virginia" (unpub. Ph.D. diss., University of Michigan, 1977).

[38] *Carter Diary*, I, 369.

[39] *Byrd Diary, 1709–12*, 285. See also ibid., 322, 291; William Byrd to Sister Otway, June 30, 1736; William Byrd to Cousin Taylor, July 28, 1728; "Letters of the Byrd Family," *VMHB*, xxxvi (1928), 216, 44.

[40] *Carter Diary*, II, 1089; *Virginia Gazette*, April 18, 1755.

persistently and deviously undercut this "reasonable" under-standing of male-female relationships, many men believed. For in the minds of men all the dangerous sexual passions were lodged uncontrollably in the female psyche. Coy, mysterious, and unpredictable, women appeared to men as a sexual threat.[41] As a result, fathers warned sons to steer clear of beautiful wom-en, who were seen as entrapments. In 1760 Charles Carroll ex-plained to his son that women should be important to him only insofar as they could "soften & Polish" his manners; he should avoid any "intimacy or familiarity with the fair Sex." Charles Carroll, Jr., apparently understood his father's view, for he con-fessed that beautiful women "are always the most powerful, at least with me. I would defy an ugly woman endowed with the sagacity of a sphinx ever to entrap me."[42]

Eighteenth-century planters were of course exceedingly mind-ful of protecting their wealth as well as their emotional health from extravagant, cunning women. One man cautioned a friend about the "power of that sex," claiming that some women "are nothing better than Moth in a garment, for they not only ruin Fortune but Constitutions, that greatest blessing."[43] Landon Car-ter, in his typically petulant manner, insisted that women had always threatened men with their sexuality. "I do believe women have nothing in the general in view, but the breeding contests at home. It began with poor Eve and ever since then has been so much of the devil in woman." Carter later complained that he had never seen "a more treacherous, interprising, Perverse, and hellish Genius than is to be met with in a A Woman."[44] And Jefferson worried about unrestrained female sex drives, which he believed could only be subdued by marriage.[45]

[41]See Peter Gay, *The Enlightenment: An Interpretation: The Science of Freedom* (2 vols., New York, 1969), II, 33–34, 199–205.

[42]Charles Carroll of A to Charles Carroll of C, August 30, 1758, Charles Carroll of C to Charles Carroll of A, Jan. 29, 1760, CARP.

[43]William Reynolds to George Norton, Sept. 9, 1771, Mason, ed., *John Norton and Sons*, 187.

[44]*Carter Diary*, II, 713, 1103. For another view of women as competitive breed-ers, see William Byrd I to Warham Horsmander, June 5, 8, 1685, *Byrd Correspond-ence*, I, 39, 43.

[45]Winthrop Jordan, *White over Black: American Attitudes toward the Negro, 1550–1812* (New York, 1968), 462–64.

Men and women had constructed a world in which outside of marriage there was no legitimate means for the expression of sexual desires. But men could not always deny the existence of these feelings. Thus, fearful of their own ungovernable passions, men often projected their largely suppressed sexual feelings onto women, to whom they were so clearly attracted. As a result, male-female relationships were frequently adversary ones, reflecting the emotional estrangement between the sexes.

The emotional segregation of men and women is evident in the rather distant manner in which girls responded to their male admirers. Reared almost exclusively among women, adolescent girls may have found boys a somewhat alien group. Consequently, relationships during courtship were often stilted and formal, with an elaborate code of grandiloquent "addresses" and "favors." This came about largely because the separation of sons and daughters in the family since childhood made informal and relaxed contact between young men and women exceedingly difficult.[46]

With such emotional differences separating the sexes, it is perhaps not surprising that young men and women often clashed during courtship. Some women, in fact, were quick to criticize the men who sought their "favors." Maria Tilghman of Maryland wrote of one such instance in which she refused a man's bold addresses. "The Creature has actually taken it into his head that he is handsome and because I have happened to be of a different opinion, and have occasionally given him a few Lectures on decorum and propriety, he has called me a prude, and twenty other shocking names." Maria attributed her suitor's arrogance to "the effects of a disappointed vanity."[47] Elizabeth Cocke gave an admirer "a very pathetical reproof" for his "ill Conduct" toward her.[48] And one man's intentions were stifled by a girl who was

[46]For examples of grandiloquent "addresses" see the following: Joseph Nourse to Maria Bull, Sept. 22, Dec. 27, 1783, June 17, Feb. 10, 1784, NFP; Jonathan Boucher to Mrs. James, March 9, 1767, "Letters of Jonathan Boucher," *MHM*, VII (1912), 341–43; St. George Tucker to Frances Tucker, Jan. 15, 1778, March 2, 31, 1778, TCP.

[47]Maria Tilghman to Anna Maria Tilghman, 1780, HFP.

[48]Thomas Jones to Elizabeth Cocke, n.d., JFP.

"pettishly severe & keenly poignant in her Sarcasms," which permitted him only a "sneaking kind of Regard for her."[49]

The most extreme form of these conflicting temperaments between the sexes in courtship suggested, on the one hand, an arrogant and exaggerated masculine ethos projected by young men, and, on the other, a coquettish but easily offended demeanor in women. Unable to communicate comfortably with the opposite sex, young men sometimes tried to win favor through elaborate displays of daring and strength. A particularly revealing illustration of this clashing style among young men and women is contained in the diary of Frances Baylor Hill of King and Queen County, Virginia, in 1797. While visiting her cousins, Francis and Tom Taylor, she was introduced to two young men from Kentucky, apparently relatives of her cousin. Immediately she was struck by the boys' brash conduct around her. "I never saw two people have more assurance in my life than they had." Much to her dismay, Frances and another cousin, Betty Taylor, were in for a couple of raucous nights with their escorts, Tom Taylor and Billy and John Meaux. In one memorable evening the girls

> play'd at cards with the gentlemen romp'd and play'd a great deal more than I wish'd but they were so wild & full of their tricks they would not let us rest. Miss Betty the two Meaux's Tom Ta——r & myself walk'd to the mill and then Tom Ta——or would insist on our going to Beargarden to drink tea with him, we went and had a very disagreeable tiresome walk. The gentlemen made an old Negro woman drunk and then she turn'd out and shew'd Capers dancing & mineuvering about, we staid an hour or two and return'd, Tom Ta——r had his horse got for us to ride but we were affraid as he was very gaily, John Meaux shot a gun directly over my head and frighten'd me very much, when we got back found the Doctr there Billy Meaux wear'd me allmost out of my life I never was so tir'd of any body." ["The Diary of Frances Baylor Hill," 21–22]

If that first evening of carousing slowed Frances down, the next day finished her off. In her second—and last—day together with

[49]Thomas Davis to St. George Tucker, Oct. 3, 1779, TCP.

the Meaux boys and Tom Taylor, she reported that John Meaux sang a song "over & over about an hundred & fifty times," while Tom Taylor "was intoxicated" and "pull'd & holl'd me about in such a manner that I wish'd I had never seen him, nothing would do but we must dance Billy play'd on the Fiddle Miss Betty on the Harpsicord, at it we went dancing away as hard as we could. . . . "[50]

In all of these instances we have described, more was involved than simply acting out a courtship ritual in which men made bold advances and women remained as aloof as possible, for rituals such as these were rooted in important social experiences.[51] It was the widely divergent socialization of boys and girls—which emphasized independent action and forceful participation in the world for males and passive, "agreeable" deportment for females—that led to relationships in which spontaneity and the open expression of emotional regard were difficult.[52]

Intimacy and friendship among girls and adult women, on the other hand, developed in an easier and more natural fashion. The strong emotional ties between women were forged out of a positive, lifelong contact with each other. Since childhood girls had grown up alongside their mother and other women, learning the duties of housewifery and motherhood and a variety of domestic skills. Traveling to dances and balls for entertainment, attending weddings, caring for other female kin in sickness and sharing their sorrow in death, helping in the continuing female cycle of pregnancies, lyings-in, and births, and above all, simply visiting other women—all of these activities helped to shape distinct female identities and bound women together in intimate friendships that often persisted after marriage.

[50]"The Diary of Frances Baylor Hill," 21–22.

[51]For a treatment of male-female relationships as simply ritualistic, see Edmund S. Morgan, *Virginians at Home: Family Life in the Eighteenth Century* (Charlottesville, Va., 1952), 35–37.

[52]In a broader study of sex roles in nineteenth-century America, Carroll Smith-Rosenberg has found this same link between divergent socialization processes for boys and girls and subsequent emotional estrangement between the two sexes by adolescence. See "The Female World of Love and Ritual: Relations between Women in Nineteenth-Century America," *Signs: Journal of Women in Culture and Society,* I (1975), 1–30.

It is difficult to determine exactly when strong female friendships became common in Chesapeake society. Evidence about these female alliances begins in scattered form during the latter third of the eighteenth century and proliferates in the early nineteenth century.[53] It is likely that the same phenomenon was occurring much earlier in the eighteenth century, but because there are very few extant diaries or letters of women (sources essential for investigating this question) until well into the century, it is impossible to establish this for certain.

Strikingly absent from the correspondence of female friends was any strong concern for men. Sometimes girls traded stories about prospective beaux or men seen at a recent ball, but most of these friendships between young women were characterized by the communication of mutual affection.[54] For instance, a girl from New Kent County, Virginia, identifying herself as "P Davenport" wrote longingly to her friend Elizabeth Pelham in May of 1791, imploring Elizabeth to consider her as a deep friend, "one who sincerely wishes your happiness, who can enter into and highly interest herself, in all that concerns you, in your every Sentiment, and who wou'd with transport do anything in her pow'r to serve you." "P" insisted on a relationship with Elizabeth that was devoted to an "affection of the Heart." In defining this friendship, "P" wrote with a directness of expression few girls could have managed with men. Elizabeth was told "if you love me, write very soon, and if you wish for my constant affection—be invariable in your for me—for never can I; 'tis not in my Nature, to love *anybody*, that does not love me."[55] Eighteen-year-old Lucy Lee Orr of Chantilly, Virginia, was left in a state of melancholy over the distance that separated her and her friend Polly. Writing in 1782, Lucy noted that it had been "a year since the morning I parted from you and how long, very long will it be before I clasp

[53]Rosenberg, 10, dates the emergence of close female friendships to around 1760.
[54]Molly Tilghman to Polly Tilghman, May 8, 1789, "Molly and Hetty Tilghman Letters," *MHM*, XXI (1926), 239, and P. Davenport to Elizabeth Pelham, Feb. 24, 1791, May 17, 1791, "Pelham Letters," *WMQ*, 2d ser., IX (1929), 265–66.
[55]P. Davenport to Elizabeth Pelham, May 17, 31, 1791, ibid., 266, 268.

you to my breast. I am deprived even the consolation of hearing from you. Adieu, my love."[56]

Religion also served to bind young women in deep, affectionate relationships. Indeed, the spiritual often blended with the sensual in forming lasting bonds of friendships between women. These kinds of relationships became more pronounced after 1800, but we can glimpse the religious dimension in the closeness of two South Carolina girls, Martha Lauren and Elizabeth Brailsford, whose correspondence is one of the few among Southern girls before 1800 to survive. In her late teens or early twenties in the 1770s, Martha became profoundly disturbed when Elizabeth moved away from Charleston. "I never knew how much I loved you," she wrote. "The Loss of your company pains me exceedingly"; "From my first acquaintance I have been attached to you, and every month has beheld you growing in my esteem; but in the last week which I spent with you, you have entirely finished the conquest, and imprinted on my soul your beloved image, in characters so indelible, that neither time nor absence can ever erase them." That the two girls shared a common bond in Christianity which deepened their relationship was uppermost in Martha's mind in her rhapsodic letter to Elizabeth: "I trust too, that our regard for each other is founded on a noble basis; and that united by Christian bonds, our friendship will be eternal. I glory in an intimacy with one who seems so sincere, a lover of the Lord Jesus, and with whose conversation I have been so often delighted and refreshed; and the very thought of our Treading together the narrow way that leads to bliss, rejoices me beyond expression."[57]

Many of these female friendships continued after marriage, especially during the early nineteenth century. Carroll Smith-Rosenberg, in a very perceptive study, has suggested that the close emotional and sensual relationships between women made

[56]Lucy Lee Orr, *Journal of a Young Lady in Virginia, 1782* (Baltimore, 1871), 34–35.

[57]Martha Laurens to Elizabeth Brailsford, n.d. (sometime in the 1770s), in David Ramsay, *Memoirs of the Life of Martha Laurens Ramsay*, 2d ed. (Charleston, S.C., 1812), 217–18.

it difficult for them to adjust to marriage, since they remained rather distant and formal in their dealings with men.[58] Little evidence exists from the eighteenth-century Chesapeake to shed light on such a matter, but the experience of Lucy Orr indicates that female friendships were more than momentary alliances of adolescent girls. The recent marriage of Lucy's close friend Hannah had disturbed Lucy, who felt she was losing Hannah to her new husband. Lucy explained to her friend Polly how they should not allow marriage to disturb the life of their friendship. "This said Matrimony alters us mightely. I am afraid it alienates us from every one else. It is, I fear, the bane of Female friendship. Let it not be with ours, my Polly, if we should ever Marry."[59]

"A Kind of Lethregie": Adult Women and Plantation Life

The character of the female experience in the eighteenth-century Chesapeake did not significantly change once girls made the transition to adulthood. In a sense, girls were already little women at an early age, for their domestic apprenticeship, begun in childhood, trained them for the same adult responsibilities.[60] Moreover, women had always been defined relationally—as someone's daughter or sister—and marriage simply enlarged their kin-based status. Having grown up surrounded by other females, adult women continued the process of female socialization, helping *their* nieces, daughters, and grandchildren to understand the duties and cultural role of women in a plantation society.

An important responsibility of adult women, in addition to their own domestic work, was to aid their female friends and relatives in times of sickness. In the early stages of illness women usually treated each other and provided the emotional reassurance and encouragement for recovery. More important, women

[58]Rosenberg, 20–21, 28.
[59]Orr, 28.
[60]Ariès, 332.

were frequently called on to manage the almost exclusively female business of lying-in, childbirth, and recovery.[61]

In their leisure hours, most women—whether wives, widows, or spinsters—continued to seek out other female friends and relatives for companionship and emotional support. Sisters, cousins, nieces and aunts, mothers and daughters, as well as friends, frequently visited each other for days, even weeks at a time. When a man was away from home for court days or to see business friends, his wife often left the plantation to stay with a sister or daughter. Elderly women (those whose children had grown up and left home, as well as widows) devoted much of their time to maintaining contact with their expanding network of kin.[62]

For some women, traveling to see other women became almost a daily preoccupation. Elizabeth Dulaney, for example, wrote enthusiastically of the large number of female friends she saw in eastern Maryland. "As soon as my breakfast is clearly down my throat away I go—and generally make an engagement to spend the Evening before I return so that I am very little at home unless with company." Another Maryland woman was also pleased with her "very agreeable Society" of women "that I can gossip with by the Hour."[63]

Men seemed to understand the female need for sociability. Theodore Bland, Jr., knew that his wife Patsy spent her time in visits ("both of friendship & ceremony") to close friends and relatives. When Bland's sister Frances Tucker was left alone at home while her husband St. George was fighting during the Revolution, he hoped she could find several of her friends to

[61]See, for example, *Byrd Diary, 1709–12*, 404; Molly Tilghman to Polly Tilghman, April 13, 1786, Jan. 29, 1788, "Molly and Hetty Tilghman Letters," 138, 232; and Martha Jefferson Carr to Lucy Terrell, Aug. 9, 1794, CTFP. See also Edward M. Riley, ed., *The Journal of John Harrower* (New York, 1963), 124.

[62]Susan Thompson to Suzanne Lewis, Jan. 15, 1798, Lewis Papers, University of Virginia Library; FTD, May 29, Sept. 19, 1797; *Byrd Diary, 1709–12*, 490–91; Molly Tilghman, April 3, 1785, April 13, 1786, "Letters of Molly and Hetty Tilghman," 35, 137; Elizabeth Tucker to St. George Tucker, Nov. 25, 1779, Aug. 14, 1789, TCP.

[63]Elizabeth Dulaney to Catherine Belt, Nov. 9, 1798; Catherine Belt to George Fitzhugh, Sept. 4, 1792, DP.

"amuse" her at Bizarre plantation. "Cou'd you persuade your Friends who used to *flock* to you at Matoax to visit you at Bizzar?"[64] David Meade, who moved his family from Virginia to Kentucky in 1795, realized that he had to do something to help his wife and daughters overcome their longing for their former home. He decided to rent a place in Lexington where he could "fix our females for a few weeks in as large a society as possible to divert their thoughts" from what "they had left behind in Virginia."[65]

What men and women both recognized was that regular visiting among women was sometimes necessary to relieve the tedium of plantation life. Often isolated miles away from other plantations, some women attempted to cure their "indifference" and boredom by traveling to see female friends. In May of 1787 Mary Dulaney complained of "a Kind of Lethregie" that she hoped to alleviate with a trip to Annapolis to see three married women she knew.[66] Others tried to absorb themselves in the details of domestic duties. Elizabeth Maynadier commiserated with a friend about "the feelings of listlessness & lassitude" that women experienced on the plantation. But she had to guard against falling into a "resignation," she claimed, and advised her friend "to busy yourself as much as possible in the House, Garden &c. it is a matter of great consequence to have the attention always engaged." Concentrating on her daily work responsibilities saved Elizabeth from ennui. "The highest of my employment is setting Hens & the highest of my ambition to have them hatch well." The whole point was to "have some object in pursuit, something that engages the present time & prevents

[64]Theodore Bland, Jr., to Patsy Bland, Nov. 1777, BP; Theodore Bland, Jr., to Frances Tucker, March 30, 1781, TCP.

[65]David Meade to Joseph Prentis, 1796, WPC.

[66]Mary Dulaney to George Fitzhugh, May 3, 1787, DP. For other evidence of women battling boredom on the plantation, see P. Davenport to Elizabeth Pelham, May 17, 1791, "Pelham Letters," 267; Frances Tucker to St. George Tucker, Oct. 14, 1781, TCP; Catherine Belt to Polly Fitzhugh, Nov. 2, 1794, DP; Margaret Saunders to Margaret Parker, April 17, 1785, PFP. Even urban life could mean idleness for gentry wives. See "The Diary of Mrs. William Thornton, 1800," *Columbia Historical Society Records*, x (1907), 113–14.

either too much retrospect of the past or anticipation of the future."[67]

From "Widowarchy" to Patriarchy

The polarized male-female world of Chesapeake society described here had not always been so sharply defined. Indeed, the contrast between the seventeenth and eighteenth centuries reveals important changes in the nature of sex roles and female identity. The eighteenth-century Chesapeake, in fact, was in some ways peculiarly suited to the development of distinct male and female gender identities.

Perhaps the most visible social difference in Virginia and Maryland during the eighteenth century was the equalization of the sex ratio (usually defined as the number of males for every 100 females). Because of the largely male stream of white immigrants in the early Chesapeake, women remained in short supply throughout the seventeenth century, as males often outnumbered females by as much as three or four to one. Women, consequently, possessed a scarcity value that gave them considerable bargaining power with men in the marriage market. Moreover, by outliving men and acquiring their wealth through successive marriages, women created a form of "widowarchy" in the seventeenth-century Chesapeake.[68] By the early eighteenth century, however, when the influx of black slaves replaced the dwindling supply of white male servants, the sexes became more balanced. In Maryland the sex ratio fell to 157.2 in 1704, and by 1755 it was down to 113.3. Virginia experienced roughly the same equalization of the sex ratio during the eighteenth century.[69] With

[67]Eliza Maynadier to Catherine Belt, Aug. 9, May 14, 1786, DP.

[68]Edmund S. Morgan, *American Slavery, American Freedom: The Ordeal of Colonial Virginia* (New York, 1975), 407; Roger Thompson, *Women in Stuart England and America* (London, 1974), 36–39. The term "widowarchy" is from Morgan, 165–67. For an example of strategic remarriage by aging women in seventeenth-century Virginia, see the letters of William Byrd I to Nordest Rand, Warham Horsmanden, and Thomas Gower, March 31, 1685, and same to Thomas Gower, March 31, 1685, *Byrd Correspondence*, I, 32, 35–36.

[69]Allan Kulikoff, "Tobacco and Slaves: Population, Economy, and Society in Eighteenth-Century Prince George's County, Maryland" (unpub. Ph.D. diss., Brandeis University, 1975), 36.

the emergence of a balanced sex ratio in the eighteenth-century Chesapeake, women lost their earlier advantages in marriage opportunities and the accumulation of property.

Women's role in family and economic life was also shaped by changes in life expectancy and labor in the colonial Chesapeake. A high mortality rate in seventeenth-century Virginia and Maryland, which cut short the lives of most men and women by their mid-forties, produced widespread early parental loss and prevented the development of elaborate kin networks. In this high-mortality region, grandparenthood was a rare phenomenon. With the early death of fathers, seventeenth-century Chesapeake women had an important unifying role in what were often very complex households of orphans and stepchildren. And in the absence of a permanent and plentiful labor supply, women performed valuable plantation work. Family farms in the seventeenth century (except among a very few wealthy families) were true economic partnerships operated almost equally by husbands and wives, which gave women significant political and economic authority within the family.

Increasing life expectancies by the mid-eighteenth century, however, diminished the familial influence of women. As men and women survived into their mid- to late fifties, large kin groups grew up around families and longer-lived fathers helped nurture many of their children to maturity. Women, then, no longer held families together singlehandedly as they often did in the seventeenth century. Fathers, grandparents, uncles and aunts, and close friends shared child-rearing tasks with parents.

Moreover, the large-scale importation of African slaves after 1700 provided middle- and upper-class families with much of the work force needed on the plantation. Consequently, except among the poorest families, women's work became more narrowly defined as domestic labor (which they shared with house servants), as women were physically confined to the home. Small family farms dependent on the active participation of both spouses and their children had become for many families by the mid-eighteenth century large plantation communities dominated by planter patriarchs and worked almost exclusively by black slaves. Gradually stripped of economic and familial authority in the household, the eighteenth-century planter's wife increasingly served as an ornament to her husband and family.[70]

These changing demographic and economic conditions also reinforced certain psychological aspects of female identity in the eighteenth-century Chesapeake. The increasing likelihood that fathers and mothers would survive to see their children to maturity allowed parents to exert a longer shaping influence in their childrens' lives. Thus, the emotional bonds between mother and daughter may have become more solidly established throughout childhood and adolescence, providing girls with a stronger personal identification with their mother. In psychological terms, girls whose mothers were around them during all their maturing years and beyond could more fully internalize a feminine ego structure.[71] The enlarged kin network that grew out of the lengthening life spans in the eighteenth century created for the first time an intergenerational world of relatives who helped socialize children. Hence, girls from infancy were embedded in a network of relationships with other female servants and kin—grandmothers, aunts, cousins, and sisters—whose presence near or in the household also accentuated sex-role learning. Girls in eighteenth-century Virginia and Maryland, then, came to accept a more limited role in family and economic life than had seventeenth-century women, but in the process deepened their ties to other women and became more self-consciously "ladies" in an increasingly male-dominated world.[72]

[70]I am drawing on the perceptive essay of Lois G. Carr and Lorena S. Walsh, "The Planter's Wife: The Experience of White Women in Seventeenth-Century Maryland," *WMQ*, 3d ser., XXXIV (1977), 542–71. See also Wilson, 389, 393–94, 416–17, 430–31.

[71]See the illuminating work of Nancy Chodorow, "Family Structure and Feminine Personality," in Michelle Rosaldo and Louise Lamphere, eds., *Woman, Culture and Society* (Stanford, 1974), 43–66. The experience of mothering gave women an even stronger sense of their gender identity. As Helene Deutsch wrote, "in relation to her own child, woman repeats her own mother-child history." See Deutsch, *The Psychology of Women* (2 vols., New York, 1944), I, 205.

[72]For an interesting if somewhat forced view of the declining female image in an increasingly "bourgeois" society of early modern England, see Margaret George, "Female Image in Bourgeois Culture," *Science and Society*, XXXVII (1973), 152–77.

Chapter Three

Fathers and Sons

The Meaning of Deference and Duty in the Family

Boys matured into men in Chesapeake society under the powerful influence of their fathers. Indeed, the shaping force of paternal values was so strong that planters' sons often demonstrated and gave expression to a lifelong sense of duty and gratitude toward their fathers. It was not an authoritarian paternal presence, however, that commanded such obedience and respect. Instead, dutiful behavior emerged out of a relatively permissive mode of child-rearing which emphasized the development of self-confidence, autonomy, and the reciprocal obligations of fathers and sons.

The Independence of Plantation Life

In many respects boys grew up on their own in the eighteenth-century Chesapeake, with little parental intrusion into their early years. Religious instruction for children, though advocated by ministers and authors of child-rearing manuals, appears to have been largely nonexistent in most Anglican planter families.[1] Childhood autonomy was permitted in other ways as well. Except among the poorest families, especially those without any slave labor, there were few work responsibilities for sons under the age of twelve or thirteen. When labor became scarce,

[1]For a discussion of religion in Chesapeake families, see Chapter 1, note 68.

boys might help plant corn, sucker tobacco, or pick peaches in late summer and fall.[2] In general, however, parents allowed their sons to run freely about the plantation with their sisters and "playfellows," composed usually of brothers and friends and relatives who lived nearby.[3] Despite the distance between plantations, boys often visited their cousins, and frequent barbecues and balls, especially in the summer, gave them the opportunity to mix with children throughout the neighborhood.[4] Planters' sons also made companions of slave children, though parents began to discourage this interracial contact when their sons reached puberty.[5]

While parents did not control their sons' preadolescent years (roughly, the years between six and thirteen), fathers did begin to suggest, at least by example, what roles would be expected of their sons at maturity. From the time boys were first dressed like men in breeches and shirts—at around five or six—fathers gradually drew their sons away from home and began to show them a part of the adult male society in which they would participate. For example, planters carried their young sons with them on social visits to other men. Fathers seem to have considered these trips important in their sons' early understanding of a man's world beyond the family.[6] Independence of movement by horse or boat

[2]Charles Carroll of A to Charles Carroll of C, Oct. 4, 1775, CARP; FTD, Sept. 8, 1796, Jan. 27, 1797; Lorena S. Walsh, "'Till Death Us Do Part': Marriage and Family in Seventeenth-Century Maryland," in Thad W. Tate and David Ammerman, eds., *The Chesapeake in the Seventeenth Century: Essays on Anglo-American Society and Politics* (Chapel Hill, N.C., 1979), 126–52.

[3]*Byrd Diary, 1739–41,* 122–23, 130.

[4]See FTD, Aug. 31, Sept. 13, 14, 1794; William Wirt Reminiscences 1825, Wirt Papers, Library of Congress.

[5]See Samuel Thornley, ed., *Journal of Nicholas Cresswell, 1774–1777* (New York, 1924), 30; Henry Hollyday to James Hollyday, May 17, 1777, HFP; and H. D. Farish, ed., *Journal and Letters of Philip Vickers Fithian, 1773–1774* (Williamsburg, 1943), 82, 94, 250.

[6]The Reverend Robert Rose, for example, took his two sons, ages four and six, with him to eat dinner with six other men. RRD, July 5, 1747. But fathers were sometimes careful not to impose these new experiences on very young children. The grandson of Landon Carter, George Carter, took a boat trip in February of 1770, accompanied by his grandfather and two other men. When the water got a little rough, however, the men guided the boat back to shore, as they were, according to Carter, "unwilling to frighten him [George] on his first trip by water." *Carter Diary,* I, 362.

to neighboring farms and taverns and to church and county court, where men gathered for business and conviviality, was an essential dimension of adult life.[7] The close contact and emotional bond between a planter and his son helped to gradually dissolve the boy's ties to his mother and to give him an accurate idea of his physical skills, responsibilities, and values as a male in a plantation society.[8]

When sons were old enough to handle a horse well—usually by their early teens—parents used them as messengers between plantations. As they matured, it was not uncommon for boys to take long trips alone to visit relatives or conduct business for their father. The experience of Henry Hollyday and his sons of the Eastern Shore of Maryland illustrates this point. Henry's eldest son, Jimmy, in his early teens, shuttled news between the home plantation and his uncle's farm in Talbot County. In September of 1781, Hollyday sent his nineteen-year-old son Thomas to a friend's home to exchange some paper money for specie. Frequently, "Tommy" left home for weeks at a time to visit his uncle and friends in a neighboring county, while his father remained "uncertain when he will be at home again."[9]

The freedom of movement that planters' sons enjoyed may have shortened the gap between childhood and adulthood. One traveler in late-eighteenth-century Virginia commented on this early mobility of sons: "A Virginia youth of 15 years is already such a man as he will be at twice that age. At 15, his father gives him a horse and a negro, with which he riots about the country, attends every fox-hunt, horserace, and cock-fight, and does

[7]By contrast, young daughters remained at home much of the time, except when courting. They rarely travelled "abroad" unescorted by a servant, brother, or some other adult. Julia C. Spruill, *Women's Life and Work in the Southern Colonies* (New York, 1938), 89–90; *Byrd Diary, 1739–41*, 68, 87, 105; Frances Tucker to Theodorick Bland, Jan. 21, 1784, TCP; Henry Hollyday to James Hollyday, Dec. 21, 1781, Jan. 2, 1782, HFP. An apparent exception to this pattern of limited mobility for girls was Landon Carter's granddaughter, Lucy, who, according to Carter, was almost always gone "gaddy abroad." *Carter Diary,* I, 356, 369, 492; II, 652, 659–60.

[8]See Tess Forest, "The Paternal Roots of Male Character Development," *Psychoanalytic Review,* 54 (1967), 86–87.

[9]Henry Hollyday to James Hollyday, Sept. 17, June 25, 1781, HFP.

nothing else whatever." Nicholas Cresswell was even more force-fully struck by the independence of Virginia youth. "If they have any genius, it is not cramped in their infancy by being overawed by their parents. There is very little subordination observed in their youth. Implicit obedience to old age is not among their qualifications."[10]

Undoubtedly a key dimension in the independence of planters' sons was the presence of black slaves on the plantation. Observing their fathers' daily disciplining of the slaves and exercising their own authority over house servants surely inured young men to the "command experience" and gave them a measure of autonomy and assertive power that sons elsewhere in early America did not possess. Jefferson worried about these lessons of dominance learned in planter households. "The parent storms, the child looks on, catches the lineaments of wrath, puts on the same airs in the circle of smaller slaves, gives a loose to his worst passions, and thus nursed, educated, and daily exercised in tyranny, cannot but be stamped by it with odious peculiarities."[11] The strong-willed, self-confident character of the planter gentry derived in part from their almost lifelong experience as masters.

The Power of Paternal Approbation

Despite the generally unrestricted plantation environment, which encouraged autonomy and self-reliance, most young men from planter families grew up profoundly dependent on their parents—especially their fathers—for their sense of identity and emotional security. Many sons seem to have been deeply attached to their fathers, finding in them strong male figures with whom they could easily identify. To a large extent, these deep emotional bonds had been nourished in infancy and early child-

---

[10]Johann David Schoepf, *Travels in the Confederation, 1783–4* (Philadelphia, 1911), 94–95; *Journal of Nicholas Cresswell*, 270. For other examples of boys' early independence of movement, see *Carter Diary*, II, 662, 753; *Byrd Diary, 1739–41*, 148.

[11]Thomas Jefferson, *Notes on the State of Virginia*, William Peden, ed. (Chapel Hill, 1955), 162.

hood when parents lavished attention and affection on their offspring. Respect and filial devotion came much easier to sons secure in the knowledge that their parents derived pleasure from their presence.[12]

The origins of deference and duty of course can also be located in more practical matters. As boys matured into young men, they doubtless recognized that in an agrarian society their economic success depended largely on the generosity of their fathers. With little liquid capital available and few alternatives to farming, especially in the first half of the eighteenth century, most sons could begin careers and marry only with paternal consent and financial aid either by gift or inheritance. Many children were naturally disposed to try to please parents who had provided them with affection and considerable freedom since childhood. And fathers owned the family land and personal property, which in general they distributed evenly among dutiful sons.[13]

Dutiful behavior required a strong dependence on parental values. The central message fathers tried to convey to their sons was the fundamental importance of achievement and self-government. Because they felt confident of their sons' continuing devotion to them, parents, particularly fathers, were able to encourage in their sons these seemingly conflicting values of autonomy and deference. And planters were careful to link all the achievements they expected—and sometimes demanded—of their sons to the essential requirement of filial duty.

We can see this paternal message at work most clearly in the early correspondence between young boys and their fathers. The

[12]The emotional security of children in father-dominated households such as those in the Chesapeake has been studied by psychologists, but always with the assumption that the deference and sense of duty children showed toward their father grew out of fear and developed into a "castration complex." I am suggesting that planters nurtured strong superegos in their sons, but under a rewarding, affectionate form of paternal discipline, not through authoritarianism. See Therese Benedek, "Fatherhood and Providing," in E. James Anthony and Therese Benedek, eds., *Parenthood: Its Psychology and Psychopathology* (Boston, 1970), 167–84.

[13]Inheritance patterns will be discussed in Chapter 7 above. See also C. Ray Keim, "Primogeniture and Entail in Colonial Virginia," *WMQ*, 3d ser., xxv (1968), 545–86.

St. George Tucker family of Virginia provides a vivid illustration of how father-son relationships revolved around the twin virtues of deference and self-improvement. During the Revolution, Tucker was separated from his family, but he often wrote to his stepsons offering them paternal advice on hard work and obedience. Receiving these letters from their soldier-father seemed to deeply affect the Randolph boys, strengthening their self-image as young men. Whenever the boys heard from him, Mrs. Tucker explained, "They fancy they are Men." The drive for self-improvement and to match paternal expectations grew strong in Tucker's children. Richard Randolph, St. George's stepson, expressed his commitment to paternal values: "I have been very negligent of my grammar, which I am very sorry to say, but be assured, I shall have my Syntax at my fingers end when you return. I know you give us good advice for our advantage, as no good can arise from it to you, but that you wish to see us all clever men, which I firmly believe." Paternal affection that flowed freely to infants and small children had to be earned by maturing sons through self-discipline and dutiful behavior. Tucker's stepsons appeared to grasp this lesson well. John Randolph seemed grateful for the paternal advice he had received, for, as he explained to his stepfather, "I will try all I can to be a good Boy & a favorite of Mamas & when you come home I hope shall be one of yours."[14]

The central assumption governing parent-child relationships was that a child's ultimate happiness and self-worth depended on his knowledge of parental approbation. Fathers were occasionally explicit about this expectation. Thomas Jefferson, for example, insisted that his daughter use his letters to her so that "you may always have present in your mind those things which

[14]Frances Tucker to St. George Tucker, May 25, 1779; Richard Randolph to Tucker, May 25, 1779; John Randolph to Tucker, July 10, 1781, TCP. See also Theodorick Bland Randolph to Tucker, July 9, 1781, TCP. Paternal uncles often played extremely important roles in the rearing and education of young men. One can observe as well the effort of boys to seek their uncles' approval through achievement. Henry St. George Tucker wrote to his uncle in August of 1781: "I obey with Pleasure, tho conscious how unequal my Performance will be to his Wishes & your Expectations." Ibid.

will endear you to me."[15] Children recognized that parental love was now conditional, requiring evidence of self-improvement and achievement. As a result, sons quite literally performed for their fathers to demonstrate their worth to watchful parents. Some fathers regularly arranged to have their sons read aloud before them, after which the boys might learn if their father had been "highly pleased with their performance."[16] Fathers also examined their sons' writing for signs of intellectual progress and expressions of filial duty. Consequently young boys penned their early letters with considerable apprehension. In 1782, Littleton Tazewell wrote to his father promising to obey him "in all things" and to "shew a good example to my dear sister and Aunt so as to merit your Praise."[17] Ten-year-old Keith William Pratt presented himself in writing to his mother in November of 1731: "This is my first Performance, & I hope you will be so good as to Excuse my Imperfections, assureing you, I will Endeavor to Improve my Self, in everything which may make my Self Acceptable to you." To be sure, some boys employed such deferential language as much out of strategy as conviction in dealing with their parents, but Keith Pratt genuinely feared his mother's displeasure. The boy's tutor told Keith's mother that he "shed tears upon his being suspected of wanting Duty & Love for so good a Mother."[18]

In Their Own Images:
The Educational Goals of Chesapeake Planters

Paternal influence intensified when sons began to prepare for their careers. Schooling and apprenticeship experience, like marital decisions, strongly affected a young man's economic and

[15]Thomas Jefferson to Martha Jefferson, Nov. 28, 1783, in Sarah N. Randolph, ed., *The Domestic Life of Thomas Jefferson* (New York, 1939), 69–70. See also ibid., Dec. 11, 1783, 71.

[16]Edward M. Riley, ed., *The Journal of John Harrower* (New York, 1963), 91, 104. See also *Byrd Diary, 1739–41*, 125, 133.

[17]Littleton Tazewell to Henry Tazewell, Oct. 28, 1783, TFP.

[18]Keith William Pratt to Elizabeth Jones, Nov. 20, 1731, Philip Dorey to Elizabeth Jones, Nov. 9, 1737, JFP.

political opportunities, and fathers guided their sons through these important decisions. Sons became in a very real sense "projects" of their fathers.[19] Planters spent years trying to shape sons into adults who either reflected or surpassed paternal accomplishments and reputations. Much of this paternal shaping is a common dynamic in families at all times. What is striking about these eighteenth-century gentry households is the large measure of success fathers seemed to enjoy in creating sons in their own images. The impact a father had on his son's work and learning experiences differed widely, depending on the family's wealth. In the absence of public-supported schools, children from poor families could expect little formal schooling, a few years in grammar school at most. Small farmers rarely possessed enough assets in land and personal property to provide an education for all their sons. Thus they sometimes chose to bind a son out for four or five years to merchants, artisans, or to other planters, where he might acquire a craft or learn how to manage a plantation and eventually earn a respectable living. Even children of small farmers usually did not leave home until the age of fourteen or fifteen, a fact suggesting that eighteenth-century planters in Virginia and Maryland may have become more protective of their offspring than were previous generations. Elsewhere in seventeenth-century Anglo-America, parents often bound out their children at around the age of ten.[20]

[19]The term "projects" was first suggested by R. D. Laing in analyzing the psychological "operations" of family relationships. See his *The Politics of the Family* (New York, 1969), especially 77–87. See also D. H. J. Morgan, *Social Theory and the Family* (London, 1975), 217.

[20]See Alan Macfarlane, *The Family Life of Ralph Josselin: A Seventeenth-Century Clergyman* (Cambridge, 1970), 210; Joseph E. Illick, "Child-Rearing in Seventeenth-Century England and America," in Lloyd de Mause, ed., *The History of Childhood* (New York, 1974), 321; and Edmund S. Morgan, *The Puritan Family: Religion and Domestic Relations in Seventeenth-Century New England* (New York, 1966, rev. ed.), 68. For a discussion of apprenticeship in eighteenth-century Virginia, see Morgan, *Virginians at Home: Family Life in Eighteenth-Century Virginia* (Williamsburg, Va., 1952) 22–25; Michael L. Nicholls, "Origins of the Virginia Southside, 1703–1753: A Social and Economic Study" (unpub. Ph.D. diss., College of William and Mary, 1972), 163, 165.

Apprenticeship accomplished several things for parents unable to give their children a formal education. Young men and women were given "Sufficient Meat, Drink, Washing, and Lodging and apparill"; they acquired a functional literacy (usually the ability to read well in the Bible); and most important, they learned a marketable skill, "so that they may know how to get their living."[21] That apprenticeship should lead to economic independence was the expectation of the community as well as of the parents, for local officials insisted that apprenticed orphans not become burdens on the parish or county.[22]

Wills testify to the importance of apprenticeship for fathers with small or modest estates. A York County man in 1767, for example, instructed his wife that since "theirs [his sons' legacies] is but small, I would have them bound out to proper Trades as soon as they are fit."[23] Even men like Benjamin Clifton, who owned six slaves in 1728, could not afford to school his daughter and two sons. Instead he asked that his sons be placed in the hands of merchants between their sixteenth and twenty-first birthdays and provided his fifteen-year-old daughter a one-year apprenticeship in a friend's house.[24] Some small planters who were not burdened with numerous children put their limited assets to work in order to educate one or two sons. Dedman Stedd, whose estate was worth less than fifty pounds at his death in 1726, required that his executor carefully supervise his sons and give them four years of schooling. Other fathers charged their wives with the duty of overseeing their sons' education, or at least, as one man put it, "give him what learning she could."[25]

[21]George Hume to James Hume, Aug. 22, 1754, in "A Colonial Scottish Jacobite Family," *VMHB*, xxxviii (1930), 231.

[22]See, for example, the Petsworth Parish provisions for an apprenticed orphan on July 6, 1719, in C. G. Chamberlayne, ed., *Vesty Book of Petsworth Parish, Gloucester County, Virginia, 1677–1793* (Richmond, 1933), 144. Labor demands and educational opportunities for orphans often depended on the size of their estate: orphans with relatively large estates worked less and learned more in their apprenticeship than those less fully provided for. See Lorena Walsh, "'Till Death Us Do Part'."

[23]York County Wills and Inventories, XXI, 1760–1771, 377, Va. St. Lib., Richmond.

[24]Ibid., XVI, 1720–29, 549–50, 607–8.

[25]Ibid., 413, 100. See also ibid., 219–20, 595–96.

Those few children from poorer families who did receive some schooling could expect little more than a rudimentary training in grammar and arithmetic at a neighborhood school. Since boys from these families were needed to help work in the field several months of the year, schooling had to be structured around family labor needs. The early experience of Devereux Jarratt, who grew up in New Kent County, Virginia, in the 1740s, illustrates the meager and haphazard educational training boys from relatively poor families received. Jarratt's father, a carpenter, died when Jarratt was six years old. Under his mother's guidance, Jarratt began attending a local grammar school when he was about eight. Despite numerous interruptions in his schooling—probably due to seasonal farm work and the scarcity of teachers—Jarratt continued in the school until the age of twelve or thirteen, when his mother died, and, Jarratt noted, "no further care was bestowed on my education." He spent the next four or five years doing odd jobs for his older brothers on their plantations. In grammar school Jarratt had been taught to read the Bible, to perform some elementary arithmetic, and "to write a sorry scrawl." The purpose of such an education was completely pragmatic. "To understand figures well," Jarratt explained, "we reckoned the height of learning. Philosophy, Rhetoric, Logic, &c. we never heard of. There were no books on such subjects among us. *Arithmetic* was all and all."[26]

For boys like Jarratt, labor and not learning shaped most of their early years. Helping their sons get a respectable living was what small planters were concerned about. Given the limited educational opportunities for the poor, one suspects that paternal expectations were minimal for young men growing up in these households. Fathers probably did not intrude so directly into their sons' emotional and moral life as did wealthier, more prominent planters, especially since many sons left home as apprentices by their early teens. These poorer men asked only that their sons work hard and become independently settled. We can

[26]"The Autobiography of the Reverend Devereux Jarratt," *WMQ*, 3d ser., IX (1952), 363–66.

glimpse in Jarratt's autobiography (one of the few extant records of family and social life among the poorer people in the eighteenth-century Chesapeake) the nature of parental aspirations for sons in these farm families: "My parents neither sought nor expected any titles, honors, or great things either for themselves or children. Their highest ambition was to teach their children to read, write, and understand the fundamental rules of arithmetic. I remember also, they taught us short prayers, and made us very perfect in repeating the *Church Catechism.* They wished us all to be brought up in some honest calling, that we might earn our bread, by the sweat of our brow, as they did."[27]

Educating sons of the planter gentry involved a much broader set of parental responsibilities and higher expectations. Men with large estates and influential positions in the county had reputations as well as property to protect. Providing a complete education for their sons was essential for preserving the family name and social status in the next generation. Uneducated sons would become failures and embarrassments in their careers, parents believed. One mother considered schooling her son in England, for she was "fully sensible from Experience as well as observation how Essential a Liberal Education is to that Sex and the Indifferent figure they make in the world without it."[28] That relatives felt that ill-educated sons damaged family reputations is indicated in the reaction of Nathaniel Burwell in 1718 when he heard that his younger brother Lewis was neglecting his studies at William and Mary. Lewis, his brother maintained, showed little ability to read or write (he could not "give one letter a true Shape" nor spell correctly) and was "altogether ignorant of Arithmetick." The result of such ignorance, Burwell concluded, was that Lewis appeared "noways capable of the management of his own affairs & unfit for any Gentlemen's conversation, & therefore a Scandalous person & a shame to his Relations."[29]

[27]Ibid., 361.
[28]Jane Swann to Thomas Jones, March 8, 1756, JFP.
[29]"Letter of Colonel Nathaniel Burwell," *WMQ*, 1st ser., VII (1898), 43–44. See also Stephen Bordley to Elizabeth Bordley, Jan. 22, 1728, SBL.

The medical and legal professions expanded during the eighteenth century, and planters developed elaborate educational plans to elevate their sons into these callings, especially when family land was insufficient to distribute among a large number of sons. The following letter from Richard Ambler to his two sons studying in England suggests that these plans could be class-conscious decisions: "I shall think the expense I am at (tho' great) well laid out provided you make proper use of it and acquire such an Education as may set you above the common level & drudgery of Life, of which be mindfull. You are now entering into Years which will enable you to reflect, that many Children capable of learning, are condemn'd to the necessity of Labouring hard, for want of ability in their Parents to give them an Education. You cannot, therefore, sufficiently Adore the Divine Providence who has placed your Parents above the lower Class and thereby enabled them to be at the expence of giving you such an Education (which if not now neglected by you) will preserve you in the same Class & Rank among mankind." Aware of his own inadequate education, Ambler became all the more determined to provide the proper schooling for his boys who could then become complete gentlemen. "You have at present an advantage which was never in the power either of my Father or my Self, I have often heard Him lament his want of Learning, and I my self am very sensible of my own defects and have frequently condemn'd myself for neglecting the opportunity I once had! for how stinging is the [affliction?] when we fall into the Company of the learned, we cannot bear a part in the conversation for want of Learning."[30]

Efforts of fathers like Richard Ambler to provide a classical education for their sons grew in part out of an effort among larger planters to emulate the values of the English gentry in the first half of the eighteenth century. Learning was an integral part of

[30]Richard and Elizabeth Ambler to Edward and John Ambler, Aug. 1, 1748, May 20, 1749, in Lucille Griffith, ed., "English Education for Virginia Youth: Some Eighteenth-Century Ambler Family Letters," *VMHB*, LXIX (1961), 14–16.

the life style of the cultured gentry, toward which many planters and their sons aspired.[31]

Until the late eighteenth century, sons from middle- and upper-class families appear to have had little choice as to what sort of careers they would be trained for. Fathers who "introduced" sons into the adult world expected them to follow carefully designed educational plans that would bring "honor & reputation" to the family.[32] This strong paternal influence was reflected in the education of young Stephen Bordley of Maryland in the 1720s. Before his father died, Bordley learned from him that he was "fittest" to study law. "The Law is what my father pitch'd upon me," he confided to a friend in 1728. Fortunately, it was a career that also suited Bordley's own inclinations. As he contemplated the future, Bordley clearly understood that others would be more likely to measure his success against his father's reputation than to evaluate him as an individual man. He quoted the following verse from Cato:

> My father's merit setts me up to view
> And Shows me in the fairest point of light.
> To make my virtues or my faults, conspicuous.
> [Stephen Bordley to Mother, Feb. 15, 1728][33]

Well-to-do fathers with several sons to place in Chesapeake society designated a specific calling for each one and a particular educational program to prepare them for their careers. Richard Henry Lee was only one of many planters who tried to mold their sons into successful gentlemen. Like other prominent planters in the eighteenth century, Lee educated his sons in England. He gave detailed instructions on the proper schooling of his two boys to his brother William, who was to supervise them. "I propose Thomas for the Church, and Ludwell for the Bar." Ludwell, age twelve, was to be entered at the Inns of Court by age fifteen and to

[31]Jack P. Greene, "Search for Identity: An Interpretation of the Meaning of Selected Patterns of Social Response in Eighteenth-Century America," *Journal of Social History,* III (1970), 189–219.

[32]Henry Tucker to St. George Tucker, Aug. 21, 1784, TCP.

[33]Stephen Bordley to Mother, Feb. 15, Aug. 16, 1728; same to John Beale, June 22, 1728, SBL.

begin studying law there at eighteen, so that he might graduate by twenty-one. Ludwell's training was to emphasize the study of "eloquence," which, Lee believed, would lay a strong foundation for the practice of law in America, "the ready way to honor & to fortune."

The American Revolution, however, led Richard Henry Lee to reconsider the career of his elder son, Thomas. The war convinced him that a young man needed to be placed more directly in the service of his country than Thomas's preparation for the ministry promised to do. In 1777, five years after his sons first arrived in England, Lee informed William that he now wanted Thomas to become a merchant and Lee apprenticed him as a clerk to his uncle in France. "Instead of Church, I would now have him as knowing [as much] as possible in Commerce, as well the theory as the practical part." Lee told Thomas to study and become fluent in French for the father anticipated that France would be a major trading partner of America after the war. He explained the practical benefits of this new plan for his son. If Thomas performed well as a factor for his uncle's business in France, Lee pointed out, "there is no doubt but on your return to your own Country, you will be so trusted to conduct the business of foreign Merchants, as to be very useful to them, & profitable to yourself."[34] Sons like Ludwell and Thomas Lee began their careers in their father's shadow.

For sons of the gentry, paternal shadows fell on a relatively wide social landscape. In a society where literacy conferred some distinction, these young men were offered educational opportunities that all but insured them economic security and social prominence.[35] Throughout the colonial era, planters such as

[34]Richard Henry Lee to William Lee, July 12, 1772, Jan. 25, 1778, Lee to Arthur Lee, April 20, 1777, Lee to William Lee? May 10, 1777, Lee to Ludwell and Thomas Lee, May 10, 1777, in James C. Ballagh, ed., *Letters of Richard Henry Lee* (New York, 1970), I, 72, 384, 280–88.

[35]Kenneth Lockridge has recently suggested that at most two-thirds of all adult males in eighteenth-century Virginia were literate—or at least could sign their names to wills—and that it is possible that by the end of the century, as many as one-half of middle- and lower-class men could not sign their names. See Lockridge, *Literacy in Colonial New England: An Enquiry into the Social Context of Literacy in the Early Modern West* (New York, 1974), 77–78.

Richard Ambler tended to view education as a way for their sons to acquire the mark of a gentleman—one who was conscious of and comfortable with his superior social status—rather than as a pragmatic self-improvement program that could be exploited for economic advancement. Many men continued to educate their children from a desire to maintain family honor and status, but increasingly during the late eighteenth century, fathers conveyed a more competitive ethic to sons receiving a formal education. What mattered most to parents by the 1780s and 1790s was that their sons should seize on their privileged educational opportunities and make the most of them. Fathers who had cleared a wide and promising path for their sons emphasized to them that a wise and diligent use of time and their innate talents would certainly bring economic success. A considerably brighter and more expansive set of parental aspirations shaped young men from these gentry families than had influenced sons from all families in the seventeenth and early eighteenth centuries. The possibilities for achievement and self-advancement were clearly laid out by St. George Tucker in 1787 for his stepsons, who were studying at Princeton.

I need not I am sure repeat, what I have from your earliest infancy endeavoured to inculcate in your minds, that every man is respectable in society in proportion to the Talents he possesses to serve it. A Blacksmith, a Cobler, a Wheelwright, if honest men are respectable Characters in their proper Spheres—but a man of Science, a Philosopher or a Legislator, as they have talents to be more eminently and extensively useful, so are they more eminently and generally respected. The world is a circle about every man, exactly of such a size as his Abilities make it. —It is very well known five miles about Petersburg that Mr. Booker is a good Chair-maker—that Alexander Taylor is a very tollerable Cabinet-maker. —It is known for a circle of an hundred Miles that Doctor Strachas is a good Physician—It is known throughout Virginia & perhaps through America that Mr. Baker & the present Governor are eminent pleaders at the Bar—but it is known all over the civilized World that General Washington is a great General—that Doctor Franklin is a great Philosopher & Politician, and that Mr. Rittenhouse is a great mathematical Genius. It is in your election at present whether you will have a world like Mr. Booker's & Alexander Taylor's worlds, or a world like General Washington's, Doctor Franklin's and Mr. Rittenhouse's: for neither of these eminent Characters let me tell you possessed half your advantages at your time of Life. —Let me therefore conjure you not omit any thing that can contribute to your improvement in virtue or in understanding—without the former the latter is only a curse. [St. George Tucker to John and Richard Randolph, June 12, 1787][36]

This was a paternal ideology of confidence and mobility. Self-improvement, based on virtue and wisdom, led to personal success and great achievement. Tucker was articulating the essentially modern, secular point of view that success and influence depended solely on talent, not on ascribed status or divine authority. It was in part, of course, his growing wealth and prestige as a prominent planter and lawyer in Virginia that allowed him to paint such a bright future for his sons. Nonetheless, his commitment to values of self-improvement and self-advancement— even beyond the achievements of one's parents—suggests a relatively fluid society, at least among the middle and upper classes, in which men competed with each other for material success and influence. Indeed, by the late eighteenth century, Virginia and Maryland—and perhaps most of American society—had shed some of its hierarchical class structure. Wealth and political power were no longer lodged in the hands of a few important families. The world in which Tucker's children grew up *did* contain more opportunity for self-advancement in political and economic life than what Devereux Jarratt or even the Ambler boys encountered forty years before.[37] Tucker, like most parents,

[36]St. George Tucker to John and Richard Randolph, June 12, 1787, TCP. See also Robert Carter Nicholas to Bryan Fairfax, Feb. 13, 1763, quoted in Victor Galladay, "The Nicholas Family in Virginia" (unpub. Ph.D. diss., University of Virginia, 1973), 198.

[37]At both the county and state levels, economic and political opportunities were significantly wider by the 1780s and 1790s than ever before in the century. See Daniel B. Smith, "Changing Patterns of Local Political Leadership: Justices of the Peace in Albemarle County, Virginia, 1760–1820," *Essays in History* (University of Virginia), XVIII (1973–74), 52–85; Jackson T. Main, "Government by the People: The American Revolution and the Democratization of the Legislatures," *WMQ*, 3d ser., xxii (1966), 391–407. For a thoughtful analysis of the growth of individualism and the competitive ethic in the late eighteenth century, see Rowland Berthoff and John M. Murrin, "Feudalism, Communalism and the Yeoman

mediated his culture's central values, and thus he passed on to his children the importance of personal achievement, which for many had become increasingly possible in the late eighteenth-century Chesapeake.[38]

Deference and Gratitude: The Response of Dutiful Sons

Paternal influence extended into all areas of a son's educational experience. Throughout the seventeenth and early eighteenth centuries, many sons of wealthy planters were educated abroad, and fathers, with the aid of kin and friends, closely watched their moral conduct and intellectual progress. Boys studying in other colonies or in England were often lodged near the home of an uncle or friend of his parents who acted *in loco parentis*. In the summer of 1698, William Fitzhugh arranged for his merchant friend George Mason in Bristol, England, to supervise the schooling and upbringing of his eleven-year-old son. Fitzhugh asked Mason to provide the boy with books, clothes and pocket money (for which Fitzhugh promised to reimburse him) and "do by him as if he were a Child or relation of your own."[39]

Richard Ambler tried to monitor from Virginia the school experience and maturation of his two sons studying in England. Letters of introduction were sent out to merchant friends and "kinsmen" who could be used as contacts and hosts for the boys while they looked for places to live. Ambler left unsealed letters

Freeholder: The American Revolution Considered as a Social Accident," in Stephen G. Kurtz and James H. Hutson, eds., *Essays on the American Revolution* (Chapel Hill, N.C., 1973), 281–88.

[38]For a discussion of how parents act as mediators of environmental information and norms for children, see Robert A. Levine, "Culture, Personality and Socialization: An Evolutionary View," in David A. Goslin, ed., *Handbook of Socialization Theory and Research* (Chicago, 1969), 503–41.

[39]William Fitzhugh to George Mason, July 21, 1698, in Richard Beale Davis, ed., *William Fitzhugh and His Chesapeake World: The Fitzhugh Letters and Other Documents* (Chapel Hill, N.C., 1963), 361–62. English merchant friends were not always successful as surrogate parents in caring for planters' sons. See, for example, Robert Carter to John Carter, Feb. 23, 1720/1, in Louis B. Wright, ed., *Letters of Robert Carter, 1720–1727: The Commercial Interests of a Virginia Gentleman* (San Marino, Calif., 1940), 79–83.

to his friends and kin, he told his sons, "for your perusal and to regulate your conduct by." To strengthen kinship ties, Ambler directed the boys to visit their paternal uncle and aunt and cousins when possible, but not to bring uninvited school friends with them, "for it may give trouble to the Familie." Travel could be salutary for their minds and health, but, the boys were cautioned, trips should be "useful" ones in which they could make "profitable observations or some improvements, but to be too long and too often from your Studies will relax and unbend your minds too much," and perhaps, "give way to Pleasures and diversions, which will quite pervert my end and design."[40]

The extent to which paternal authority and emotions were invested in a son's career is evident in the response of Charles Carroll of Annapolis upon hearing that his son Charley was growing tired of being away after years abroad studying for a legal career and wanted to come home. If he were to permit his son's return to Maryland before finishing school, Carroll asked Charley, "wou'd not that Consent make us ridiculous in the eyes of thinking men?" The idea of a son defying his paternal authority and possibly squandering a "Liberal Profession" that a father's generosity and careful plans had made possible both astonished and angered Charles, Sr.: "Are six years of your life to be flung away? If that should be the Case I have done my duty, you will too late Repent your not Corresponding with my will & intention."[41]

Living away from home gave boys an opportunity to test their habits of self-discipline and frugality. Planters were exceedingly concerned that their sons learn to resist the temptations for indulgence and extravagant spending—evils that destroyed good character and virtuous conduct. Most fathers supervised their sons' spending habits, often requiring that they regularly submit a complete balance sheet of their traveling and school expenses.[42]

[40]Richard Ambler to Edward Ambler, Oct. 31, 1751, Ambler to Edward and John Ambler, May 20, 1749, "Some Eighteenth-Century Ambler Family Letters," 22, 15–16.
[41]Charles Carroll of A to Charles Carroll of C, July 24, 1762, CARP.
[42]See, for example, Richard Randolph to St. George Tucker, July 15, 1787, TCP; and Charles Carroll of C to Charles Carroll of A, Feb. 4, 1758, CARP.

Richard Ambler allowed his boys some flexibility in their new environment but like many fathers insisted that they guard against overindulgence, which he believed led to permanent moral and intellectual weakness. As long as the boys were "hunting after knowledge and learning," Ambler advised, "I shall not grudge your Expense, nor would I debar you from a moderate Expence on Eating and drinking sometimes such things as are not to be found amongst the Provisions of Your House but by no means give way to too great an endulgence of your appetites, this will cloud and darken your natural Faculties, and pervert the End and aim of sending you where you are, which was to improve and brighten them."[43]

Such paternal supervision of the daily habits and moral life of sons rarely provoked resistance or tension between fathers and sons. On the contrary, sons absorbed these parental values of self-improvement and virtue and self-consciously sought to demonstrate their gratitude for paternal concern through adherence to these norms. For sons who had grown up under a father's affectionate and guiding presence, paternal approbation remained the most precious reward.[44]

[43]Richard Ambler to Edward and John Ambler, May 20, 1749, "Some Eighteenth-Century Ambler Family Letters," 15. See also George Gilmer to Thomas W. Gilmer, June 4, 1790, Gilmer Letters, University of Virginia.

[44]The prevailing view of many historians runs counter to what I am arguing here. For a different perspective on father-son relationships in eighteenth-century Virginia, see Gordon S. Wood, "Rhetoric and Reality in the American Revolution," *WMQ*, 3d ser., XXIII (1966), 3–32; Emory Evans, "Rise and Decline of the Virginia Aristocracy in the 18th Century: The Nelsons," in Darrett B. Rutman, ed., *The Old Dominion* (Charlottesville, Va., 1964), 62–78; and Jack P. Greene, *Landon Carter: An Inquiry into the Personal Values and Social Imperatives of the Eighteenth-Century Virginia Gentry* (Charlottesville, Va., 1965), 76–83. These historians suggest that many third- and fourth-generation sons of the gentry squandered the family estate, led dissipated, overindulged lives, and generally ignored paternal values. But there is a serious problem of evidence on this matter. In Wood's perceptive article, for example, he simply repeats the evidence from the Nelson and Carter families as presented by Evans and Greene, respectively, in their essays. In the case of Robert Wormeley Carter, Landon Carter's rebellious son, much of the conflict grew out of an unusual three-generational living arrangement in Sabine Hall. This problem is discussed at length in Chapter 5. The falling stature of the Nelsons seems to have centered more on the financial mismanagement of third- and fourth-generation sons than on any sort of overt rebelliousness or indifference to paternal authority and norms. Then as now, of

The letters of sons studying away from home to their fathers reveal the deep imprint of paternal authority and values. This correspondence suggests that throughout most of the eighteenth century boys remained extremely deferential and fearful of impertinence toward their parents, often addressing them in reverential terms such as "my honoured father and mother."[45] In some instances, of course, these expressions of dutifulness and respect may have been a form of posturing, but that there was an intense desire to receive parental approval cannot be overlooked.

Sons, like fathers, recognized that an education abroad provided a chance for strong character development as well as intellectual growth. Thomas Robins, while studying in Scotland in the late 1750s, complained of the "debauchery" he saw among his classmates and asserted that he "was sent here to preserve my morals."[46] Few sons more openly displayed a strong sense of filial duty than Charles Carroll of Carrollton. Sent at an early age to France and England for his education, Charles spent his childhood and early adult years under the forceful influence of his father, albeit at a distance. The lifelong bond between him and his father, as reflected in their voluminous correspondence, was but a slight exaggeration of the general pattern of paternal dominance and deferential conduct in sons that prevailed in most gentry families until the late eighteenth century. Charles Carroll, Sr., decided early that his son should become a lawyer and arranged for his education at the best schools in France and England. The elaborate and expensive educational plans Carroll had laid out for Charley left him with a sense of deep indebtedness and devotion to his father. "I can easily see," the young Charles wrote in the spring of 1750, "the great affection you have

course, ne'er-do-wells existed in Chesapeake families, but the dominant pattern in gentry households, I am suggesting, was toward deferential conduct and acceptance of paternal values.
   [45]Henry Hollyday to James Hollyday, Oct. 23, Dec. 10, 1740, HFP; Elizabeth Holloway to Elizabeth Jones, June 9, 1752, JFP. In a recent study of childhood in eighteenth-century America, John F. Walzer found a similar usage of deferential language toward parents. Walzer, "A Period of Ambivalence: Eighteenth-Century American Childhood," de Mause, ed., *The History of Childhood*, 362–63.
   [46]Thomas Robins to James Hollyday, Oct. 15, 1757, HFP.

for me by sending me hear to a Colege, where I may not only be a learned man, but also be advanced in piety & devotion." So that he might retain paternal insights and instructions, Charley corresponded with his father several times a year ("as you commanded me") and made detailed financial accounts of each year's expenses for his father to judge "wether I have spent foolishly or no." Even in his early twenties, Charley sought guidance from his father on all aspects of his social life. Once he considered visiting an old Maryland acquaintance who was living in London, but fearing that his father disliked the man, Charley hesitated. "I shou'd not care to pay such a compliment as a visit to any person you don't like or esteem."[47]

Because many young men depended so greatly on paternal approbation for their motivation and inner sense of worth, the withdrawal of such paternal support could release in them a flood of anxiety followed by effusive efforts to regain their parents' respect. Failure to live up to a father's expectations implied a lack of gratitude for the psychological and economic investments parents had presumably made in their children. Sons who had given evidence of "foolish dissipation" and "inconsistent" behavior while in school—usually associated with a love of "diversions" and ill-managed spending habits—worried incessantly about paternal rebukes. For example, William Quynn of Maryland, a medical student in Philadelphia, was apparently guilty of these youthful excesses, which, Quynn realized as he explained to his father, "incurred your displeasure." He reassured his father that these "follies of youth" would end and promised to "be useful to myself" and "a Pleasure to you."[48]

[47]Charles Carroll of C to Charles Carroll of A, March 1750, Nov. 13, 1759, Sept. 16, 1760, Sept. 24, 1750, Nov. 13, 1759, CARP. See also *Carter Diary*, II, 686. Stephen Bordley also sought to maintain friendships in the same families his father had been close to in Maryland. Thus, Stephen urged his "school fellow" to write him so that "we may thereby become as great men & good friends as our fathers were." Stephen Bordley to William Tilghman, Jan. 22, 1728/9, SBL.

[48]William Quynn to Allan Quynn, Oct. 23, Dec. 9, 1782, Nov. 12, 1783, March 6, 1784, in Dorothy Macky Quynn and William Rogers Quynn, eds., "Letters of a Maryland Medical Student in Philadelphia and Edinburgh (1782–4)," *MHM*, xxxi (1936), 185, 189, 195, 203.

When John Carter, who was apprenticed to a merchant in London, overspent the allowance his father provided him, he begged for paternal forgiveness of his "past extravagances." The extravagant use of time and money was particularly galling to parents, for it suggested a lack of the self-control necessary for a virtuous life. The behavior of John Carter angered his father precisely because it revealed in his son an inability to monitor his own impulses. Carter accepted his son's apologies for the moment, but warned him that if such overindulgence continued, "I must be so plain to tell you I shall have little dependence upon what you say hereafter in relation to the government of yourself."[49]

Although mothers in the colonial Chesapeake exercised considerably less influence than fathers over their sons' intellectual and moral development, it is a testimony to the growing intimacy between mothers and their offspring that by the 1780s and 1790s sons became increasingly dependent on maternal approbation of their progress in school and general moral conduct. The correspondence of Richard Randolph and his mother Frances Tucker reveals an intense concern for her approval as well as for his stepfather's. During Richard's schooling in Williamsburg and Princeton in the late 1780s, Frances carefully noted his behavior and continually tested his devotion to her. When Richard learned that she had become "anxious" about the friends ("connections") he had made at William and Mary, he attempted to reassure her that these were innocent relationships. According to Richard, there were "one or two idle dissipated young men here but these are intirely separated from those of a more discreet turn of mind. I can assure you I am intimate with none but the latter, or if they are dissipated, I am ignorant of it, being always in my Room in those hours which are by some taken up in dissipation and debauch."

Dissatisfied with the program at William and Mary, St. George and Frances Tucker sent Richard to Princeton in the summer of

[49]Robert Carter to John Carter, July 13, 1720, Wright, ed., *Letters of Robert Carter*, 7–8. See also Stephen Bordley to Thomas Wilgress?, 1730, SBL.

1787. Frances scrutinized Richard's letters for expressions of affection, gratitude, and duty to her. When he began to develop close relationships with his schoolmates, she complained that the friendships interfered with his duty to her. His letters, she insisted, had grown "reserved" and reflected dwindling affection and interest for his mother. Richard responded with an obsequious display of dutiful rhetoric: "my most honored, most loved of Parents! Were I ever to forget for a moment your unequalled Tenderness, were I to be so ungrateful as not to pay the most assiduous and constant attention to your happiness and wishes, I should not deserve the blessings I enjoy from the bountiful disposer of all human happiness! I should not deserve the caresses and tender fondness of an indulgent mother nor the unwearied and never ceasing watchfulness and attention of an affectionate Father!" "You are," Richard insisted, "my best friend." He had not written her about the balls he had attended and the friendships he had formed because he could not "confess a Thing which I knew of directly opposite to your wishes and opinions, which I knew would incur your highest displeasure and ridicule, which I was certain . . . would lessen me in your eyes." But Mrs. Tucker wanted more than a "constrained letter of duty" from Richard; she expected open feelings of affection and love commensurate with the intimate relationship she hoped existed between her and her sons. At the end of Richard's painful apologia to his mother, he concluded: "I have now unbosomed myself in the most open unreserved manner—I never again shall be ceremonious or reserved to my dearest Parent."[50] It is not that sons, when away from their parents, observed all their admonitions in a continuous show of deference and duty. Clearly they did not, as the experience of Richard Randolph and others suggests. The important point, though, is the extent to which young men felt compelled to demonstrate their self-worth to parents and to receive their approval.

[50]Richard Randolph to Frances Tucker, April 12, March 8, 1787; Randolph to St. George Tucker and Frances Tucker, July 15, 1787; Randolph to Frances Tucker, Oct. 28, 1787, TCP.

Affection over Authority:
The Problem of Control in Planter Families

Frances Tucker's fervent attempt to maintain a close emotional bond with her sons was indicative of the increasingly affectionate, child-centered family life that characterized the Chesapeake after the middle of the eighteenth century. Parents and children addressed each other in more tender, expressive language, which symbolized the growing intimacy of personal relationships within the family.[51] Along with deep parental attachments to children came a more cautious, protective attitude toward educating young men. Anxious to remain close to their maturing sons and to supervise their moral as well as intellectual growth, parents increasingly chose to educate them closer to home, rather than send them abroad as wealthy planters had frequently done in the seventeenth and early eighteenth centuries.

This strong concern of parents for their children bothered such schoolmasters as Walker Maury, who complained in 1783 of insufficient enrollments at his school, for "such is the fondness of the parents of this country for having their sons near them."[52] And those parents who still chose to educate their sons abroad did so with considerable ambivalence. One father who had just sent his two young sons to England reflected the tension between paternal affection and the felt need to provide the best education for his sons: "poor dear fellows! I have a Thousand & a Thousand Heart-aches about them. You will perhaps wonder how I cou'd have parted with them at so early an Age. I wonder at it myself, but I hope that my Anxieties will be amply rewarded in the Advantages they will derive from a good Education."[53]

[51]Frances Baylor signed her letter to her son, "Your Doating Mother," in Oct. 14, 1802, BFP. For other evidence of maternal authority over sons and expressions of duty and affection to mothers, see Theodorick Bland, Sr., to Theodorick Bland, Jr., Feb. 14, 1763, BP; Elizabeth B. Carroll to Charles Carroll of C, Sept. 8, 1756, CARP; Farish, ed., Journal of Fithian, 128, 154. The growing impact of maternal love on family life and the kin network will be explored in Chapters 5 and 7.

[52]Walker Maury to St. George Tucker, April 1, 1783, TCP.

[53]Thomas Tudor Tucker to St. George Tucker, April 14, 1784, ibid. See also Jane Swann to Thomas Jones, March 8, 1756, JFP.

An apparently deteriorating moral climate in eighteenth-century English society also contributed to this growing tendency among parents to protect their children by educating them closer to home. Reports of dissipation and extravagance in English schools, which began in the 1730s and 1740s, convinced many planters that their sons might be corrupted rather than educated if sent abroad to study. In 1756, John Page refused to send his son to England because, his son later recalled, "several Virginians, about this time, had returned from that place . . . so inconceivable illiterate, and also corrupted and vicious, that he swore no son of his should ever go there in quest of an education."[54] Placing a son in a fashionable school like Eton or Cambridge was considered by many parents "very hazardous," for it left "a youth, quite removed from his Parent's eye."[55] Moreover, the estrangement of the colonies from Great Britain during the 1770s and early 1780s obviously prevented most men from sending their children to England for their schooling. By the time of the Revolution, few parents were inclined toward an English education for their children. The hostilities between the colonies and the mother country clearly narrowed the educational choices well-to-do planters could make for their sons.

Changing demographic and economic conditions also encouraged some men to consider alternative educational plans for their sons. The growth in family size during the eighteenth century—the consequence of increased life expectancies, longer marriages, and reduced infant and childhood mortality—often left planters

---

[54]"Reminiscences of John Page," *Virginia Historical Register*, III (1850), 146.

[55]John Frere to John Baylor, March 1, 1796, Oct. 2, 1797, and William Bonds to John Baylor, Jr., Aug. 17, 1793, BFP. To Richard Henry Lee, the level of dissipation at William and Mary was even worse than in English schools: "so little is paid either to the learning or the morals of boys that I never could bring myself to think of Wm & Mary." Richard Henry Lee to William Lee, July 12, 1772, Ballagh, ed., *Letters of Richard Henry Lee*, 70–71. See also William Nelson to John Norton, Feb. 27, 1768, Mason, ed., *John Norton and Sons*, 39. A study of the Carter family in the eighteenth century shows that less than one-fourth of the fourth generation of Carter sons (a cohort born around 1710) were educated abroad, whereas over four-fifths of the Carter boys in the seventeenth and early eighteenth centuries had been sent abroad for their schooling. Katherine Kubayashi, "Colonial Virginia Children Abroad: A Case Study of the Carter Family," unpub. seminar paper, Johns Hopkins University, 1974.

with four or five sons for whom they sought to provide some schooling.[56] Moreover, the practice of partible inheritance, which had prevailed throughout the colonial era, gradually fragmented family land so that by the late eighteenth century relatively few planters possessed the wherewithal to send their children to prestigious European or English schools.[57] Although he managed to send his sons abroad, Richard Henry Lee understood the burden of educating several sons with limited land and personal property. "With 5 children & another it may be, two, on the Stocks, a small estate must part with nothing unnecessary."[58]

By the latter third of the eighteenth century, then, the combination of shrinking family estates, fear of dissipation abroad, Anglo-American hostilities, and increasingly affectionate parent-child relationships induced many planters to school their sons closer to home. Neighborhood schools were established in areas where planters pooled their resources to hire a teacher, usually on a yearly basis. Sometimes a small group of parents contracted with the local minister to teach their sons for a few years.[59]

If their financial circumstances allowed, however, most planters in the late eighteenth century preferred to hire a private tutor to educate their children. A tutor was usually a young man in his twenties with college training who was brought in to instruct a planter's children—especially the sons—in grammar, mathematics, and languages.[60] Choosing a tutor was an important decision

[56]Allan Kulikoff, "Tobacco and Slaves: Population, Economy, and Society in Eighteenth-Century Prince George's County, Maryland" (unpub. Ph.D. diss., Brandeis University, 1975), 44; Karen Dawley, "Childhood in Eighteenth-Century Virginia" (unpub. M.A. thesis, University of Virginia, 1972), appendix.

[57]The average cost for schooling and boarding a student in Virginia was thirty to forty pounds in the late eighteenth century, which was too high for many middle-class planters. According to one man, this cost could "deterr many poor & some men of moderate living from attempting anything at all." Joseph Prentis to Francis Prentis, Nov. 2, 1786, "Some Letters of Joseph Prentis," *WMQ*, 2d ser., II (1921), 45–46; "The Autobiography of Devereux Jarratt," 380.

[58]Richard Henry Lee to William Lee, July 12, 1772, Ballagh, ed., *Letters of Richard Henry Lee*, 72.

[59]"Page Reminiscences," 146. See also the discussion of schooling in the eighteenth-century South in Richard Beale Davis, *Intellectual Life in the Colonial South, 1585–1763* (3 vols., Knoxville, 1978), I, 299–313.

[60]"Page Reminiscences," 146; Morgan, *Virginians at Home*, 13–14.

for family and kin. Members of the Taylor family of Orange County, Virginia, for example, helped arrange and pay for the schooling of the various sons of the Taylor brothers in the county. Reuben Taylor "bargained" with a Mr. O'Neill to teach his son Billy in exchange for O'Neill's free boarding. Reuben's brother Francis agreed to pay for the tuition and boarding of Reuben's other son, Frank.[61]

A tutor's most important responsibility, however, probably lay in the child-rearing process, for he helped to provide discipline and moral guidance for the boys under his care. Indeed, the central virtue of the tutoring system was that the tutor relieved a father of the disagreeable job of disciplining his sons, a job which seems to have grown especially difficult by the late eighteenth century because of the strong affectional ties that developed between many fathers and sons. But unlike apprenticeships, which separated children from their parents, the tutoring system, with the teacher usually living on the plantation, allowed parents to remain closely attached—but not excessively so—to their children. Thus the bond of trust and affection established in early childhood between fathers and sons could be maintained during the often trying years of adolescence with less risk of intergenerational tension.[62]

That parents considered a tutor a valuable aid in the child-rearing process is suggested by the experience of couples who had to discipline their children themselves. Adults recognized the ill consequences for children who grew up in the care of overindulgent parents.[63] St. George Tucker confided to his eldest son in 1787 that he worried about his younger children, who had no one at home to discipline them. "I must get a tutor for them soon or they will be quite spoilt." In raising her sons, Frances

[61]FTD, Oct. 26, 1797, Sept, 8, 1798, Jan. 1, April 23, 1790.
[62]Over 30 years ago Edmund Morgan speculated that parents put their children out because they "did not trust themselves with their own children" and "were afraid of spoiling them by too great affection." See his *The Puritan Family*, 77. Since then, historians of the family have simply repeated his insight or found evidence to support it. See, for example, Macfarlane, 92; John Demos, *A Little Commonwealth: Family Life in Plymouth Colony* (New York, 1970), 74.
[63]See Peter Fontaine to Moses Fontaine, Nov. 4, 1749, in Ann Maury, ed., *Memoirs of a Hugenot Family* (New York, 1907), 336.

Tucker had also emphasized the need for a tutor to control unruly children. Her boys, she explained, were "like all other children who are without employment, [they] are grown quite Idle & troublesome for want of a Tutor. . . ."[64] A tutor occupied a strategic position with the family, for he was to combine the authority of a father with the friendly familiarity of an elder brother. This, one suspects, is why planters usually chose relatively young men as tutors, since they were old enough to act as surrogate fathers, but sufficiently young to serve as an example of virtue to planter sons.[65] The diary of Philip Vickers Fithian, a tutor at Robert Carter's Nomini Hall in 1773 and 1774, provides an unusually intimate glimpse of authority and discipline in a gentry family.

Fithian, a young graduate of Princeton, learned to evaluate the character and special disposition of each of the children under his care. And he understood the proper position of a tutor vis-à-vis a planter and his sons. A tutor, Fithian explained, should place himself "at a perfect equidistance between the father & the eldest son. Or let the same distance be observed in every article of behavior between you & the eldest Son . . . between the eldest Son, & his next youngest Brother." This meant that when "abroad" with his charges at horse races, cockfights, or balls, a tutor ought to join in the activities like an elder brother. Ideally, he would befriend one of the older sons and provide an example of mature, responsible behavior for him to emulate and in turn demonstrate to the younger brothers. In fact, Fithian did become close to Colonel Carter's eldest son, Ben. Fithian and Ben shared the same room in the school house and they rode horses together and sometimes traveled with Mr. Carter on business.[66] But since a tutor was also a surrogate father in the schoolhouse, it was

[64]St. George Tucker to John and Theodorick Randolph, June 12, 1787; Frances Taylor to St. George Tucker, June 4, July 19, 1781, TCP. In 1766, Richard Corbin wrote a London friend: "I am greatly in want of a Tutor for my children, it gives me pain to see them misspending the precious moments of their youth." Quoted in Morgan, *Virginians at Home*, 13.
[65]"Page Reminiscences," 145–46.
[66]Farish, ed., *Journal of Fithian*, 64–66, 212, 189, 230, 238. See also Riley, ed., *Journal of John Harrower*, 46.

important that he make a firm show of authority on occasion and distance himself from the boys to gain and maintain their respect and obedience.

Fithian's chief concern in governing the moral conduct of the Carter sons was the control of their "liberty," the freedom to leave the plantation. In his tenure at Nomini Hall, Fithian tried to strike a balance between confining the boys at home and allowing them to "go much abroad." Excessive "liberty," he felt, would hurt their studies and promote immoral conduct that could "scandalize their family." If such misbehavior occurred, the tutor would be held responsible, since the parents would claim they had given the boys "no license relying wholly on your [the tutor's] Judgment & prudence."[67]

To compel obedience, Fithian usually employed shame and persuasion. The assertiveness of the Carter boys often challenged the authority Fithian tried to maintain. "My Duty seems to require my Presence pretty constantly," he observed, "& I am forced to produce an Example for what I find it necessary to enforce on our Boys, in order to do it with some face, for they always call upon me for a Reason for every one of my precepts." When reason failed, corporal punishment became the discipline of last resort. After a violent quarrel between Bob and Nancy Carter, for example, Fithian decided to simply admonish both of them "for better behavior." Unconvinced by Bob's repentance, however, Mr. Carter sent word to Fithian later that day to give Bob a whipping. The threat of paternal correction was the ultimate form of discipline at a tutor's disposal. Fithian cautioned Bob three times in one day about his misconduct—which often involved using "imprudent language" or appearing "impertinent in school"—but gained his obedience only by threatening to send Bob to his father for correction, "which had so strong an Effect on him (as all the Children are in remarkable subjection to their Parents) that he firmly p[r]omised to attend to my advise."[68]

Robert Carter's use of the whip—administered occasionally by himself, but more frequently by Fithian—was confined to his

[67]Farish, ed., *Journal of Fithian*, 218–19.
[68]Ibid., 170, 46–47, 205, 245, 264, 66, 86, 114, 155, 157–58, 173.

recalcitrant son, Bob. Indeed, it is likely that in most gentry families in the eighteenth century only unusually disrespectful or abusive sons were whipped by their fathers. Most men chose to use rational persuasion and the powerful psychological device of paternal disfavor to discipline their sons. The experience of St. George Tucker, who was not an especially permissive father, may have been typical of many planters. In recalling the difficulties of raising his stepson Theodorick Bland Randolph, he noted, "I tried various experiments upon him (except the Rod which he never felt in his life or even a slight slap of my hand)."[69]

It may be conjectured—and the extremely limited evidence permits nothing firmer than speculation—that parents in the seventeenth and early eighteenth centuries were less reluctant to punish their children physically than parents in the late eighteenth century. We know that whippings were common in the William Byrd household, for example. Both house servants and children suffered numerous whippings. Byrd frequently beat his servant boy Eugene for "neglecting his business."[70] And Byrd's wife came to accept such routine whippings of her son. At first she couldn't bear to see her children punished, Byrd explained, but she soon became "such a Stoick that she can endure the pain of even her son being the victim." Byrd advised his sister to accustom herself in the same way to corporal punishment of her children, "to hear the dismal news" of her child being whipped, "without any other emotion, than only the concern that he may have been naughty enough to deserve it."[71] Some of Byrd's contemporaries doubtless preferred persuasion to corporal punishment in disciplining their children, just as Robert Carter of Nomini Hall was not alone in his use of the whip in the late eighteenth century. But given the growing emotional bonds

[69]Quoted in Morgan, *Virginians at Home*, 7. See also "Self-Portrait, Eliza Custis, 1808," *VMHB*, LXI (1953), 94; Charles Carroll of C to Charles Carroll of A, Oct. 19, 1772, CARP; Jean Blair to Mary Blair, Oct. 14, 1769, in Frederick Horner, *The History of the Blair, Banister and Braxton Families* (Philadelphia, 1898), 49.

[70]*Byrd Diary, 1709–12*, 84, 113, 119, 192, 224, 240–41, 295, 338, 412, 462, 501, 514, 550–51, 573, 579, 583, 585. For a discussion of Byrd's brutality to his house servants, see Gerald W. Mullin, *Flight and Rebellion: Slave Resistance in Eighteenth-Century Virginia* (New York, 1972), 64–67.

[71]Quoted in Morgan, *Virginians at Home*, 7.

between parents and children during the eighteenth century, it is reasonable to suggest that parents increasingly chose reason over force in dealing with disobedient sons. As we have seen, the development of the tutoring system was in large part a reflection of parents' acknowledged tendency toward indulgence of their children.

Some planters openly bargained with their children to encourage the achievement of parental goals. Sons who distinguished themselves in their studies, for example, received rewards for their dutifulness. Upon attaining honors in his exams at Princeton in 1787, John Randolph wrote to his mother: "I expect the watch you promised me." St. George Tucker used the threat of paternal displeasure to coax his son Henry into a closer attention to his reading. If Henry did not work harder at his book, Tucker insisted, "I shall not permit him to sit by me at Table."[72]

Planters clearly accepted the notion that discipline could best be accomplished through well-reasoned persuasion rather than paternal fiat. An ungovernable temper was a serious character flaw to most adults. When Landon Carter realized his grandson Landon, Jr., was given to outbursts of temper, he decided to speak to him about it. Carter tried to persuade the boy that his fiery temper created unhappiness in others and would cause Landon to be "dispised by all his relations." The boy feared a scolding; thus Carter tried to appeal to Landon's reason and common sense in governing his emotions. Carter noted that in counseling young Landon, he was "earnest to advise him to imploy his good sense which god had blessed him with, and not to sacrifice that to a temper which must in the end make him miserable. At last he seemed to listen, and indeed shed tears at what I said. I hope in God then he will learn to behave better."[73]

[72]John Randolph to Frances Tucker, Sept. 27, 1787; St. George Tucker to Frances Tucker, April 7, 1787, TCP. See also Theodorick B. Randolph to St. George Tucker, May 6, 1787; St. George Tucker to Frances Tucker, April 6, 1787, ibid.

[73]*Carter Diary*, II, 578, 869. Carter believed that his grandson's problems stemmed from an overly permissive childhood: "had this youth been Properly flogg[ed] when young nothing of this would have happened." Ibid., 895–96, 702–3.

The use of moderate, common sense persuasion in regulating a young man's behavior not only minimized family conflict but also provided an example to children of how they should solve their own quarrels with others and eventually with their own children. While small children learned only by example, adolescents could understand the principles behind discipline and proper conduct. As Charles Carroll of Annapolis told his sixteen-year-old son Charley in 1753, he could now "enter into the reason of the rules & lessons" he was learning. "Children," Carroll pointed out, "learn like parrots, memory and practice aid them chiefly, but men of sense do not content themselves with knowing a Thing, but make themselves thoroughly acquainted with the reasons on which that knowledge is founded."[74]

In the pursuit of family harmony, fathers sometimes encountered unusually wayward sons whose conduct and temperament seemed ungovernable and dangerous to family stability. As difficult to manage as recalcitrant sons might have been, planters nevertheless seem to have reacted with considerable restraint and patience in dealing with open rebellion against paternal authority. One very striking illustration of paternal moderation amid what appears to have been a serious emotional problem in the household was the deteriorating situation of Henry Hollyday and his family in the 1770s and 1780s. Hollyday, a well-to-do planter in Queen Anne's County, Maryland, was the father of six daughters and three sons, the youngest of whom was Thomas. The family correspondence suggests that perhaps from his early teens, Tom Hollyday was given to extreme mood shifts and, on occasion, irrational displays of violence and anger toward those around him. In 1778, when the boy was about seventeen, his father observed that he was "unable to determine in my own

[74]Charles Carroll of A to Charles Carroll of C, Oct. 10, 1753, CARP. Parental use of reason in child-rearing gives a child experience in self-evaluation and provides him with internal resources for judging his own behavior and in making moral judgments. This is the "internal monitor" eighteenth-century parents sought to implant in their children. See Wesley C. Becker, "Consequences of Different Kinds of Parental Discipline," in Morton L. and Lois Hoffman, eds., *Review of Child Development Research* (New York, 1964), I, 169–208.

Judgment whether his said Conduct and Deportment proceed from any Injury he may have Sustained in his Intellects, or are the Effect of an obstinate and undutiful Temper of Mind."[75]

By the time he was twenty-two, Tom's condition had worsened. In an elaborate lamentation to his brother James Hollyday, who often served as an adviser to Henry and his boys, Henry tried to describe the troublesome nature of Tom's emotional difficulties and the chaos his behavior produced in the Hollyday household. Because of the letter's detailed description of a subject rarely discussed in eighteenth-century correspondence, it is worth quoting at length.

From the unaccountable conduct of this unhappy child we have past the greater part of the last three or four months in a State of wretchedness not easily to be expressed. His manners, towards the whole family, but especially to his mother & Sister Sally, have been rude beyond measure: his temper peevish, childishly capricious, and, to the Servants, so ill natured that few days pass without his beating some of them, upon no other pretence than that there was something in their looks or manner of speaking to him, that was insolent. In short the instances of his absurd & undutiful behaviour are too numerous & too various to be inserted in a Letter; and I am really afraid his intellects are injured. I have for some time intended, as soon as I should be able, to ride up & advise with you what I should do with him; for if these dispositions should, as they have for some time done, continue to grow upon him, I must of absolute necessity endeavour to get him removed out of the family. Tho his behaviour is so notorious in the family that I suspect it must be known abroad, yet it is so tender a point that I have not given the least intimation of it to anybody except Davison, whom at his instance I sent for about a month or five weeks agoe to come down & see him: and yet his health appears to be perfectly good & his appetite really great. I entreat you to be without seeming to be so, attentive to his behaviour whilst he is at your House, & see if you can discover any marks of insanity. I will as soon as I can, tho it will be some time first, ride up & disclose to you more particularly the circumstances on which my apprehensions are grounded. [Henry Hollyday to James Hollyday, Feb. 23, 1783][76]

[75] 1778 Codicil to 1773 Will of Henry Hollyday, HFP.
[76] Henry Hollyday to James Hollyday, Feb. 23, 1783, HFP.

Besides taking advantage of the good counsel and warm friendship of Tom's uncle, James Hollyday, Henry also saw to it that the boy's "outrageous behavior" in front of the family would be minimized. Rather than threaten physical punishment, Hollyday tried to contain the outbursts of his troubled son by placing him "under an injunction not to enter the parlor or come into company." This step was taken in 1785 after "some instances of very gross language to his mother & some of his Sisters ... have wounded his Mothers spirits exceedingly." Keeping Tom away from company and other family members, Hollyday reasoned, would quieten the rumors "abroad" of Tom's rebelliousness, as well as promote some measure of peacefulness in the household. Despite the relative restraint with which Hollyday operated in managing his youngest son, Tom objected to his treatment at home. Hollyday reported in November 1785 that his wife's admonition to Tom about coming into the parlor "offended him so much that he immediately declared he would leave the house & she imagines, is now preparing to do it, and which I have no intention to discourage."[77]

Given the apparently unsteady and irrational character of Tom's mental condition, Henry Hollyday's most perplexing problem was exactly how to settle his youngest boy on family property. In a series of wills and codicils drawn up between 1778 and 1785, Hollyday carefully restricted the landed property he was passing on to Tom. Originally, he gave him all the land that the boy's grandfather had placed in Henry's hands, if Tom was "restored to sound mind & understanding"—in the opinion of the judges of Maryland's General Court (a stipulation that was changed from "the opinion of my friends"). In the final codicil, Hollyday revoked the land initially given to Tom and instead granted him another parcel of his own property on the Chester River under the trusteeship of two friends. The purpose of this arrangement, of course, was "to preserve" the land "from being destroyed or burned" due to the neglect or mismanagement of a troubled young man. After Tom's death, Hollyday stipulated,

[77]Same to same, March 16, Dec. 3, Nov. 16, 1785, HFP.

the trustees were to give the land to Tom's first son or first surviving son.[78]

Clearly the rather vague understanding in the eighteenth century of mental illness or emotional problems in general limited
the effectiveness of planters like Hollyday in trying to control
irrational or unruly behavior in the "great house." Nevertheless,
what was remarkable about the problem in the Hollyday home
was the combination of restraint and careful monitoring of Tom,
while avoiding any kind of direct father-son confrontation or
overt displays of paternal authority. Indeed, except to forestall
violence, Henry Hollyday constantly assumed a hands-off policy
in dealing with the boy. He confided as much to his brother James
in 1784. Because Tom had "renounced in terms my Authority as a
Parent," Henry wrote, "I have forborn to exorcise any, unless to
restrain his violence to any of the family; and I consider myself as
possessing no legal authority over him, other than what is essentially necessary to protect my family from his abuse & acts of
violence."[79]

As extreme as Henry Hollyday's family problems were, they
point up the widespread parental conviction among the
eighteenth-century gentry that paternal authoritarianism was
not the way to the well-ordered household, and that in fact
children flourished best in a relatively open, flexible home environment. Overbearing parents, some men feared, would stifle
their children's innate talents. A child needed nourishment and
good parental examples for emulation, but otherwise he was to
be given freedom to mature through the strength of his own
unique qualities and abilities. Landon Carter bemoaned this
permissive trend in child rearing: "Nothing [is] so common as to
hear Parents say 'to curb their children is to spoil their genius.'"[80]

---

[78]Separate wills and codicil were drawn up in 1778, 1783, and 1785, HFP.
[79]Henry Hollyday to James Hollyday, Dec. 6, 1784, HFP.
[80]*Carter Diary*, II, 997. Carter was probably right in observing that most parents
tried to promote an independent, even self-assertive spirit—albeit, not disrespectful to themselves—in their sons. Thomas Tudor Tucker of South Carolina
boasted to his brother St. George of his son's arrogance and pride: "Jack is the
most conceited Coxcomb in the World—By the bye, St. George, there is no Harm
in having a good opinion of ourselves—in my little Commerce with Mankind I

Indeed, there was a growing belief among sons in the late eighteenth century that an individual's natural instincts and special disposition could compete with paternal authority in making decisions about careers, marriages, and general conduct in the family. While fathers continued to dominate most aspects of family life throughout the eighteenth century, in the 1780s and 1790s young men increasingly began to assert the primacy of their own aspirations, sometimes in contradiction to paternal values and expectations. This was a significant change in father-son relationships, but not a revolutionary one. For as we shall see, deference and duty remained integral to the psychological well-being of most sons.

William Quynn was studying medicine in Edinburgh in the early 1780s, against his father's advice. Quynn insisted on marking out his own professional path despite his father's protests, defending his actions on the grounds that a man's career ought to be based on his own interests and unique abilities, not on the predilections and designs of his father. Quoting from Alexander Pope and the *Spectator*, Quynn argued that "particular Geniuses [are] adapted to particular Professions" and that it was important for young men to follow their own "natural disposition" wherever it may lead them. Thus his decision to study medicine, Quynn announced, "was my own choice so it will be my own fault if I omit the present opportunities that offer to Qualify myself for the Practice of my Profession."[81] However assertive Quynn appeared in making his own career choice, he remained, as we noted earlier, dependent on his father for moral guidance.

This difficulty in reconciling youthful self-determination with the need for parental approbation was painfully apparent to Theodorick Bland, Jr., in the winter of 1771. As it was his father's wish that he should become a doctor, Theodorick spent most of his adolescence and early adult life studying medicine abroad.

---

have had frequent Occasion to observe, that it goes a great Way towards persuading other People to have a good Opinion of us." Thomas Tudor Tucker to St. George Tucker, April 14, 1784, TCP. See also *Journal of Nicholas Cresswell*, 129.

[81]William Quynn to Allen Quynn, March 4, 1784, "Letters of a Maryland Medical Student," 202.

But at age twenty-eight, two years after beginning his practice in Virginia, he decided to give up his medical career and become a farmer. A naturally weak constitution, Bland explained to his father, led him to abandon medicine. The "immense fatigue, labor, toil, and trouble," he feared, "would put a period to my existence." "Would it then be more pleasing to my parents to see me a lifeless carcass in one or two years" of practicing "physic" than forego the debilitating profession, Bland asked? He preferred a "calm, quiet, and philosophical life in a rural situation." A strong sense of family responsibility also led Bland to reconsider his future. Because of his "precarious state of health," he claimed he had a great obligation to his wife, "who is more immediately dependent on me for protection [than] to those whom I owe my existence."

Despite the independent course Bland had followed in leaving medicine for farming, his mind was riddled with fears of parental "disapprobation" of "my future manner of life." Indeed, Bland's persisting sense of duty would not permit him to feel comfortable in his decision until he eliminated, through a well-reasoned explanation, any hint of parental disfavor: "my duty points out to me, the necessity of abating if possible that displeasure." In effect, Bland was arguing that sons should always remain close to and respectful of their parents, but make their own career decisions. "I hope no apology to a parent, for any error in judgment (when he is assured, that the heart is full of duty and respect), is necessary."[82]

Increasingly in the late eighteenth and early nineteenth centuries, sons came to decisions similar to those of William Quynn and Theodorick Bland, that in selecting a career their own innate talents, interests, and personal feelings could outweigh predetermined parental designs. Parental control diminished as well in marital decisions of the late eighteenth century, as sons and daughters began to choose marriage partners on the basis of

[82]Theodorick Bland, Jr., to Theodorick Bland, Sr., Jan. 12, 1771, BP. See also George Hume to John Hume, Aug. 22, 1754, "A Colonial Scottish Jacobite Family," 89.

companionship rather than accept matches arranged by parents.[83] Part of this democratization of authority in the family grew naturally out of a relatively permissive child-rearing style that encouraged the development of self-confidence and assertiveness. Moreover, these new youthful sentiments reflected a shift from the rational, orderly world eighteenth-century planters had created to a growing eagerness to give expression to suppressed instincts and emotions.[84]

These more equitable relationships between fathers and sons were also linked to a corresponding leveling influence in political and economic opportunity in postrevolutionary Chesapeake society. The gentry's firm hold on economic resources was yielding to a wider distribution of land and personal property by the 1780s and 1790s. The rapid population expansion into the interior regions of the Chesapeake during the mid-eighteenth century absorbed much of the land that in earlier times had been patented by planters eager to expand their holdings. As the number of landowners increased, the size of farm units shrank. Moreover, the large estates of wealthy planters were parceled out among numerous children over several generations, leaving young men by the late eighteenth century only modest land and property holdings with which to begin their careers. In addition, years of intense tobacco cultivation had in many cases exhausted the soil, forcing second- and third-generation planters to consider alternative ways of sustaining themselves.[85]

[83]Marriage patterns will be analyzed in Chapter 4. See Daniel Scott Smith, "Parental Power and Marriage Patterns: An Analysis of Historical Trends in Hingham, Massachusetts," *Journal of Marriage and the Family,* XXV (1973), 419–28.
[84]The career and identity crisis Nathaniel Beverly Tucker experienced in the early years of the nineteenth century suggests the conflict between a son's personal feelings and a father's controlling design. See Robert J. Brugger, "Heart over Head: The Antebellum Persuasion of Nathaniel Beverley Tucker" (unpub. Ph.D. diss., The Johns Hopkins University, 1974), 60–68, 71–72, 89–90. The much more volatile and expressive emotional world of Southerners after 1800 is clearly documented in Jan Grimmelmann, "This World and the Next: Religion, Death, Success and Love in Jefferson's Virginia" (unpub. Ph.D. diss., University of Michigan, 1977).
[85]Jackson T. Main, "The Distribution of Property in Post-Revolutionary Virginia," *Mississippi Valley Historical Review,* XLI (1954), 241–59; J. R. Pole, "Repre-

As a result of these dwindling family estates, planters commanded less economic authority within the family than had landed elites earlier in the century. Unlike their ancestors, many upper-class planters simply could not establish most of their sons in large plantations where they might remain under parental control. Beckoning to young men instead were the newly opening lands in the West, especially Kentucky, and rising opportunities in the legal and medical professions.[86] Frequently these pursuits required a geographic mobility that prompted autonomy at the expense of paternal authority.

Although paternal influence over a son's marital and career decisions lessened in the late eighteenth century, the ties of affection between fathers and sons did not weaken, and in fact, may have grown stronger. Indeed, the fragmentation of estates that gradually undercut paternal authority in the family may have also fostered a growing intimacy between fathers and sons. That a stronger emotional bond developed between them as a result of these leveling social and economic conditions was perceived by Alexis de Tocqueville in the early nineteenth century: "perhaps the subdivision of estates that democracy brings about contributes more than anything else to change the relations existing between a father and his children. . . . In proportion as manners and laws become more democratic, the relation of father and son becomes more intimate and more affectionate; rules and authority are less talked of, confidence and tenderness more often increased, and it would seem the natural bond is drawn closer in proportion as the social bond is loosened."[87]

sentation and Authority in Virginia from the Revolution to Reform," *Journal of Southern History,* XXIV (1958), 16–51. On economic mobility see Peter J. Albert, "The Protean Institution: The Geography, Economy, and Ideology of Slavery in Post-Revolutionary Virginia" (unpub. Ph.D. diss., University of Maryland, 1976), 64–66.

[86]Daniel Calhoun, *Professional Lives in America* (Princeton, 1971); Authony F. Upton, "The Road to Power in Virginia in the Early Nineteenth Century," *VMHB,* LXII (1954), 259–80. Robert Ireland found many Virginians among the early political leadership in Kentucky. See his *The County Court in Antebellum Kentucky, 1799–1850* (Lexington, Ky., 1972).

[87]Alexis de Tocqueville, *Democracy in America,* ed. Phillips Bradley (New York, 1945), II, 194–95.

Duties and Obligations:
The Politics of the Planter Family

Despite the growing autonomy of young men in the last third of the eighteenth century, parents and children continued to feel a deep sense of duty to one another. In short, parental authority was reciprocal, not authoritarian in nature, for fathers and sons shared an obligation for care and respect throughout their lives.[88] Above all, parental duty required fathers to teach their children the principles of self-reliant, virtuous conduct and to make financial provisions sufficient to insure their economic independence. These two obligations were interdependent, for men strongly believed that virtue and self-respect came only after the achievement of financial autonomy.

A few years after starting his own family, Richard Terrell bought some land along the Ohio River as "a fund" for his children. Terrell's brother-in-law, Peter Carr, praised him for the paternal decision for he recognized that this land "will make them independent, and you happy—for your happiness will certainly be increased by the reflection that they are independent. When this is attained, nothing is wanting to constitute earthly felicity but the steady and undeviating practice of virtue."[89] Parents agonized over the possibility that they might fail in their responsibility to see their sons "well settled in the world."[90] "My

[88]Alan Macfarlane also contends that reciprocity, not paternal authoritarianism, characterized the Josselin household in seventeenth-century England. See his *The Family Life of Ralph Josselin*, 118–25. The notion that fathers ruled over a subservient, fearful household comes from historians of the antebellum South. Eugene Genovese insists that paternal authoritarianism—over disobedient children, women, and slaves—was a necessary part of the whole slave system. See his *Roll, Jordan, Roll* (New York, 1974), 73–75. See also Anne Firor Scott, *The Southern Lady: From Pedestal to Politics, 1830–1930* (Chicago, 1970), 17. If this is a correct description of antebellum Southern family life—and the question is far from resolved—it certainly does not square with the evidence from the eighteenth-century Chesapeake. The difference may lie in the fact that eighteenth-century slaveholders were less conscious—though not unmindful—of a white and black family community on the plantation than antebellum planters and thus possessed only an ill-defined patriarchal self-image.
[89]Peter Carr to Lucy Terrell, Feb. 10, 1803, CTFP.
[90]Peter Fontaine to Moses Fontaine, April 17, 1754, Maury, *Memoirs of a Hugenot Family*, 343.

121

children are dear to me," James Mercer explained to his brother in 1783, "& it is so much *my Duty* to preserve them from the distresses of want, that I must stand *self-condemned* to risque it any longer."[91] It was also a conspicuous sign of personal success and family honor for planters to have their sons well placed in the world. Landon Carter, for example, was obviously proud of "the care I have taken of my family, the paying off children's fortunes, and putting out 3 sons with an Estate very well to pass in the world, still maintaining a large family at home, and all this without being in debt but a very trifle." Emphasizing the importance of a family's continued economic independence, Carter claimed that his central task as a parent had been "to leave those descended from me a reasonable subsistance to provide for those they shall be the instrument of birth to."[92]

A son's duty to his parents involved more than just obedience and was often perceived as a lifelong obligation. Just as a father's principal responsibility was to guarantee the economic independence of his children, a son's essential task was to maintain that sense of self-reliance and financial autonomy. Despite the close kin networks that had grown up around most Chesapeake families by the mid-eighteenth century, an independently settled young man could rarely justify any sustained reliance on his parents or relatives for financial support. When he failed to make his own way or became heavily indebted, a son relinquished any claim to self-respect and confidence in his father's presence. The confrontation between Robert Bladen Carter and his father Robert Carter the Councillor in 1786 suggests how a misspent early career could reduce a young man to abject fear of his father. Having squandered the profits from an estate his father had given him, twenty-six-year-old Robert Bladen Carter approached his father asking for help: "This morning I waited on you in Your Library with an intention of asking you for some employment. It has and ever will be the case I am afraid, when

[91]James Mercer to John Francis Mercer, Jan. 20, 1783, in "Letters of James Mercer to John Francis Mercer," *VMHB*, LIX (1951), 92. See also the laments of Henry Hollyday to James Hollyday, Dec. 23, 1781, HFP.
[92]*Carter Diary*, I, 447–48; II, 733.

before you; in any serious reflections, I have observed a stoppage in my throat and intellect vastly confused: What it proceeds from God only knows—It is my wish if you should choose to be imployed by you. Every exertion of body and mind will I exert in your behalf."[93]

Becoming a burden on one's parents was an especially troubling familial sin, for it contradicted the proper expression of filial devotion: that sons were to provide comfort and aid—financial aid, if necessary—for their parents during their declining years. When a young man became dependent on his aging parents, it robbed them, as one son put it, of "those calm and peaceable enjoyments which old age and infirmity require."[94] In the seventeenth and early eighteenth centuries when short life expectancies all but precluded the development of an elderly generation, few sons incurred this kind of family obligation. But clearly by the late eighteenth century caring for the aged—which by eighteenth-century standards meant those over fifty or fifty-five— became an increasingly common responsibility that sons were expected to accept.

In a society where protection against illness and financial loss was minimal, children were viewed in part as a form of economic and emotional security. As a result of the close bonds that developed between parents and children during the eighteenth century, parents came to expect that their children—especially their sons—would continue to provide pleasure and comfort to them in their "declining years."[95] Aging fathers sometimes arranged for sons to manage the family estate. George Hume of

[93]Robert Bladen Carter to Robert Carter, June 9, 1786, quoted in Louis Morton, *Robert Carter of Nomini Hall: A Virginia Tobacco Planter of the Eighteenth Century* (Charlottesville, Va., 1941), 225.
[94]Theodorick Bland, Jr., to Theodorick Bland, Sr., Jan. 12, 1771, BP. See also Charles Carroll of C to Charles Carroll of A, Dec. 19, 1760, CARP.
[95]See Eliza Tucker to Frances Tucker, May 29, 1783, TCP; George Walker to Mrs. Courtenay Walker Norton, Feb. 14, 1779, in Mason, ed., *John Norton and Sons*, 418–19; William Byrd to Franky Otway, Feb. 16, 1740, *VMHB*, xxxvii (1929), 33. Charles Carroll of Carrollton understood his lifelong obligation to his parents' emotional security: "If my wishes were fulfilled a long and happy old age wou'd be the least blessing; God grant you may life to see me at present your hope and joy, the comfort of your declining age." Charles Carroll of C to Charles Carroll of A, Dec. 28, 1757, CARP.

Spotsylvania County, Virginia, at the age of fifty-three and with failing eyesight, grew especially dependent on his son for his economic well-being. "I thank God I have now a son (George) who does my business for me and when he leaves me I hope to have another (Francis) ready."[96]

The strong paternal influence in planter families explored here was in part a consequence of demographic changes in the eighteenth-century Chesapeake. Short adult life expectancies— to about the mid-forties for adult men—created by the endemic malarial environment of early Virginia and Maryland compressed the life cycle and disrupted family life. Early parental death and consequent orphanhood were common experiences for many families, often confining the contact between fathers and sons to only a few years. Under these circumstances, many sons grew up with little sustained paternal guidance. As life expectancies rose in the eighteenth century—to about the mid-fifties for adult males—families grew in size and strength and parents established firmer control over their children. Increasingly, fathers and mothers could expect to see their children to maturity and to convey successfully to them important cultural and parental values. Perhaps for the first time in the Chesapeake, most fathers could gradually shape their sons in their own images.

But as we have seen, eighteenth-century planters did not try to crush the willful, autonomous tendencies in their sons. Indeed, rather like modern parents, Chesapeake fathers insisted that their sons become self-reliant, competitive, and economically independent. The modernization of the Chesapeake family, however, was far from complete, especially with respect to father-son relationships. However much planters encouraged autonomy in their sons, there was little interest in the "rugged individual" we associate with modern America, who made a total

[96]George Hume to Mrs. Isabell Hume, Sept. 15, 1751, "A Colonial Scottish Jacobite Family," 211. See also *Carter Diary,* I, 545.

separation from his father, withdrawing psychologically as well as financially from paternal control.[97] Individualism had limits in the farm families of the eighteenth-century Chesapeake, for land, transmitted through inheritance or parental gift, linked generations together in an expanding network of kin. And even the growing number of young men in the late eighteenth century who did not depend on family land and personal property for their economic security retained strong emotional commitments and obligations to their fathers and mothers.

[97]For a provocative theoretical assessment of the personality structures created in preindustrial and modern families, see Fred Weinstein and Gerald M. Platt, *The Wish To Be Free: Society, Psyche, and Value Change* (Berkeley and Los Angeles, 1969), 178–92.

Westover, William Byrd's home. Library of Congress Collection.

The Johnson brothers, painting by Charles Willson Peale, ca. 1774. Maryland Historical Society, Baltimore.

Mrs. Richard Tilghman and sons, painting by Charles Willson Peale, 1789.
Maryland Historical Society, Baltimore.

Governor Thomas Johnson and family, painting by Charles Willson Peale. Courtesy of the owner.

The Edward Lloyd family, painting by Charles Willson Peale, 1771. Courtesy, The Henry Francis du Pont Winterthur Museum.

Mrs. Samuel Chase and daughters, painting by Charles Willson Peale, ca. 1772–75. Maryland Historical Society, Baltimore.

Mrs. Isaac Hite, Jr., and son, painting by Charles Peale Polk, ca. 1800.
Maryland Historical Society, Baltimore.

Mrs. Joseph Nicholson and granddaughter, painting by Rembrandt Peale, ca. 1798. Maryland Historical Society, Baltimore.

Rachael Weeping, painting by Charles Willson Peale, 1772–76. Philadelphia Museum of Art. Given by the Barra Foundation, Inc.

The Peale family, painting by Charles Willson Peale, ca. 1770–73 to 1808. Courtesy of The New-York Historical Society, New York City.

Sabine Hall, home of Landon Carter. Library of Congress Collection.

Chapter Four

Vowing Protection and Obedience

Husbands and Wives in a Planter Society

Men and women of well-to-do families in the colonial Chesapeake came to marriage through a particular combination of property, kinship, and romantic interests. Whenever possible parents shaped their children's marital decisions with an eye toward economic status and family standing. Sons and daughters, on the other hand, generally paid closer attention to qualities of friendship, virtue, and mutual affection in selecting a marriage partner. These often conflicting approaches to marriage reached a clear resolution by the mid-eighteenth century in favor of the autonomy of choice for young men and women. As children increasingly married according to personal preferences, romance and sentimental love flourished, at least among the elite.

The growing assumption that marriage should be based on companionship and love, however, did not always lead to an agreeable marital life for couples. Husbands and wives had to work out a life together in a society that rigidly defined power and social and economic roles according to sex. This chapter inquires into the images and realities of courtship and marriage.

Immigration and Mortality:
The Demographic Conditions for Marriage

The preponderance of males among immigrants to Virginia and Maryland in the seventeenth century produced a society in which men outnumbered women by as much as three and one half or four to one. This surplus of males meant that some men simply could not marry while others did not marry until relatively late in life. Indeed, most immigrant men had reached their late twenties before their first marriage. With an excess of eligible men, women acquired a scarcity value that gave them bargaining power in their relationship with the opposite sex, but despite the plentitude of males, immigrant women could not expect early marriages. Most single females arrived in the seventeenth-century Chesapeake as indentured servants, usually in their early twenties. The majority of these women remained unmarried for four or five years while completing their terms. As a result most immigrant women did not marry until their mid-twenties.[1]

Native-born men and women, however, managed more youthful marriages, largely because of the high adult mortality rates in the early Chesapeake. Early parental death left many children who, as orphans, received their inheritance upon attaining their legal majority — usually eighteen for women and twenty-one for men. These young adults were able to establish their own households without waiting for parental approval.[2] Despite the short-

[1]Lorena S. Walsh, "'Till Death Us Do Part': Marriage and Family in Seventeenth-Century Maryland," in Thad W. Tate and David Ammerman, eds., *The Chesapeake in the Seventeenth Century: Essays on Anglo-American Society and Politics* (Chapel Hill, N.C., 1979), 126–52; Russell R. Menard, "The Demography of Somerset County, Maryland: A Preliminary Report," unpub. paper presented to the Stony Brook Conference on Social History, Stony Brook, New York, June 1975; Roger Thompson, *Women in Stuart England and America* (London, 1974), 36–39; Edmund S. Morgan, *American Slavery, American Freedom: The Ordeal of Colonial Virginia* (New York, 1975), 165–67. Arthur Blackamore to Father, Feb. 25, 1714/15, in Martha W. Hiden and Harry M. Darjan, eds., "John Gibbon's Manuscript Notes Concerning Virginia," *VMHB*, LXXIV (1966), 16.

[2]Daniel Blake Smith, "Mortality and Family in the Colonial Chesapeake, *Journal of Interdisciplinary History,* VIII (1978), 403–27; Darrett B. and Anita H. Rutman, "'Now-Wives and Sons-in-Law': Parental Death in a Seventeenth-Century Virginia County," 153–82, in Tate and Ammerman.

age of women in the seventeenth century, native-born men usually married by the age of twenty-three or twenty-four, and native-born women could expect to marry much earlier, often in their late teens.[3] Native-born women were usually much younger than their spouses. Most could expect to survive their husbands and, given the abundance of eligible men, to remarry quickly. A woman might go through several husbands in her lifetime and gradually accumulate considerable weath, which became a powerful attraction to suitors. A man could expect fewer marriages because of his later marriage age and shorter life expectancy.[4]

By the mid-eighteenth century, marriage patterns had stabilized. A more balanced sex ratio developed in the Chesapeake, especially in the Tidewater; for the first time the odds were not stacked against men seeking marriage partners. If they survived to maturity, males had a good chance to marry. And the chances of reaching adulthood increased significantly as infant and childhood mortality declined considerably in the eighteenth century. An important result of these improved demographic conditions was that growing numbers of parents now lived to see their children to maturity and exercised some parental influence over at least the timing of their marital decisions. With the family unit intact for a longer period of time, the mean age at marriage for men and women tended to converge in the eighteenth century. Men continued to marry at around the age of twenty-three, and women, who were no longer so scarce, also tended to wait until their early twenties before getting married.[5]

As marriage became increasingly feasible for men as well as for women in the eighteenth century, the prospect of remaining

[3]Smith, "Mortality and Family in the Colonial Chesapeake"; Menard, "The Demography of Somerset County, Maryland." One piece of literary evidence attests to the early age at marriage for native women in the early eighteenth century. In 1728, William Byrd pointed out that his twenty-year-old daughter Evelyn was the most "antick Virgin" he knew. William Byrd to Charles, Earl of Orrery, Feb. 3, 1727/28, *VMHB*, XXXII (1924), 30.

[4]Morgan, *American Slavery, American Freedom*, 165–67.

[5]Allan Kulikoff, "Tobacco and Slaves: Population, Economy, and Society in Eighteenth-Century Prince George's County, Maryland" (unpub. Ph.D. diss., Brandeis University, 1975), 439, 32, 34.

single grew less acceptable. While young men had to weigh the "Noise and ill Humours of a dangerous Wife" against the possibility of a "virtuous, good natured Wife," they had enough incentive to marry because of the "Care, Respect, and Attendance . . . paid to the Master of a Family."[6] Men (and some women) became more suspicious and occasionally contemptuous of bachelors and spinsters, especially the latter, whose single status to them usually indicated an unstable personal life and a dependence on relatives or friends for economic support. Single women rarely performed important economic functions outside the household, except for some widows who ran family businesses.[7] Thus, the failure of a woman to marry seemed to many men a violation of her central social responsibilities: to bear and raise children and to manage the domestic affairs in a family. At the least spinsters—unwanted dependents—were often considered misanthropic by married men. The *Virginia Gazette* gave the following "Picture of an Old Maid" in 1772: "Mrs. Mary Morgan has lived to the Age of fifty-five unmarried, but she merits no Blame on Account of her Virginity, for she certainly would have entered into the Marriage State if any Man had thought proper to make his Addresses to her. Nature has bestowed on her no Beauty, and not much Sweetness of Temper; the Sight of every pretty Woman, therefore, is very offensive to her, the Sight of a married One hardly supportable. . . . Inwardly tortured with her own ill Nature, she is incapable of any Satisfaction but what arises from teasing others. . . . She has read just enough to render her distinguishingly pedantick, but too little to furnish her Mind with any useful knowledge."[8]

---

[6] *Virginia Gazette*, Feb. 10–27, 1737. In 1777, Nicholas Cresswell was struck by the early marriages and the paucity of "old maids" he had found in Virginia. He noted that unlike in England where population growth was slow due to poverty and late marriages, in Virginia "there are no fears" of poverty "and with the least spark of industry, they may support a family of small children." Cresswell's claim, however, that most Virginia women married between sixteen and twenty-two is probably too low. Samuel Thornley, ed., *Journal of Nicholas Cresswell, 1774–1777* (New York, 1924), 271.

[7] Julia C. Spruill, *Women's Life and Work in the Southern Colonies* (New York, 1938), 74–76, 293.

[8] Quoted in ibid., 138.

"Paying Addresses" and Winning Favor: The Pattern of Courtship

Finding a marriage partner, at least for men, was an easier process in the eighteenth century than in earlier times. The expanding population and growing wealth of most planters in eighteenth-century Virginia and Maryland created more neighborhood communities and increased leisure time among the more well-to-do farmers and planters, which enhanced courtship opportunities for young men and women. Planters frequently organized barbecues, for example, that were attended by perhaps fifty or more adults and young people.[9] These festive affairs, with an abundance of food and drink, dancing, horse-racing and card-playing, often lasted for several days and provided an important form of entertainment and diversion for planters and their young. In 1784 one man described for an English friend a typical plantation celebration in Virginia. The company dined "under a large shady Tree or an harbour made of green bushes under which we have benches & seats to sit on when we dine sumptuously all this in an old field, where we have a mile Race Ground & every Horse on the Field runs, two & two together, by that means we have a deal of diversion, and in the Evening we retire to some Gentle's House & dance awhile after supper, & then retire to Bed, all stay at the House all night (its not like in your country) for every Gentleman here has ten or fifteen beds which is aplenty for the Ladies & the Men Ruffs it, in this manner we spend our time once a fortnight & at other times we have regular Balls as you have in England."[10]

Dancing was especially popular in Chesapeake society. Parents sent daughters to dancing school and regularly held "balls" for them and their friends.[11] Young men were eager to learn dancing

[9]See Hunter D. Farish, ed., *Journal and Letters of Philip Vickers Fithian, 1773–4* (Williamsburg, 1943), 70, 75–77.

[10]Lawrence Butler to Mrs. Anna F. Cradock, Oct. 15, 1784, *VMHB*, XL (1932), 266–67. See also "The Frances Baylor Hill Diary of 'Hillsborough,' King and Queen County, Virginia (1797)," in *Early American Literature Newsletter*, II (1967), 34, 37, 40.

[11]See Agan Blair to Mary Braxton, 1769?, in Frederick Horner, *The History of the Blair, Banister and Braxton Families: A Collection of Letters* (Philadelphia, 1898),

too, for it was an important means of social contact between the sexes. Through the dance—especially the jig, in which partners of each sex gave solo performances—young men and women competed for each other's admiration and personal favor.[12] The country dances at Virginia balls shocked some travelers, including Nicholas Cresswell, who considered them "more like a Bacchanalian dance than one in a polite assembly. Old Women, young wives with young children in the lap, widows, maids and girls come promiscuously to these assemblies which generally continue till morning."[13] At dances such as these courtship began for many couples.

Kin groups became particularly influential in promoting courtship in the eighteenth century. As population density and life expectancy increased, neighborhoods of kin and friends emerged in many areas of the Tidewater and Piedmont.[14] Young men visited uncles and cousins, especially in the summers, who introduced them to eligible girls and organized special gatherings for youth. James Taylor of Orange County, Virginia, for example, invited a group of "young people" to his house for a party in January of 1791. "No married people but his brothers invited," it was noted.[15]

51–52; Joseph C. Cabell to David Watson, April 6, 1801, in "Letters to David Watson," *VMHB*, xxix (1921), 279; FTD, Aug. 10, Nov. 14, 1795; John Hanson to Philip Thomas, July 23, 1782, Hanson Papers, Maryland Historical Society; Farish, ed., *Journal of Fithian*, 47; Frances Norton to John H. Norton, June 23, 1771, in Frances Norton Mason, ed., *John Norton and Sons, Merchants of London and Virginia (Being the Papers from Their Counting House for the Years 1750 to 1795)* (Richmond, 1937), 162; and Andrew Burnaby, *Travels through the Middle Settlements of North America*, 3d ed. (New York, 1970), 58.

[12]See Burnaby, 58; Farish, ed., *Journal of Fithian*, 177; and Jane Carson, *Colonial Virginians at Play* (Williamsburg, 1965), 21–35. For a perceptive view of the symbolic importance of leisure activities among the Virginia gentry, see Rhys Isaac, "Evangelical Revolt: The Nature of the Baptists Challenge to the Traditional Order in Virginia, 1765 to 1775," *WMQ*, 3d ser., xxxi (1974), 352.

[13]Thornley, ed., *Journal of Nicholas Cresswell*, 53.

[14]Kulikoff, "Tobacco and Slaves," 10–34.

[15]FTD, Jan. 4, 1791. Francis Taylor's nephews William and Jonathan of Botetourt County visited their Orange County kin in the summer and fall of 1795. William's contact with the neighborhood girls during his visit proved successful, for he married a friend of Francis Taylor in November of that year. Ibid., Aug. 10, Nov. 6, 7, 9, 11, 13–14, 18, 22, 25–26, 1795. See also James Parker to Margaret Parker, Feb. 20, 1779, PFP; Hetty Tilghman to Polly Tilghman, April 3, 1785?, in "Molly and Hetty Tilghman Letters," *MHM*, xxi (1926), 36.

Young people, of course, devised their own ways of meeting one another, apart from dances and parties arranged by parents and kin. Landon Carter observed that adolescent boys and girls roamed the neighborhood and broke windows in Sabine Hall, which, he lamented, was "always the Case when men and women go acourting."[16] In some cases parents recognized that young men and women needed to mix with their peers away from parental control. Henry Hollyday was one planter who pointed out the importance of youth as a distinct age group: "many of my Children during the last Seven years have grown up into Men & Women, and at that season of life it is but a reasonable expectation that they Should be able to associate with those of their own rank, with ease and satisfaction to themselves."[17]

The absence of parental control over much of the courtship process is suggested in the brief engagements before marriage. Often it was only a matter of weeks or a few months between a young man's first "addresses" to a woman and their marriage. James Wallace of Port Tobacco, Maryland, informed his brother Michael of King George County, Virginia, that if he intended to pay "any addresses to young ladies" in Maryland, "I must tell you as a friend" to be quick about it, "for the ladies in general on this side [of] the River are very abrupt in Matrimonial affairs." The advice was apparently well taken, for in only a little more than two months Michael had courted and married a Maryland girl.[18] One Baltimore man wasted no time arranging for his marriage in the summer of 1796. William Pitt ate breakfast one morning with William Faris and his wife and declared his intentions toward their daughter Nancy. Faris noted that "neither of us had any objection to him therefore I suppose it will not be long before they are married." The wedding took place less than three weeks later.[19]

[16]*Carter Diary*, II, 1009.
[17]Henry Hollyday to James Hollyday, Dec. 23, 1781, HFP.
[18]James Wallace to Michael Wallace, April 26, July 6, 1775, WP.
[19]FD, June 19, July 7, 1796. See also ibid., March 11, 1794; FTD, Sept. 21, Oct. 30, Nov. 1, 1786. Weddings could end abruptly too. Captain James West's marriage to Peggy Whittaker was canceled when West found out that Peggy's sister had a mulatto or black husband. FD, Dec. 31, 1795.

The ideal courtship was a more elaborate, stylized affair, and girls from gentry families sometimes purposely prolonged the engagement period. In a society in which women remained distinctly subordinate to men throughout most of their lives, some women relished their power to accept or reject an admirer's advances. In this view the engagement process resembled a "long siege" in which a girl took the time to evaluate a young man's wealth, moral character, and eloquence in courtship. Molly Tilghman commended her cousin Ana Maria Tilghman for not "surrendering at the first Summons" when a suitor proposed. "That wou'd have been cowardly indeed." Molly obviously enjoyed the courtship, for she also praised the young man for not giving up despite several "repulses." She saved her greatest admiration for a friend who married a man after a three-year courtship, a "brilliant reign." "It is a nice point," she commented on the occasion, "for a Belle to know when to marry and one in which they are very apt. She understood the matter."[20]

Despite a tendency toward the emotional segregation of the sexes, which developed out of sharply divergent socialization experiences for sons and daughters,[21] young women admired and found themselves attracted to genteel suitors. Men who cut a graceful figure at balls and who demonstrated intellect and moral character especially commanded the ladies' attention. One girl confided to a friend that she was awed by "a very elegant Washington beau" named Cummins, "one of the handsomest, most elegant, sensible and accomplish'd young men I ever knew; extremely rich" too.[22] Molly Tilghman was likewise enamored with "the ever agreeable Major Forman" whose "equal is not to be found." She marveled at his ability to quote from *The Spectator* with ease and his "superior knowledge," but also observed that he was "to be bought" for £20,000.[23]

[20]Molly Tilghman to Polly Tilghman, Aug. 5, 1785, April 13, 1786, Jan. 29, 1789, "Molly and Hetty Tilghman Letters," 132–33, 137–38, 235.

[21]See Chapter 2.

[22]Harriet Wilson to Maria Roy, Aug. 13, 1811, BFP.

[23]Molly Tilghman to Polly Tilghman, April 13, 1786, "Molly and Hetty Tilghman Letters," 137–38. See also P. Davenport to Elizabeth Pelham, June 4, 1791, "Pelham Letters," *WMQ*, 2d ser., ix (1929), 269.

Women certainly considered a man's physical appearance. As Elizabeth Holloway observed about her daughter's unattractive suitor, "she can't love a man that's like a munkey."[24] But since men would dominate the household after marriage, women sought to find a mate whose authority would be tempered by good character and fondness for his spouse and children. Such a man, Molly Tilghman pointed out concerning one of her friend's admirers, might be "extremely agreeable, not very handsome, but [have] an animated countenance, and [be] a very good person, which is enough for a Man."[25] Lucinda Orr always took note of the attractive beaux she met, but she came to respect good-natured men who were "truly Amiable," though "not handsome." "But how preferable," she wrote in 1782, "is good sense and affability to Beauty: more pleasing a Thousand times!"[26]

It is perhaps not surprising that young men were even more concerned with physical beauty in the opposite sex than were women. Robert Carter's son Bob, for example, kept a list of names of local girls and an assessment of each. One girl, he observed, had "d———n'd ugly Freckles in her Face, otherways She is handsome & tolerable." Another girl was "very pretty" and one he called "a beautiful young Lady." Men often described women as "nymphs," which suggested both their innocent beauty and graceful manner, but they remained wary of coquettes—those who lured men with their beauty and charm for their own purposes—and generally preferred cheerful, sensible, and industrious women who would make pleasing wives and good domestic managers.[27]

[24]Elizabeth Holloway to Elizabeth Jones, n. d. [1750?], JFP.

[25]Molly Tilghman to Polly Tilghman, July 7, 1788, May 8, 1789, "Molly and Hetty Tilghman Letters," 229, 240. Molly often took a condescending view of her suitors. She once noted that the only potential beau for her was "the serene Hugh Sherwood," who was "what the Philosophers have so long been in search of, a perfect Vacuum." Molly to Polly, Aug. 5, 1785, ibid., 131.

[26]Lucy Lee Orr, *Journal of a Young Lady in Virginia, 1782* (Baltimore, 1871), 35.

[27]Farish, ed., *Journal of Fithian*, 179–80; William Byrd to John Custis, July 29, 1723, *VMHB*, XXXVI (1928), 36–37; Jonathan Boucher to Mrs. Jones, March 9, 1767, "Letters of Jonathan Boucher," *MHM*, VII (1912), 341–43; Eliza Harleston to St. George Tucker, Jan. 2, 1784, TCP; Charles Carroll of C to Charles Carroll of A, Feb. 19, 1763, July 26, 1764, CARP and *Carter Diary*, II, 728.

Following the "Impulses of the Heart":
Romance and Sex in Gentry Courtship

The letters and diaries of young men and women in the middle and upper strata of eighteenth-century Chesapeake society, especially after 1750, clearly reveal a strong belief in romantic love. Sentimental and sometimes passionate male-female relationships reflected the growing importance in marriage during the eighteenth century of companionship and the declining significance of property and family lineage. Increasingly, men and women perceived each other in the more emotional terms of friendship: a mutual admiration of the virtue, knowledge, and pleasing nature each possessed. The growth of privacy and affectional ties in family life by the mid-eighteenth century probably encouraged this interest in romantic intimacy.[28]

The sharp division of sex roles in the colonial Chesapeake, however, often made simple, direct expressions of mutual affection difficult for young men and women; consequently, especially during the early eighteenth century, men couched their feelings in gallant displays of rhapsodic language that contrasted their weaknesses as men with an idealized image of women. Thomas Jones characterized this grandiloquent approach when he was pursuing Elizabeth Pratt in 1725: "If my Heart could take a flight from the imprisonment of a worthless Carcasse little better than dirt, it should whisper to you in your Slumbers the Truth of my soul, that you may be agreeably surprised with the Lustre of Celestial Visions surrounding you on every side with presents of joy & Comfort, in one continued sleep 'till the Sparkling Rays of

[28]For a discussion of the rise of romantic love in the eighteenth-century West, see Edward Shorter, *The Making of the Modern Family* (New York, 1975), 121–58; Lawrence Stone, *The Family, Sex and Marriage in England, 1500–1800* (New York, 1977), 270–404. According to Stone and Shorter, the growth of romantic courtship had begun by the mid-eighteenth century. Jerry Frost sees a decline in religious love and a surge of sentimentalism in courtship and marriage among middle- and upper-class Quaker families after 1760. This was reflected in the growing number of Quaker marriages to outsiders ("marrying out") after 1740. See Frost, *The Quaker Family in Colonial America* (New York, 1973), 164–67. See also Barry J. Levy, "The Light in the Valley: The Chester and Welsh Tract Quakers in the Delaware River Valley, 1681–1750" (unpub. Ph.D. diss., University of Pennsylvania, 1976), 71–73.

the Sun puts you in Mind with Him to Bless the Earth with your Presence Then may contentm't attend you as near in similitude as near as ever possible to those happy favourites of Heaven."[29]

Even someone as strong-willed as William Byrd II engaged in this self-effacement while courting. In 1703, for example, Byrd proclaimed Lady Betty Cromwell "the only darling object of my Thoughts." She rejected his advances, but he continued to write her long, florid love letters, "in spite of all the pride, a man ought to have upon being neglected."[30]

By the late eighteenth century, however, one detects more intimate personal relationships among young couples. Men and women in love saw each other as close friends. "P" Davenport of Williamsburg, for instance, told her girlfriend that she and a Mr. Ash had become "just so terrible intimate Friends, and in a mutual interchange of sentiment" which gave them "the most refin'd pleasure." Being with him led "P" to "hate folly in every form" and to widen her thinking, "as he converses freely on every subject that may tend to open the understanding and inform the mind."[31]

In this view love was a rational, sensible commitment to another based upon genteel accomplishments. The head clearly governed the heart in these relationships, but affection was important. In the spring of 1767 Jonathan Boucher described for a friend the qualities he most admired in the girl he had been courting. She was "sprightly & animated" and had a "fire of Wit ... Tempered & chastened by a happy Judgment & the purest Benevolence." His love for her, Boucher insisted, was well grounded in reason, for he would not have cared for her so much "had not her Merit entitled her to it."[32]

[29]Thomas Jones to Elizabeth Pratt, Oct. 11, 1725, JFP. See also same to same, Oct. 5, 7, 14, 15, 1725, ibid.

[30]William Byrd II to Lady Betty Cromwell, Aug. 25, 1703, *Byrd Correspondence*, I, 233. See the entire collection of letters from Byrd to Lady Cromwell in ibid., 216–44.

[31]P. Davenport to Elizabeth Pelham, June 14, 1791, "Pelham Letters," 269.

[32]Jonathan Boucher to Mrs. Jones, March 9, 1767, "Letters of Jonathan Boucher," 341–43. See also Charles Carroll of C to Charles Carroll of A, Oct. 11, 1763, CARP.

The mutual approbation of "mental and personal Accomplishments" was essential to Joseph Nourse and Maria Bull of Virginia. In trying to win the favor of Maria, Nourse explained to her what they shared in common. "A similarity in Taste," he wrote in 1784, "appears necessary to mutual happiness." He admired the "purity and elegance" of the letters she wrote him (unlike those of most women, which were "illspelt, badly written & devoid of sentiment"), and the "enlivening Company" she always provided. Nourse assured Maria that his love for her was built on the strong foundation of "Truth, Honor and Virtue" and that time "will only serve to repeat how equally my Mind is formed with your Own, for domestic happiness." Until they were married, Nourse claimed he would have to live on "the flattering expectation that I shall meet your approbation." But he also asked that she send him a lock of her hair which he would "wear next to my Heart."[33]

Many young men and women in the late eighteenth century gave expression to emotional and passionate language that suggested a full flowering of romantic love unchecked by reason. When John Hatley Norton became romantically involved with Sally Nicholas in 1771, his friend reported to Norton's brother that John's "regard for Miss Nicholas is too deeply rooted to be eradicated."[34] St. George Tucker conducted a passionate courtship of Frances Bland Randolph in the winter of 1777–78. Tucker apologized for writing her so often but insisted that it was the "Impulse of my Heart, which leads me to trouble you with my Nonsense." His deep feelings for Frances ("Fanny") overcame

---

[33]Joseph Nourse to Maria Bull, Jan. 17, Feb. 10, 1784, Sept. 22, Dec. 27, 1783, NFP.
[34]William Reynolds to George Norton, Sept. 9, 1771, Mason, ed., *John Norton and Sons,* 186. The rise of romantic language between men and women as reflected in American literary magazines in the late eighteenth and early nineteenth centuries is traced by Herman R. Lantz, "The Pre-Industrial Family in America: A Further Examination of Early Magazines," *American Journal of Sociology,* LXXIX (1973), 581. See also William Ronald to James Parker, Oct. 14, 1769, PFP; Henry Callister to Robert Whitfield, Nov. 16, 1749, CALP. One girl confessed that romantic love tended to upset her emotional equilibrium. Thus she admired a friend who had "nothing of the romance in her" and was "much happier without it. I wish to Heaven I had as little." Orr, 9.

his commitment to a well-regulated emotional life. "Whatever Restraint I may be under in Company, the [?] Satisfaction of beholding you is a pleasure which my heart now pants-after." Tucker's sentiments constantly battled his reason over Frances, and in the end Tucker desperately wanted her to reveal her feelings for him just as he had done for her. "If the Ardor of my Affections and the sincerity of a heart wholly devoted to you can inspire you with a Tender Sentiment towards me suppress not the Emotion." Marriage required the union of hearts as well as minds, Tucker claimed, and any compromise would eventually destroy their relationship. "Reason for a moment has resum'd her long deserted Empire, and Tells me that your hand, without the entire possession of your heart, will only serve as a perpetual source of Misery to us both."[35]

Conspicuously absent from most of these love letters is any hint of erotic passion. Indeed the eighteenth-century emphasis on rational love almost excluded sensual desires. The ideal woman was defined in asexual terms: propriety, decency, modesty, and delicacy were the constituents of female virtue. But the very effort to conceal sexual feelings in male-female relationships exposed the preoccupation with these impulses. Richard Steele pointed out that the prude and the coquette were alike in that they have "the distinction of sex in all their thoughts, words and actions."[36] In a slave society such as that of Virginia and Maryland, the European double standard became fully developed: men could indulge their sexual passions with black women while insisting on the purity and virtue of their white women. Because erotic feelings had to be controlled for the stability of family and society, men and women stressed the possibilities of rational

[35]St. George Tucker to Frances Tucker, Dec. 19, 1777, 1778?, Jan. 15, March 2, 31, 1778, TCP. Tucker considered love the great leveler: "Love may really be compared to Death—it subdues us all & gets all Man upon the same Level—It is the True Republican Principle; no wonder than, if Should be inculcated in such Governments as Virginia, where, by the Constitution all Distinctions of persons are abolished." Same to same, March 31, 1778, ibid.

[36]Quoted in Ian Watt, *The Rise of the Novel* (Berkeley and Los Angeles, 1957), 170.

friendships, reserving marriage as the only permissible means of sexual expression.[37]

The social reality in the eighteenth-century Chesapeake, however, contradicted all of this. Premarital sexual contact was probably common on Chesapeake plantations, and not only between planters' sons and slave women.[38] White men and women frequently engaged in sexual activity before marriage. John Harrower, a tutor at the Dangerfield plantation in Virginia during the 1770s, took note of the sexual life of young Anthony Frazier, a white servant, and Lucy Gaines, a white housekeeper. They slept together each night in the schoolroom, which Harrower observed with some amusement. "Lucy at school Hugg & Hugg with Tony untill verry late and had not a nigger wench staid out for her wou'd have been allnight in the same position." Harrower referred to the couple as the "Lucy friggat" and the "Anthony Man of War" who were frequently "Moored there in Blanket Bay."[39]

But was this kind of sexual behavior on the Dangerfield plantation typical of Chesapeake society in general? Recently, demographic historians have suggested that premarital sex (as reflected in pregnancy at marriage), which had been relatively common especially among immigrants in the seventeenth-century Chesapeake, reached its height during the late eighteenth century. Daniel Scott Smith and Michael Hindus have shown, for example, that between 1749 and 1780 from one-fourth to one-third of all brides in Kingston Parish, Gloucester County, Virginia, were pregnant on the day of their first marriage. The rise in premarital pregnancy throughout much of eighteenth-century America developed largely because of growing seculari-

---

[37]See Peter Gay, *The Enlightenment: An Interpretation: The Science of Freedom* (New York, 1969), II, 199–205; Keith J. Thomas, "The Double Standard," *Journal of the History of Ideas*, xx (1959), 195–216. The only extensive discussion of sexual attitudes in the colonial South is in Winthrop Jordan, *White over Black: American Attitudes toward the Negro, 1550–1812* (New York, 1968), 136–78, 457–75.

[38]See, for example, the sexual behavior of Ben Carter on the Nomini Hall plantation, in Farish, ed., *Journal of Fithian*, 115, 246, 248.

[39]Edward M. Riley, ed., *The Journal of John Harrower* (New York, 1963), 143–44.

zation and waning community and parental authority.[40] The gap between sexual attitudes and behavior was but one of several ambiguities in eighteenth-century family and social life.

Companionship and Choice in Marriage

The ability to choose a marriage partner is a fundamental aspect of personal autonomy. But few sons and daughters in early America exercised this independence of choice. In the farm communities that dominated colonial America, the possession of land was the principal asset necessary for a young man to seriously consider marrying and setting up his own household. But fathers controlled this important source of wealth and until at least the mid-eighteenth century used their leverage as owners of family land and property to supervise and frequently to arrange their children's marriages. The *Whole Duty of Man,* one of the most widely read advice books in the colonies, emphasized the significance of parent-controlled marital decisions. "Children are so much the goods, the possessions of their Parents, that they cannot without a kind of theft, give away themselves without the allowance of those that have the right in them."[41]

One of the leading patriarchal figures of the colonial South, William Byrd II, was in full agreement with these parent-dominated marriages. In 1723 he rejected the intentions of his daughter Evelyn to become engaged to a baronet. He counseled her "never more to greet, speak, or write to that gentleman, or to give him an opportunity to see, speak or write to you. I also forbid

[40]Daniel Scott Smith and Michael S. Hindus, "Premarital Pregnancy in America, 1640–1971: An Overview and Interpretation" *Journal of Interdisciplinary History,* v (1975), 563, 556–59, 564. Premarital pregnancy engendered some criticism in the community, but as long as marriage followed as soon as possible there was no sense of public disgrace. The Reverend Robert Rose married Thomas Murray, who "was obliged to correct for his ruiness and immorality." RRD, Oct. 15, 1748. It was only when a couple waited a long time to marry after the pregnancy was detected that public ridicule emerged. William Faris noted that "The Town," Annapolis, Maryland, gossiped and criticized a man's marriage to his pregnant fiancée because "he should have marryed her soon as she is with Child." FD, May 9, 1792. See also ibid., Aug. 12, 1792.
[41]*The Whole Duty of Man* (London, 1684).

you to enter into any promise or engagement with him of marriage or inclination." Byrd's rationale for preventing the relationship was simple: it was, he wrote to his daughter, because of "the sacred duty you owe a parent, & upon the blessing you ought to expect upon the performance of it." If Evelyn evinced only a weak sense of duty to her father, then Byrd had more powerful leverage with which to exercise his will. She was "not to look for one brass farthing," Byrd declared, "if you provoke me by this fatal instance of disobedience. Nay besides all that, I will avoid the sight of you as of a creature detested. Figure then to yourself my dear child how wretched you will be with a provokt father & a disappointed husband."[42]

During most of the colonial era, marriages were usually more an economic merger between two families than a union based on companionship. Good matches were those that brought together two people representing families of similar economic and social status. The focus on fortunes rather than sentiments in marriage among gentry families is revealed in a typical wedding announcement published in the *Virginia Gazette* in 1738: "We hear from *Henrico* county, that on *Thursday*, the 13th Instant, the Rev. Mr. *William Stith* was married to Miss *Judith Randolph*, Sister of *William Randolph, Esq., of Tuckahoe,* an agreeable Lady, with a very considerable Fortune."[43]

The obsession with balance and a well-ordered family government presided over by a patriarchal father gave way gradually during the eighteenth century to a view of family life that prized intimacy, affection, and even a measure of passion. Moreover, with the emergence of child-centered families during the century, in which parents attributed greater powers of reason to their offspring, parental domination of marriages began to subside. Increasingly, parents believed that if children were raised in an environment that stressed self-government and rational disci-

---

[42]William Byrd II to Evelyn Byrd, July 20, 1723, *Byrd Correspondence,* I, 343.

[43]*Virginia Gazette,* July 28, 1738, Nov. 5, Oct. 29, 1736. That fathers controlled the courtship process as well is reflected in Byrd's effort to "pay addresses" to Lucy Parke by first convincing her father of his good intentions. See William Byrd II to Daniel Parke, circa 1705/6, *Byrd Correspondence,* I, 256–57.

pline, they would learn to make sensible decisions on their own, including appropriate marriage choices. Especially important at this time was the growth of sentimental, romantic love, nurtured in part by an increasingly intimate family life, which led most couples to value mutual affection and companionship over economic concerns in choosing a mate.[44]

That romantic love could easily outweigh reason and financial considerations worried some parents, who recognized the risks of youthful marriages forged solely out of emotion. The upcoming marriage of sixteen-year-old Anne Randolph to her nineteen-year-old cousin Richard Randolph troubled Anne's mother.

It has never been my wish to keep my Daughters single 'till they were old enough to form a proper judgment of Mankind well knowing that a Woman's happiness depends entirely on the Husband she is united to; it is a step that requires more deliberation than girls generally take, or even Mothers seem to think necessary; the risk *tho* always great, is doubled when they marry very young; it is impossible for them to know each others disposition; for at sixteen and nineteen we think everybody perfect that we take a fancy to; the Lady expects nothing but condescencion, and the Gentleman thinks his Mistress an Angel. As young people cannot have a sufficient knowledge of the world to teach them the necessity of making a proper allowance for the foibles to say no worse of Humanity, they are apt to be sour when the delirium of Love is over and Reason is allowed to rescend her Throne; and if they are not so happy as to find in each other a similarity of temper and good qualities enough to excite esteem and Friendship, they must be wretched, without a remedy. [Anne Randolph to St. George Tucker, Sept. 23, 1788][45]

By the latter half of the eighteenth century, a pattern of marriages in which the partners chose each other was clearly established in the Chesapeake, at least among middle- and upper-

---

[44]Lawrence Stone calls this growth of companionate marriages and romantic love in the late eighteenth century "affective individualism." See his discussion in *The Family, Sex and Marriage*, 270–404. See also Shorter, 148–49.

[45]Anne Randolph to St. George Tucker, Sept. 23, 1788, "Randolph and Tucker Letters," *VMHB*, XLII (1934), 49–50.

class planter families.[46] Daughters frequently married without or against the advice of their parents and kin. One girl from Richmond County, Virginia, decided on a private wedding ceremony in Maryland because she married a man over her father's objections.[47] William Byrd III was surprised and upset to learn in 1765 that his niece, Maria Carter, had chosen to marry without informing most of her family. "I wish it had been agreeable to you to have given some of your friends here Notice of it, because we think ourselves interested in your happiness." A few years earlier, however, Byrd himself had displayed the same independence from his mother, for he married a girl from Philadelphia in 1760 and told his mother about it only after the ceremony. "I was so surprised," his mother responded, "as to cry out Good God is my Son Married & never acquainted me with it!"[48] This decline in parental authority over marriage was not confined to the Chesapeake. One recent quantitative study seems to indicate that by the latter third of the eighteenth century, personal autonomy carried more significance than parental desires in Massachusetts marriages.[49]

Although parents were deeply concerned about whom their children married, they attached increasing importance to companionship and free choice in marital decisions. Lasting and happy marriages, many parents came to believe, depended more on a couple's personal feelings than on economic considerations. One father in 1757 made this point abundantly clear: "all marriages ought to be entirely from the free choice of each party & that want of Fortune in either ought to be no objection provided

[46]It is reasonable to assume that with less family property and reputation at stake, sons and daughters of small planters may have experienced the same marital autonomy, perhaps even earlier.
[47]General Hooe to Michael Wallace, Oct. 3, 1785, WP.
[48]William Byrd III to Maria Carter, Nov. 25, 1765, "Family Letters of the Eighteenth Century," *VMHB*, xv (1908), 435; Mrs. Maria Byrd to William Byrd III, Feb. 17, 1761, "Letters of the Byrd Family," *VMHB*, xxxviii (1930), 350. See also Margaret Parker to James Parker, Feb. 19, 1777, PFP; *Carter Diary*, II, 810–11, 814–15, 830; Charles Carroll of A to Charles Carroll of C, Aug. 30, 1758, CARP; *Byrd Diary, 1709–12*, 435; Richard Terrell to Patsy Minor, July 3, 4, 1791, CTFP; and "Eliza Custis, Self-Portrait," *VMHB*, lxi (1953), 93–94.
[49]Daniel Scott Smith, 419–28.

there was no other." Samuel Swann was especially optimistic about the future of his daughter's upcoming marriage, for the couple had "a natural regard for each other Which is the best Prognostick of their future Happiness." Theodorick Bland, Sr., was likewise pleased with his daughter's marriage in 1763, "as it is a choice entirely of her own making."[50]

Even a father as domineering and contentious as Landon Carter refrained from interfering too frequently in matters of matrimony. When his daughter Lucy accepted the addresses of William Colston in the fall of 1775, Carter articulated his paternal policy on marriage: "as a Parent I never took any Liberty with a Child but to dissuade where I thought I had reason so to do; but in no instance Whatever to Persuade, therefore her approbation must Proceed from his own conduct and her good liking."[51] Many fathers considered it actually harmful to arrange a marriage between two unwilling individuals and believed that, except for unusually dubious cases, parental involvement should amount to little more than blessing the union after the couple had made the decision. At the marriage of his nephew in 1785, George Washington clearly outlined this view of limited parental participation in marital decisions:

> It has ever been a maxim with me through life, neither to promote, nor to prevent a matrimonial connection, unless there should be something indispensably requiring interference in the latter. I have always considered marriage as the most interesting event of one's life—the foundation of happiness or misery. To be instrumental therefore in bringing two people together, who are indifferent to each other, and may soon become objects of disgust,—or to prevent a union which is prompted by the affections of the mind, is what I never could reconcile with reason, and therefore neither directly, nor indirectly have I ever said a syllable to Fanny or George, upon the subject of their intended connection, but as their attachment to each other seems of early growth, warm, and lasting

[50]Jane Swann to Elizabeth Jones, Sept. 7, 1757; Samuel Swann to Thomas Jones, Sept. 8, 1757, JFP; Theodorick Bland, Sr., to Theodorick Bland, Jr., Feb. 14, 1763, BP. See also Mary Dulaney to Walter Dulaney, Aug. 7, 1783, DP.
[51]*Carter Diary*, II, 939.

it bids fair for happiness. [George Washington to Burwell Bassett, May 23, 1785][52]

Marital decisions for some young men were not always such unambiguous matters of free choice. The close bonds of affection and deference between fathers and sons sometimes made it difficult for a young man to consider marrying a woman if his father disliked the match. Even if most fathers did not actually forbid their sons to marry certain women, the prospect of earning parental disfavor by entering an unapproved engagement was disturbing enough to give many young men pause. This was especially true in exceptionally wealthy families, in which sons were particularly mindful of marrying women of equal status who understood the importance of keeping the family estate together.

The tensions between a desire for personal autonomy in choosing a wife and the familial obligations imposed by great family wealth and a watchful father are revealed in the courtship experience of Charles Carroll of Carrollton. Like most sons in the late eighteenth century, Charles insisted on the right to select his own marriage partner. Paternal control of this crucial event, he wrote his father in 1763, was "the highest cruelty a father can be guilty of." "I had rather be disinherited," he announced, "than obliged to marry against my inclination." But young Carroll's almost obsessive devotion to his father tempered such stridency, for he ended the same letter with the promise "never to marry without your full & free consent & approbation."[53]

In addition, the young man's responsibility as heir of his father's huge landed estate in Maryland weighed heavily in Carroll's marital plans. He worried about dying young—surviving beyond the age of thirty-six was problematic to him—and having

[52]George Washington to Burwell Bassett, May 23, 1785, *Virginia Historical Register*, III (1850), 224–25. An exception to this parental hands-off policy toward a daughter's marriage is evident in Martha Jefferson Carr's efforts to prevent the marriage of her daughter to Samuel Terrell. Mrs. Carr informed Terrell in the summer of 1794 that he could not marry her daughter unless he was willing to settle in Maryland, which he considered "impracticable." Martha Jefferson Carr to Lucy Terrell, Aug. 9, 1794, CTFP.
[53]Charles Carroll of C to Charles Carroll of A, Feb. 19, 1763, CARP.

his widow remarry and "carry off the greater part of the estate to another family." When Carroll was courting an English girl, his father provided him with detailed estimates of his own net worth—£88,380 in land, slaves, and investments in iron works—and ordered his son to investigate the nature and amount of the wealth of the girl's father. His fiancee's reluctance to move to the Carroll family home in Maryland eventually brought an end to the courtship. "The situation of our affairs," he explained to his father in 1764, "absolutely require[s] my residence in Maryland; and I cannot sacrifice the future aggrandisement of our family to a woman." In short, Charles Carroll believed that marriage was essentially an individual matter based on companionship and love (he broke an engagement in part because he "knew too little of her to be in love"), but since extraordinary family wealth and firm paternal plans were at stake, his father held the upper hand in marital decisions.[54]

Few sons had to contend with such an overpowering father and the responsibility of such an immense estate as did Charles Carroll, however; paternal authority over marriage was not so strongly felt in most families. Still, fathers did occasionally intercede in their sons' marital plans, rarely out of paternal power or a concern for consolidating the family fortune, to be sure, but rather to insure that sons married only after they had achieved sufficient economic independence to live with their wives in some sort of "genteel competence." Although the use of this economic leverage sometimes resembled a paternal ploy to influence a son's choice of a wife, more often it was simply an objection to the timing of the marriage.[55]

[54]Charles Carroll of C to Charles Carroll of A, Oct. 11, 1763, Jan. 10, 1764, Aug. 8, 1763, Jan. 9, 1764, May 30, 1764, CARP.
[55]It should be noted that on occasion men may have been rather capricious in rejecting the marriage plans of their daughters. Richard Henry Lee, according to Philip Fithian, insisted that neither his sister nor daughter—if he had had one—would be allowed to marry a Scot. Farish, ed., *Journal of Fithian*, 234. Robert Carter of Nomini Hall prevented his daughter Sarah from marrying Richard Bland Lee in 1790, largely because of his political stand. But in 1804, Carter claimed that he never interfered with his daughters' marital decisions. "As a Father, I never recommend either Male or Female in the Line of marriage, and my married Issue

The marriage of John Hatley Norton in 1772 is a case in point. During his first year in Virginia as a factor for his father's London-based mercantile firm, Norton became deeply involved with Sally Nicholas and decided to marry her and remain in Williamsburg. Without actually prohibiting the match, John's father pointed out that the decision showed great "unsteadiness in your Conduct," since John had promised to return to England within a year. Moreover, John Norton, Sr., explained that with six sons to support, he could not adequately provide the kind of settlement John's prospective wife would expect. "This Lady is full young to enter into the cares of Life, has been bred in a genteel way & has a right to expect to live so, can you say 'tis in your power to comply with this piece of Justice towards her?" The limited economic resources of the family, Norton counseled his son, required prudence and a sense of fairness to the other boys in the family: "What is to be sav'd out of it the profits of the family business for younger braunches who have an equal title to the sweat of their parents brow? One sixth part of the profits of the trade is all in my powr to allow you & what will that do to maintain a family without other assistance which can't be much look'd for in America at present." Having placed such weighty obstacles in his son's path, Norton asked John to decide for himself. "I must leav[e] you to your reflections & wish you may judge properly."[56]

Norton's intervention in his son's marriage plans worked, at least for a while, as the engagement was broken. But John stayed on in Virginia and two years later he resumed his "suit with Miss Nicholas." Despite prospects of only a modest portion from his father, he married Sally in January of 1772. By this time, John Norton, Sr., had given in to the independence of his son: "Far be it from me my Dear son to bias you in a matter of the greatest concern to your future happyness, it never was nor never shall be

---

chose for themselves. Convictions never troubled me on that Score." Quoted in Louis Morton, *Robert Carter of Nomini Hall: A Virginia Tobacco Planter of the Eighteenth Century* (Charlottesville, Va., 1941), 229.

[56]John Norton to John Hatley Norton, July 28, 1769, Mason, ed., *John Norton and Sons*, 98–100.

my intention. If the young Lady & her Parents approve of a Union between our Familys & you think you can live happy & content with the small provision I am able to make for you."[57]

Parenthood, however, altered John H. Norton's perspective on the freedom of choice in marriage. In 1790, eighteen years later, Warner Lewis, Jr., was pursuing Norton's daughter Nancy. Lewis was nineteen and Nancy was eighteen. Like his father, John H. Norton worried about the economic security of a youthful marriage. Lewis informed Nancy's father that he was "captivated by the charms of your eldest Daughter and overcome by the power of Love." Moreover, Lewis explained, "I have paid my addresses to her and have been so fortunate as to find that they have met with a favourable reception." And he did his best to convince Norton—through a third party, Edmund Randolph—that his father, though dubious about an early marriage, consented to the match. His father, Lewis noted, "is averse to my marrying as soon as I wish, he thinks it wou'd have been to my advantage to have waited a few years longer before I engage myself, but he thinks my choice is as good as one as I cou'd have made, and has not the smallest objection on that head." What bothered Norton, however, was whether young Lewis's career as a lawyer would be sufficiently lucrative to maintain him and Nancy independent of Lewis's father. Norton described his financial expectations of the marriage to Edmund Randolph, a friend of the Norton and Lewis families: "A genteel competency will certainly be expected by me, you & Mrs. Randolph, & must assure to us wld. render Mr. Lewis independt. of his Father otherwise the Young People may be render'd unhappy."[58]

At Norton's request, Randolph investigated the economic prospects for Warner Lewis, Jr., and reported back to Norton a

[57]Martha Goosely to John Norton, April 22, 1770; William Reynolds to John Norton, Nov. 26, 1771, May 23, 1772; William Reynolds to George Norton, May 23, 1772; John Norton to John Hatley Norton, Jan. 29, 1772, ibid., 127–28, 208, 241, 237, 215–16.

[58]Warner Lewis, Jr., to John Hatley Norton, June 21, 1790; Warner Lewis, Jr., to Edmund Randolph, Dec. 22, 1790; Lewis to John Hatley Norton, July 15, 1790; John Hatley Norton to Edmund Randolph, July 5, 1790, ibid., 491, 498, 494–95.

few weeks later. That Lewis's father, Randolph concluded, could make "an ample provision for his son, is undoubted; but what prospects from professional success W may have, independent of his father's aid, I shall not decide. The Law is overstocked already; and it will require abilities of a very respectable rank to obtain livelihood in that line." The economic uncertainties of Lewis's career uncovered by Norton and Randolph led them to postpone the marriage for two years. When he reached his legal majority at age twenty-one in 1792, Warner Lewis finally married Nancy Norton.[59]

The same kind of conflict between a young man's romantic inclinations and paternal demands for economic self-sufficiency was evident in the experience of Patrick Parker in 1786. The twenty-two-year-old son of James Parker, a Loyalist who was living as an exile in England after the Revolution, Patick established himself as a merchant in Norfolk. He quickly decided to marry his cousin, a decision which deeply disturbed his father, who believed the young couple had too little capital to make a go of it at such an early age. Patrick responded by insisting that his "industry" would overcome his "poverty." Moreover, James's hard-line position, Patrick contended, made it difficult for him to keep "that respectful and submissive manner I ought." But, however independent-minded the young Parker appeared, he still craved his father's approval. "God help me I am really to be pitied," he wrote James in 1786. "My duty to my Parent—my own personal Interest leading one way—and on ye other an affection and esteem which I never shall be able to surmount."[60]

Apparently James was right in predicting financial trouble for Patrick and his bride, as the young couple spent the early years of their marriage struggling for economic security while slipping in and out of debt. The knowledge that he had followed his own poor judgment against the better advice and natural authority of his father haunted Patrick continually. In his father's letters,

---

[59]Edmund Randolph to John Hatley Norton, July 24, 1790, March 13, 1792, ibid., 495, 500–01.
[60]Patrick Parker to James Parker, March 20, 1787, May 1787, PFP.

Patrick confessed to James, he could "clearly see . . . that you are quite disgusted with me—every error or omission of mine is repeated and magnified to a crime—upon a Cool & sincere reflection however in past transactions, every man who has acted so dramatically opposite to the commands of a Father deserves it—."

So paranoid had Patrick become over his independent marital decision that after the death of his two-day-old infant, he openly speculated to his father "that this is the method heaven takes to punish me for disobedience in marrying contrary to your inclinations." Mixed with this pattern of self-flagellation and fear was an occasional flash of anger toward his father's persistent rebukes. "For God Allmighty sake don't run me distracted with your cruell [censures] of my conduct. . . . My spirit cannot stand it nor do I deserve it—particularly from a father . . . if a son cannot make free with a Father I think it is hard indeed—."[61]

Marital decisions in the late eighteenth-century Chesapeake, we may conclude, remained largely individual matters, growing out of feelings of companionship and a commitment to independence in the selection of a mate. Parents usually stayed in the background during courtship and marriage, often because of strong convictions that parental intervention violated the "natural regard" so essential to a happy marital life. But some parents still insisted on an ultimate right to veto, especially when they felt that a prospective marriage portended serious financial difficulty.

Kinship, Ritual, and "the Matrimonial State"

Marriage in the eighteenth-century Chesapeake was often, as it is today, a very personal matter involving the private feelings

---

[61]Same to same, May 4, 1787, Feb. 21, 179[1], Nov. 4, 1791, ibid. For other examples of paternal concern over the economic viability of a son's marriage, see the father-son conflict in Robert J. Brugger, "Heart over Head: The Antebellum Persuasion of Nathaniel Beverley Tucker" (unpub. Ph.D. diss., The Johns Hopkins University, 1974), 73, 75, 92. See also John Bland to Henry Fitzhugh, Dec. 10, 1770, BP; *Carter Diary*, II, 966–97; and Elizabeth Jones to Thomas Jones, Dec. 14, 1756, JFP.

between two people. But perhaps more important, it represented a confirmation and elaboration of the family and kinship ties in planter communities. This had not been true of most marriages in the seventeenth century. Early Chesapeake society was populated mainly by immigrants; many couples who married and lived in Virginia or Maryland set up their new households separated from family and kin. Short adult life expectancies in the seventeenth century also meant that many fathers and mothers did not live to see their children reach maturity and start families of their own.[62]

With the growth after 1700 of a native population and the rise in life expectancies, Chesapeake marriages became more kin-oriented. Networks of uncles and aunts and cousins grew up around many families during the eighteenth century and provided marriage partners in a community of kin. Indeed, one study of planters in Prince George's County, Maryland, has shown that kin marriages between first cousins and other blood relatives increased significantly during the century from about 11 percent in the first third of the eighteenth century to 28 percent between 1760 and 1790. In a very direct sense, then, marriage in the eighteenth century intensified kin group solidarity.[63]

The wedding ceremony provides insights into how marriage united two families and strengthened the bonds of kinship.

[62]See Walsh, "'Till Death Us Do Part,'"; Smith, "Mortality and Family in the Colonial Chesapeake"; and Rutman and Rutman, "'Now-Wives and Sons-in-Law.'"

[63]Allan Kulikoff, "Throwing the Stocking: A Gentry Marriage in Provincial Maryland," *MHM*, LXXI (1976), 517. It is possible, however, that particularly religious parents in Presbyterian and Baptist households may have disallowed or at least discouraged kin marriages that appear to have been fairly common among Anglican planters. Peter Fontaine, for example, against the advice of friends, opposed the marriage of his daughter to her cousin James Maury in 1754. Fontaine conceived of marriage in a religious context. The purpose of matrimony, he wrote, was to join again "the strictest ties of love and duty those who are separated in many degrees by descent from our first ancestors." Over several generations people create increasingly wider circles, he explained, but at marriage "the circle meets again, and we become one flesh." The difficulty with kin marriages, then, was that it straightened out the circle too much, "making a circle within a circle, a state within a state ... which is not only of pernicious consequence to the government, but contrary to the true spirit of Christianity." Peter Fontaine to John and Moses Fontaine, April 15, 1754, in Ann Maury, ed., *Memoirs of a Hugenot Family* (New York, 1907), 341.

Weddings were above all family affairs, held in the bride's house and usually conducted by an Anglican minister. They often began early in the day, around noon, for the convenience of guests who had to ride long distances to attend. Then as now, the ceremony itself was usually brief. One woman described a marriage in Norfolk in 1785: "it was concluded [on?] very quick."[64]

The size of a wedding probably reflected the economic status and social prominence of the two families involved. Groups of twenty or so guests witnessed the marriages of families from the middle and lower ranks of society.[65] For wealthier planters, up to one hundred guests attended the wedding and the festive celebrations that followed. The marriage of Maria Beverley and Richard Randolph in 1785 attracted close to one hundred guests, and according to one observer, the scene was quite emotional: "The ceremony was really affecting and awful. The sweet bride could not help shedding tears, which affected her mother and the whole company. She was most elegantly dressed in white satin, and the bridegroom in a lead color, lined with pink satin. After the ceremony of saluting, the ladies retired."[66] A Maryland woman was also reportedly moved by the weddings she had attended, for "there was a Solemnity in the marriage ceremony that affected her as much as the burial place." Following the ceremony, the newlyweds and their guests celebrated with a sumptuous meal, drinking, and dancing, often lasting until midnight, when the couple finally slipped away.[67]

From the marriage ceremony through the celebration, which usually continued for a day or two, the newlywed couple was almost constantly surrounded by kin and friends. The guests appear to have been mainly relatives and a few unrelated close

[64]Carson, *Colonial Virginians at Play*, 17–18; Margaret Saunders to Margaret Parker, April 17, 1785, PFP.

[65]Ibid.; "The Journal of James Gordon of Lancaster County, Virginia," *WMQ*, 1st ser., xi (1903), 104–5.

[66]The marriage is recorded in VMHB, xxxiv (1926), 162. See also *Byrd Diary, 1709–12*, 437–39.

[67]Katherine Jacques deposition, May 27, 1769, in 1757 marriage in Prince George's County, Maryland, reprinted in Kulikoff, "Throwing the Stocking," 521; Carson, *Colonial Virginians at Play*, 12; *Carter Diary*, II, 1021; FTD, Nov. 8, 1787, Dec. 22, 1795, Jan. 8, 9, 1799; "The Frances Baylor Hill Diary," 20.

neighbors. [68] James Taylor's marriage to Fanny Catlett Moore in Orange County, Virginia, in 1795 was attended by "a good many of their relatives," who were all "very merry." Days or sometimes weeks after the marriage, the wedding company might visit the bridegroom's parents and the newlyweds themselves, sometimes organizing yet another "entertainment" for them, this time sponsored by the bridegroom's family. [69]

Family and friends congratulated the couple on their marriage, contrasting a "Life of Dissipation" with "a married Life with an agreeable Partner." [70] One young man in 1772 was jubilant over his brother's marriage which signaled that he was "joined in the connubial Estate with a Young Lady who by all Accounts is above the commonalty of her sex & scarcely to be parallel'd." Both of the families welcomed their "new relation" and praised both the growth of kin and the prospect for happiness in the new marriage. [71]

Marriage was also perceived as a new and potentially powerful psychological state, as well as an important merger of two families. As we have discussed earlier, young men and women grew up largely among friends of their own sex; thus it was believed that the new living arrangements in marriage could dramatically alter one's character. Frances Tucker, for example, noted that her friend Martha ("Patty") Hall "has grown tired of celibacy & is shortly to be metamorphosed into Mrs. Day." [72] Single women appear to have distanced themselves from female friends who married, as if marriage severed the ties of intimacy that bound young women together. [73]

[68]Kulikoff, "Throwing the Stocking," 519.
[69]FTD, Dec. 22, 29–31, 1795, March 14, 16, 1795.
[70]George Norton to John Hatley Norton, Nov. 3, 1772, in Mason, ed., *John Norton and Sons*, 278.
[71]George Norton to John Norton, March 30, March 25, 1772, John Norton to John Hatley Norton, March 10, 1772; Mrs. John Norton to John Norton, March 1772; Elinor Frere Fenn to John Hatley Norton, March 1769, ibid., 228, 227, 225, 229–30, 89–90; George Hume to Mrs. Isabel Hume, July 20, 1754, in "A Colonial Scottish Jacobite Family," *VMHB*, XXXVIII (1930), 226.
[72]Frances Tucker to George Tucker, May 3, 1779, TCP.
[73]This was especially true of newly married women. Orr, 15, 29, 32; Carroll Smith-Rosenberg, "The Female World of Love and Ritual: Relations between Women in Nineteenth-Century America," *Signs: Journal of Women in Culture and Society*, I (1975), 1–30.

Moreover, domineering husbands could destroy a woman's independent spirit, some women believed. As her marriage drew near, Harriet Wilson of Richmond, Virginia, worried that she was "a ficle Jade & shudders at the idea of resigning her liberty in the hands of a *husband*."[74] Molly Tilghman became alarmed at the changes she saw in her friend after her marriage. "Never did I see a Woman more alter'd." The explanation, Molly insisted, lay in an abusive husband, given to excessive drinking; "an abominable Husband is enough to break any Woman."[75] Women approached marriage with considerable apprehension as well as enthusiasm.

Men likewise foresaw uncertain but significant character changes in marriage. Fathers, not surprisingly, hoped that the "matrimonial State" would induce unstable sons to be "a little more steady."[76] But some men feared that marriage with its new economic and emotional demands might lead to a melancholy and sullen disposition. This unsettling idea of marriage bothered James Hollyday in the summer of 1763 as he reflected on a friend's recent wedding. His friend, Hollyday observed, should be happy with his "Young Wife," but if the marriage does not work out, he argued, "I dare say it will not be his Fault—if he does not continue to be the same good natured kind and agreeable Man that I knew him, I shall certainly attribute the Change to his Matrimony, wch does Sometimes strangely alter people."[77]

Love and Health

Despite these fears, there is substantial evidence that at least among literate, well-to-do families, husbands and wives found

[74]Harriet Wilson to Maria Roy, Aug. 13, 1811, BFP.
[75]Molly Tilghman to Polly Tilghman, 1785? "Molly and Hetty Tilghman Letters," 37.
[76]John Norton to John Hatley Norton, March 10, 1772, Mason, ed., *John Norton and Sons*, 225. William Byrd II thought that marriage could be agreeable enough, but "so many are shipwreckt in that sea, that it has now quite lost the name of the Pacifick Ocean." William Byrd II to John Boyle, July 28, 1730, *Byrd Correspondence*, I, 432.
[77]James Hollyday to Sarah Anderson, James Hollyday to James Anderson, July 24, 1763, HFP. See also Dabney Carr to Lucy Terrell, April 26, 1798, CTFP; William Byrd II to Mrs. Anne Taylor Otway, circa June 1729, *Byrd Correspondence*, I, 401.

marriage a very agreeable living arrangement. In their correspondence, spouses frequently expressed feelings of close, tender regard for each other, suggesting that the romantic grandilo-
quence characteristic of courtship contained more than a small
portion of genuine love. Of course we cannot know if the sentiments revealed in letters between separated spouses—almost
the only evidence available for examining the character of
husband-wife relationships—accurately reflected the kinds of
feelings most couples gave expression to in each other's presence.
By their very nature nearly all such intimate communications are
lost forever to historians, creating the problem of "assessing the
unsaid," as Alan Macfarlane has aptly put it.[78] In all likelihood,
letters and diaries, especially the former, exaggerate somewhat
the positive emotional ties between spouses. Nevertheless, the
intensity of feelings many couples revealed in writing is worth
exploring.

When Thomas Jones's wife Elizabeth spent the summer of 1728
in England to see relatives and to improve her health, Jones
deeply missed her. He sent her gifts of sweetmeats and extra
coats, but above all confessed his need for her company. Her
absence, he explained, demonstrated the "dependence . . . I have
upon you, for my part all the real enjoyment & comfort I can
expect in this World is confined to you, & if it was not for the
hopes of having your dear Conversation again, life would be but
a burthen to me." Two months later, as he grew impatient for her
to return to Virginia, Jones asked, "How is it possible for me to
live without my only Joy & Comfort?"[79]

Twenty-six-year-old Lewis Joynes of Accomack County, Virginia, expressed similar sentiments over fifty years later. Joynes
wrote his wife Anne while he was being detained in a British
prison camp in Maryland during the winter of 1780. His affection
for her suggested an even more sensual, intimate relationship

---

[78]Alan Macfarlane, *The Family Life of Ralph Josselin: A Seventeenth-Century
Clergyman* (Cambridge, 1970).
[79]Thomas Jones to Elizabeth Jones, July 8, Sept. 30, 1728, JFP. William Byrd sent
his wife a "present of blue wing" while away in Williamsburg. *Byrd Diary,
1709–12*, 241.

with Anne than perhaps was common among spouses in the early Chesapeake. Calling Anne a "loving and Virtuous woman," Lewis described how she awakened the "tender feeling of my Heart" and the "soft emotions of my soul." As a prisoner, Joynes feared that his private affections for Anne might be uncovered by those who censored the letters: "what a pity it is that what passes between a man and his wife should be so exposed." But he closed another rhapsodic love letter with the declaration: "I shall soon hold my wife in these longing arms."[80]

While away on business trips, many men regularly corresponded with their spouses to give directions for managing the plantation in their absence and to express feelings that may have been more difficult to say in their wives' company. During a visit to his uncle's house in Maryland, Horatio Belt paused to write a long letter to his wife Catherine and closed it with this note: "As I am sure you know I love you more than I can express. I shall not injure it by a profession."[81] Theodorick Bland, Jr., wrote more freely of his affections for his wife Patsy in 1777. He missed her "agreeable chat," and, one suspects, something more: "My dearest Patsy," "you will again feel your husband's lips flowing with love and affection warmth."[82] St. George Tucker's law practice often kept him away from his wife and children, but the frequent separations only heightened his emotional commitment to "Fanny." On their anniversary day Tucker became ecstatic. "Happy, happy, happy Day! The anniversary of the happiest. Event of my Life! Blest be the Day & blest ever the Event!" The next day he composed a long poem honoring their anniversary and his virtuous, stable marital life:

> And while the Rake may wish to roam,
> I'm sure to find my Heaven at Home!
> [St. George Tucker to Frances Tucker, Sept. 24, 1791][83]

[80]Levin Joynes to Anne Joynes, Feb. 9, 29, 1780, "Letters from Colonel Levin Joynes to Ann, His Wife," *VMHB*, LVI (1948), 145–47.
[81]Horatio Belt to Catherine Belt, Sept. 30, 1783, DP.
[82]Theodorick Bland, Jr. to Patsy Bland, Feb. 1777, BP.
[83]St. George Tucker to Frances Tucker, Sept. 23, 24, 1781, TCP. For other evidence of close emotional regard between husbands and wives, see Richard Terrell to Lucy Terrell, Dec. 7, 1792, April 27, July 14, 1793, CTFP.

Because adult female literacy, especially the ability to write letters or keep a diary, remained low throughout the eighteenth century, and because women were not expected to give direct expression to their passions, it is more difficult to assess how wives felt towards their spouses.[84] The few surviving letters of women in the eighteenth-century Chesapeake suggest, however, that some wives did not refrain from showing deep affections for their husbands. Elizabeth Byrd, writing her husband Col. William Byrd III in 1757, spoke of "the inexpressible Pleasure of haveing you with me & your Babes once more."[85] Another woman asked her son to give "Thy Dear Papa," when they saw each other in London, "My Tenderest Love."[86] And Fanny Tucker disclosed the "tender anxiety" she felt for St. George while he was away from home, insisting that "very few feel the attachment we do." She kept a lock of his hair, which, she explained, "has been my Bracelet & constant companion."[87]

Illness, an almost constant problem in Chesapeake households, often drew a couple closer together. Given the paucity of doctors, sickness was largely a family matter, and the cure of illness fell to husbands and wives.[88] Ministering to a sick spouse may have demonstrated an important kind of conjugal love. During William Byrd's bout with the ague in the early fall of 1711, for example, his wife gave him the cinchona bark and "looked after me with a great deal of Tenderness." And when he had a painful back, she rubbed it with a mixture of tobacco oil and balsam of saltpeter. Although somewhat less solicitous himself, Byrd frequently took "great care" of his wife when she was ill. If her being "indisposed" left her depressed, as it frequently did, Byrd was sometimes deeply affected. On March 14, 1710, he

---

[84]Adult female literacy in eighteenth-century Virginia remained at around 50 percent. See Kenneth Lockridge, *Literacy in Colonial New England: An Enquiry into the Social Context of Literacy in the Early Modern West* (New York, 1974), 77, 92.

[85]Mrs. Elizabeth Hill Carter Byrd to William Byrd III, 1757, *VMHB*, xxxvii (1929), 242–43.

[86]A. Bland to John Bland, Jr., July 9, 1758, BP.

[87]Frances Tucker to St. George Tucker, July 10, 1778, TCP.

[88]See Chapter 6.

recorded in his diary: "My wife was melancholy, which made me weep."[89]

Maintaining a modicum of good health bordered on an obsession for many planters, and a spouse's health was more important than anyone's. While he was in Philadelphia, Theodorick Bland, Jr., wrote: "For God's sake, my dear, when you are writing; write of nothing but yourself, or at least exhaust that dear, ever dear subject, before you make a transition to another; tell me of your going to bed, of your rising, of the hour you breakfast, dine, sup, visit, tell me of anything, but leave me not in doubt about your health."[90] In October of 1787, St. George told his wife that it was her health, "about which I am more concerned than the federal Government or any other Human Concern."[91]

But sickness could strain as well as strengthen marital relationships. Numerous pregnancies and miscarriages weakened the constitution of women and undoubtedly sometimes left wives with sullen, resentful feelings toward their spouses and others around them. With an average of seven or eight pregnancies, usually clustered in the first ten to fifteen years of marriage, planters' wives in the eighteenth-century Chesapeake spent between 25 and 35 percent of their entire married life and over 60 percent of their early married life—between the ages of twenty-five and thirty-five—pregnant or recovering from childbirth or miscarriage.[92] With little medical relief from the physical discomfort of repeated pregnancies, some wives remained almost constantly "indisposed" and often ill-tempered with their husbands and children. William Byrd frequently observed that his wife was "out of humor" because she was "sick with being with child" or "indisposed with breeding & very cross."[93] The emotional difficulties of pregnancy were apparent to Molly Tilghman as she

[89]*Byrd Diary, 1709–12,* 401, 197, 368–69, 371, 155, 297, 152. See also Charles Carroll of A to Charles Carroll of C, Nov. 13, 1769, CARP.

[90]Theodorick Bland, Jr. to Patsy Bland, Feb. 1777, BP.

[91]St. George Tucker to Frances Tucker, Oct. 3, 1787, TCP. See also same to same, Oct. 3, 4, 17, 1787, March 2, 1781, ibid.

[92]These figures assume ten months for each pregnancy—a nine-month term and a one-month recovery.

[93]*Byrd Diary, 1709–12,* 548.

cared for her sister Hetty during her numerous pregnancies in the 1780s. Hetty's irritability during pregnancy doubtless bothered her husband and had begun to upset Molly: "If she drags her bloated self to the Wine Mill, she thinks so prodigious an exertion entitles her to groan and complain the whole Evening. Now is it not a melancholy thing to see a young person give themselves up to such horrid ways, because they are worried?"[94]

Such an emotional and physical condition probably strained relationships between husbands and wives and may explain in part why female friends and relatives usually cared for pregnant women, who were sometimes separated from their husbands during the last few weeks before delivery. Husbands were rarely as sensitive as other women to the physical and emotional difficulties of pregnancy. Perhaps characteristic of male attitudes was that expressed by Enoch Smith of Montgomery County, Virginia, who told a friend in 1797 that his wife was in "a low state of health," but that "perhaps nine months may cure her of her complaint."[95] The pain and responsibility of child-bearing and motherhood could drain the energies and dull the sensibilities of wives while still quite young. Motherhood appeared to have taken its toll on Frances Tucker by the age of twenty-six. In 1779 she wrote her husband, "my charms were formerly embellished when contrasted with yours, but the scale is absolutely turn'd, for the young Widow is changed into an old Pumpkin faced, dropsical Mope."[96]

Power and Submission:
Sexual Politics in the Planter Family

Conjugal love was a significant aspect of eighteenth-century marriages, but marital harmony depended primarily on a clear understanding of the power relationships in the household. In-

[94]Molly Tilghman to Polly Tilghman, Aug. 5, 1785, July 7, 1786, "Molly and Hetty Tilghman Letters," 130–31, 230.

[95]Enoch Smith to Isaac Davis, Jr., May 30, 1797, IDP. See also Henry Hollyday to James Hollyday, Aug. 5, 1782, HFP; FTD, June 12, 1797.

[96]Frances Tucker to St. George Tucker, May 25, 1779, TCP.

deed, feelings of affection were often expressed in the context of ascribed roles for husbands and wives. A husband, for example, was expected to be the complete master of the house—with the exception of overseeing female domestic servants—and showed his concern for his spouse by acting as her protector and friend. A wife's conjugal role, on the other hand, required her to satisfy and please her husband by appearing submissive, obedient, and good-natured in his presence. Through selfless devotion to her husband and domestic affairs, she could elicit his affection and a certain amount of respect. In short, a good wife provided a man with a "faithful Friend" who looked after his interests and made "his Joys and Sorrows all her own."[97] Ideally, a man did not resort to a show of authority to produce this wifely obedience and agreeable conduct; rather it was a husband's "gently & easy manner" as head of the family that guided her into compliance and respect.[98]

This was the normative version of married life, according to ministers, essayists, and authors of advice literature—almost all of whom were men, to be sure. But did private experience in the eighteenth-century Chesapeake, at least to the extent that our limited evidence can suggest, comport with this ideal view of male-dominated conjugal relationships? In most respects, yes. Men and women looked for affection and close, emotional bonds in marriage, but conjugal love did not imply a democratization of authority in the household. For the most part, husbands instructed and led; wives complied and followed.

A wife's subordinate relationship to her husband was outlined by Jefferson in a letter to his daughters Martha and Mary after their marriages in the 1790s. Jefferson discussed the responsibility of Martha's "new condition" as one of an "abundance of little sacrifices" that would leave her almost powerless in the home but would create conjugal affection and harmony—the goals of all

[97] *Virginia Gazette*, Feb. 10–27, 1737; Jonathan Swift, "A Letter to a Very Young Lady on her Marriage," quoted in Spruill, 224.
[98] Benjamin Wadsworth, *The Well-Ordered Family; or Relative Duties* (Boston, 1712), 34–36.

marriages. "The happiness of your life," he told her, "now depends on the continuing to please a single person." And she should look forward to having children soon, he advised, for motherhood was "the keystone of the arch of matrimonial happiness." Since harmony was the essence of a happy married life, husbands and especially wives needed to develop "a firm resolution never to differ in will," for persistent minor struggles could build up as "every one has their pouch into which all these little oppositions are put." Avoidance of conflict, he told Mary, required a wife to resist criticizing her spouse, but if the issue was important, she should "wait for a softer moment and more conciliatory occasion" to discuss it.[99]

Many women seem to have followed the kind of marital conduct Jefferson considered essential to conjugal felicity. Perceiving themselves as inferior, helpless, and subordinate to their husbands, wives frequently apologized to their spouses for their "Womanish fears" and sought security in protective husbands.[100] One woman told her sister in 1779 that a wife should be thankful to have "a protector & Friend in an husband."[101] Wifely self-effacement was evident in the attitude of Margaret Parker, who regretted the wordiness in her letters to husband James: "I never know when to leave of[f], but I depend on your sense to make allowances for the imperfections of a poor foolish Girl, whose Study & greatest pleasure always has & shall be to please you."[102] Thomas Dawson, the president of William and Mary from 1755 to 1761, was married to "a good natured Girl," who, like Margaret Parker, "endeavours to please her Husband."[103] Pleasing a husband required above all that a wife not interfere with her spouse's

---

[99]Thomas Jefferson to Martha Jefferson Randolph, April 14, 1791, Feb. 9, 1792, in Sarah N. Randolph, *The Domestic Life of Thomas Jefferson* (New York, 1939), 100, 192; Thomas Jefferson to Mary Jefferson Eppes, Jan. 7, 1798, ibid., 246–47.

[100]Frances Tucker to St. George Tucker, March 24, 1781, April 18, 1787, TCP. For a similar assessment of female self-perceptions in eighteenth-century America, see Mary Beth Norton, "Eighteenth-Century American Women in Peace and War: The Case of the Loyalists," *WMQ*, 3d ser., xxiii (1976), 405.

[101]Isabella Hunter to Mrs. John Baylor, Jr., May 4, 1779, BFP.

[102]Margaret Parker to James Parker, Aug. 22, 12, 1760, PFP.

[103]Thomas Dawson to Lady Gooch, Jan. 11, 1758, *WMQ*, 2d ser., i (1921), 52–53.

personal freedom in his public and economic life. Frances Tucker realized that her task was to nourish as best she could her husband's career and independence, even if that meant seeing him less than she wanted. She could only ask that he maintain good health in order "to pursue the Mode of life which he think[s] will procure him ease & independence."[104]

Sexual conduct in marriage can also be understood in terms of the husband's controlling influence in the household. The fragmentary evidence available on marital sexual behavior suggests that while husbands and wives enjoyed and needed sexual contact, only men were expected to make the advances.[105] These attitudes can be glimpsed, albeit indirectly, in the correspondence between spouses. While his wife was visiting relatives in North Carolina in the fall of 1736, Thomas Jones revealed the sensual urges he felt for her. He carefully read her letters not only as a "truly kind & gentle husband, but with the pleasure of a passionate lover that flatters himself with the hopes some time or other of being possessed with his Mistress's charms."[106] Wives probably experienced the same sexual desires, but openly expressing them was another matter. The tentativeness with which women discussed their romantic and sexual interests is suggested in the letter Margaret Parker wrote her husband in 1760: "I can tell you with a great deal of truth that the moon has never made her appearance Since you left me but what I have looked at her & thought of you, & often wished to know whether or not when you was going to bed it would not have been rather more agreeable to have had me with you. I always thought it would forgive me if I'm wrong, & Suffer me to indulge a thought that gives me much pleasure."[107]

These are examples of sexual attitudes, not of actual behavior, which is exceedingly difficult to document in the eighteenth

[104]Frances Tucker to St. George Tucker, Nov. 1787, TCP.

[105]Through an analysis of divorce records, Nancy Cott arrives at the same conclusion in her study of husband-wife relationships in eighteenth-century Massachusetts. See Cott, "Eighteenth-Century Family and Social Life Revealed in Massachusetts Divorce Records," *Journal of Social History,* x (1976), 34–35.

[106]Thomas Jones to Elizabeth Jones, Oct. 22, Nov. 10, 1736, JFP.

[107]Margaret Parker to James Parker, Sept. 5, 1760, PFP.

century. Perhaps the most revealing records of sexual behavior in marriage come from the diaries of William Byrd for 1709–1712 and 1739–1741. Byrd gloried in male sexual strength, noting once that certain rams could "jump 50 or 60 sheep" in one night: "This denotes a prodigious natural vigor... how short do poor men fall of these Feats." He frequently took sexual advantage of his servants. He confessed that he had "played the fool with Sally" and had "wicked inclinations to Mistress Sarah Taylor." Occasionally, Byrd could not resist making advances toward married women. After an evening visiting with several of the neighborhood ladies, he played cards with Mrs. Chiswell and "kissed her on the bed till she was angry and my wife also was uneasy about it, and cried as soon as the company was gone." Later Byrd was somewhat remorseful. "I ought to beg pardon for the lust I had for another man's wife."[108]

According to his diary, Byrd conducted an aggressive sexual life with his wife Lucy. He took great delight in his sexual prowess, as he constantly "rogered" or "flourished" her—not always on the bed—even when she was in an advanced stage of pregnancy. Their sexual encounters, always initiated by him, often gave her, he claimed, "great ecstasy & refreshment." Byrd not only used sex to demonstrate his virility and power over his wife, but to settle their frequent marital quarrels. On July 30, 1711, he and Lucy had "a little quarrel which I reconciled with a flourish. Then she read a sermon in Dr. Tillotson to me." "The flourish," Byrd noted, "was performed on the billiard table." After becoming angry with his wife for mistreating the servants, Byrd tried to make amends and "gave her a flourish in token of it."[109] Most planters were less self-conscious than Byrd of their need to dominate women sexually. But sexual activity, however pleasing to both spouses, probably remained in control of men.

---

[108]Quoted in Gerald Mullin, *Flight and Rebellion: Slave Resistance in Eighteenth-Century Virginia* (New York, 1972), 79; *Byrd Diary, 1739–41*, 93; *Byrd Diary, 1709–12*, 337, 90, 420, 101.

[109]Ibid., 337, 330, 345, 361, 337, 210–11, 533, 209, 463. According to the diary for the years 1710–1711, Byrd had sexual intercourse with his wife at least once every two weeks.

In these seemingly constant battles of sexual politics in the Byrd household, Lucy Byrd occasionally got the upper hand. According to Byrd, Lucy sought repeated pregnancies, despite the discomfort associated with them, as a means of gaining some hold on her husband for the future, as well as for the moment. In a letter to his wife's cousin Byrd complained of this tactic: "I know nothing but a rabit that breeds faster. It woud be ungallant in a husband to disswade her from it, but it would be kind in you, to preach her upon that chapter as a freind. She was delivered of a huge boy in September last and is so unconscionable as to be breeding again, nay the learned say she is some months gone. The truth of it is, she has her reasons for procreating so fast. She lives in an infant country which wants nothing but people. Then she is apprehensive I should marry again, if she shoud start first out of this world, but is determined to prevent [that] by leaveing me to[o] great an encumbrance. Is not this a little spiteful, to en [...] my happiness when she can be no longer a sharer in it?" Byrd's response, perhaps typical of other planters faced with rapidly growing families, was a form of abstinence through separation. "I knew no remedy but to make a trip to England some times, and then she must be content to lye fallow til I come back. But then she'll be revenged of me, and redeem her lost years by having 2 at a time when I return."[110]

Domestic Discord

Wifely obedience of course broke down on more than a few occasions, when, then as now, spouses quarreled openly. In most instances these marital spats developed when women questioned their husbands' authority, an action most men in Chesapeake society were ill prepared to tolerate. With few exceptions, however, insubordinate wives eventually bowed to their husbands' will in the interest of marital harmony. Margaret Parker, for example, was often tempted to give her husband

[110]William Byrd to Jane Pratt Taylor, April 3, 1729, *Byrd Correspondence*, I, 391–92.

James "a good Scold" for his criticism and neglect of her. His failure to write when away on business particularly galled her. After one such long silence from James, she wrote him: "I though of many abusive things to Say before I sat down but have forgot them all & can only tell you that I will not excuse you on another terms than your coming home with the greatest expedition." But if he offered her a tender response, she willingly withdrew her protests. "And after quarreling with me you say you would give me a Thousand kisses if I was there, do you think I'd take them tamely from you after a scold but I find on Second thought that I would take a hundred such Scolds as yours for as many kisses."[111]

A woman's sense of inferiority compared to a man's personal authority and wider experience in intellectual and economic life doubtless led many wives to buckle under to their husbands. Margaret Parker quite openly admitted as much after a quarrel with James. "You allways had Eloquence enough to perswade me to any thing that you desired me to do, well now you See I am all Submission as good wives ought to be, & I intend to make one of that number at least I'll do what I can to be one, & if I am not perfection, & I know myself to be very far from it, I have this consolation that I've one to please whose good sense can make large allowances for the frailltys of human nature."[112] Few women so frankly revealed their feelings toward their spouses as Margaret Parker, but the urge to please through obedience appears to have been a persistent trait in most wives. When a woman "vow'd obedience" in marriage, as one wife put it, she and her husband took that part of the oath very seriously.[113] Many marital quarrels must have ended with a sentiment similar to that expressed by Elizabeth Byrd after a disagreement with her husband in 1758: "But Sir, your Orders must be obeyed whatever reluctance I find thereby."[114]

[111]Margaret Parker to James Parker, Feb. 8, 1764, Aug. 22, 1760, PFP.
[112]Ibid.
[113]Frances Tucker to Theodorick Bland, Jr., March 23, 1783, TCP.
[114]Mrs. Elizabeth Byrd to Colonel William Byrd III, May 17, 1758, *VMHB*, xxxvii (1929), 246. See also *Byrd Diary, 1709–12*, 18–19.

It may be, however, that family letters overstate the harmonious character of marital life. How husbands and wives interacted on a daily basis—amid the tension, moods, and power struggles in the household—is impossible to discern from surviving family correspondence. Again it may be useful to turn to the Byrd diaries, for they contain the only extant record of the daily rhythms of colonial Chesapeake family life. Unfortunately for our purposes, the Byrd household at Westover was not especially representative of most planter families. Few contemporaries could have matched Byrd's great wealth, cosmopolitanism, and expansive ego; moreover, Byrd's wife, Lucy Parke Custis, seems to have been an irascible, ill-tempered woman (at least in the presence of her husband), who made marital harmony a difficult achievement. But their behavior in the household, as recorded in the diaries, can help us identify some central problems in eighteenth-century married life.

The first thing that must be noted about the Byrds is that they quarreled often—almost constantly, it seems—concerning almost every subject: the treatment of children and servants, the extent of a husband's authority, wifely extravagance, assertiveness, and sullenness. According to the diary for 1710, Byrd and his wife quarreled at least once every two weeks. Indeed, Byrd took note of a month-long hiatus in their marital conflict, as he claimed in August of 1709 that he and Lucy had not fought for a "great while."[115]

Much of the conflict between Byrd and his wife appears to have been trivial. Poorly cooked cherries led to one rift. A dispute over a card game produced another. In one instance they fought over learning to sing Psalms, "in which she was wholly in the wrong," Byrd characteristically pointed out, "even in the opinion of Mrs. Dunn," who witnessed the quarrel. Other quarrels were, Byrd confessed, "about nothing." After a ten-day trip to Williamsburg, Byrd returned home and when he and Lucy went to bed, they immediately got into a "terrible quarrel about nothing

---

[115]*Byrd Diary, 1709–12,* 71.

so that we both got out of bed & were above an hour before we could persuade one another to go to bed again."[116] Lucy Byrd's frequent challenges to William's authority ignited many quarrels. She once upset Byrd for "talking impertinently" to him. On several occasions when she tried to take a book out of Byrd's library, apparently violating his private, masculine world of books, a quarrel ensued. Her insistence on following the contemporary fashion of plucking out eyebrows brought a confrontation with her husband. He demanded she stop and eventually "got the better of her, & maintained my authority."[117]

But it was in matters of child and servant discipline that Mrs. Byrd's resistance clashed most strongly with her husband's assertion of superior authority. Byrd argued with Lucy, for example, because she tried to force their daughter Evelyn "to eat against her will." The two fell into a "terrible quarrel" when, in the presence of a family friend, Mrs. Byrd tried to whip their house servant. Byrd refused to allow the punishment, designed "to show her authority before company," and his action brought on an "abundance of crying."[118]

Lucy's frustration in a role subordinate to her husband was doubtless projected onto the servants in the numerous beatings she administered to them. That Lucy's harsh treatment of the servants stemmed in part from her unhappy marriage was suggested in one particularly dramatic confrontation. On March 2, 1712, Byrd had to pull a servant girl, Jenny, away from Lucy, who was "beating her with the tongs." When Byrd interfered, Lucy threatened to strike him. "She lifted up her hands to strike me but forebare to do it. She gave me abundance of bad words & endeavoured to strangle herself, but I believe in jest only. However after acting a mad woman a long time she was passive again."[119]

[116]Ibid., 135, 137, 272, 276, 489–90, 242.
[117]Ibid., 296, 400, 461, 472, 296.
[118]Ibid., 180–81, 462.
[119]Ibid., 205, 216, 285, 307, 481, 533–34, 494. This was not the only suicide threat Lucy Byrd made in her husband's presence. After another fight, Byrd recorded that "she threatened to kill herself but had more discretion." By that afternoon,

Byrd endured these outbursts only because he interpreted them as evidence of an innate female weakness for "foolish passion" that he believed was impossible to eliminate. And while his urge to dominate surely provoked many marital quarrels, Byrd did occasionally try to ease tension in the household by taking walks with Lucy or playing games "to divert her," which, unfortunately, could themselves lead to more fights.[120]

Byrd's constant quarreling with his wife may have represented only a slight exaggeration of the central tendency among many planters to maintain their authority in the household, while insisting on a compliant, subordinate role for their wives. As we have noted, wifely submission ideally combined with a husband's "gentle & easy" manner to minimize open conjugal conflict. But when difficulties arose between spouses, the assumed superiority of the husband in marriage may have left men ill-prepared to initiate reconciliation, except perhaps through sexual advances. One suspects, then, that a planter's frequent travels to neighboring plantations, the courthouse, the tavern, and the horse races and cock fights reflected in part his solution to tense marital problems in the "great house."[121] Few men could honorably retreat from their dominant position in the household when quarreling began, but strategic absences from home may have been the best strategy some men could devise to reduce tensions.

Marital conflict rarely passed beyond the confines of the household. Planters in well-to-do families took pride in family strength and cohesion and did all they could to settle family quarrels inside the home. Local officials or ministers were seldom asked to intercede.[122] Occasionally, however, when violence erupted or chronic disputes between spouses grew intolerable, outside help was sought.

Lucy was feeling better and she and Byrd "resolved to live for the future in love & peace," ibid., 294. See also ibid., 208.

[120]Ibid., 533–34, 537, 581, 71, 75, 119, 127–28, 152, 208.

[121]For an analysis of travel and visitation patterns, see Chapter 5.

[122]This stands in sharp contrast to the pattern of neighborhood and community supervision of marital conflict in eighteenth-century Massachusetts. See Cott, "Eighteenth-Century Family and Social Life," 25–26. The boundary between family and community was also blurred in Quaker households, especially regarding domestic discord. See Levy, 71.

Not surprisingly, a powerful source of these serious marital quarrels was the control of money and family property. The turmoil in the John Custis household in 1714 illustrates how sex-related work responsibilities and contention over economic resources could lead to the estrangement of husbands and wives. In June of 1714 John and Frances Custis approached the York County Court with "some differences and Quarrels" over "some money, Plate and other Things taken from him by the sd Frances and a more plentifull maintenince for her." They worked out an agreement concerning the management of household goods and more amicable husband-wife relationships with a goal that "all animostys and unkindness may cease and a perfect love and friendship may be renewed betwixt" them. That the conflict over property had created serious personal tension in the marriage was evident in one of the clauses of the agreement. Frances was required to stop calling John "any vile names or give him any ill language" and "neither shall he give her any but to live lovingly together and to behave themselves to each other as a good husband & good wife ought to doe."

Specifically, the agreement called for Frances to return to John all the money, plate and other items "that she hath taken from him or removed out of the house" and "be obliged never to take away by herself or any other, anything of value from him again or run him in debt without his consent, nor sell, give away or dispose of anything of value out of the family without his consent." All of which was conditional on John's agreement that he would not dispose of the damask linen or plate during her life and would give these items to the children at Frances' death.

Above all, the sexual division of power and work roles had to be clear. Frances was not to interfere with John's business affairs, the agreement read, for all "business belonging to the husband's management shall be solely transacted by him." On the other hand, John could not interfere in Frances's "domestic affairs," which, correspondingly, were considered as "properly belonging to the management of the wife. ... "

To settle their quarrel over how much of the household goods Frances was to control for her and the children's use, the agreement stipulated that John had to provide an annuity to her "for clothing herself and the children with a reasonable proportion thereof" and for housekeeping and medical expenses and the education of children, "soe long as the sd Frances shall live in peace quietly with him." If Frances overspent her yearly allowance for household consumption and ran John into debt, the agreement was to be held void. John had to allow her the same four house servants she owned at the time and two others for tending the garden, running errands, and other work. Finally, she was to receive fifteen pounds of wool and flax to spin each year "for any use in the family she shall think fit," including the freedom to distribute twenty yards of Virginia cloth each year for "charitable uses"—if sufficient surpluses existed.[123]

The economic vulnerability of women in the colonial Chesapeake probably produced many marital disputes. Since by law real property (lands and houses) belonged to their husbands, married women clung tenaciously to the movable personal property in the family, part of which may have been their own in dower. Thus, the linen, plate, cash, and other household goods Frances Custis evidently "stole" from her husband and sought to preserve represented the only economic resources she could control for herself and her children.

But even if a wife owned considerable personal property, she could not sell it or control its use outside the family while her husband was alive, and some women doubtless chafed under this restriction. Elizabeth Beverley, for example, was particularly distressed at the powerlessness she felt concerning the plight of her financially troubled sister in 1745. Because Elizabeth's husband refused to dispense any of the family property or cash to her sister, Elizabeth felt "deprived of the pleasure . . . of doing a deed of Charity." As a married woman, she was stripped of the economic freedom necessary to help those she loved: "had I been a Bro' . . . I should have been more active in the affair than I believe either of you have been," she wrote in 1745, referring to her

---

[123]The marriage agreement between John and Frances Custis appears in *VMHB*, IV (1896), 64–66.

brother and husband.[124] To avoid this economic imprisonment and potential marital fights, a few women drew up contracts with their prospective husbands to safeguard the property they owned before marriage and to insure that it remained at their disposal.[125]

Domestic discord sometimes led to violence and desertion. Chesapeake newspapers contained numerous advertisements of runaway wives by irate husbands. The point of these notices was to protect a husband from the debts with which his estranged wife might charge him, but the publication of a wife's elopement was also intended to condemn her publicly for her "unseemly" behavior or for being "highly undutiful and disaffectionate" toward her spouse.[126]

Gentry families usually avoided publicizing their marital conflict so widely. Instead they looked to kin and friends to settle serious quarrels between spouses privately. A husband's excessive drinking and abusive treatment of his wife seem to have been the most common causes of violent disputes and desertions in planter families. Women feared their husbands' power over them—in both a physical and psychological sense—and running away was sometimes the only solution, especially since the courts were notoriously unreceptive to the female side of marital disputes.[127]

In 1779, Elizabeth Cottert pleaded with her cousin St. George Tucker to advise her on what she should do to escape the numerous beatings her husband, "The Doctor," gave her. "The Doctor,"

[124]Elizabeth Bland Beverley to Theodorick Bland, Sr., July 26, 1745, BP.

[125]See the marriage agreement between Theodorick Bland, Sr., and Elizabeth Yates, Sept. 22, 1784, BP; and Marriage Contract between Thomas Walker and Elizabeth Thorton, Jan. 14, 1781, Page-Walker Papers, University of Virginia. Marriage agreements, especially among the well-to-do, were not always designed to provide the wife with economic freedom, but to keep property in the family from which it came. See Spruill, 364; Kathryn Allamong Jacob, "The Woman's Lot in Baltimore Town, 1729–97," *MHM*, LXXI (1976), 283–95.

[126]For a survey of marital friction as revealed in newspaper advertisements, see Spruill, 178–84.

[127]Ibid., 340–50. Women, however, were increasingly vocal and successful in divorce settlements in eighteenth-century Massachusetts. Cott, "Divorce and the Changing Status of Women in Eighteenth-Century Massachusetts," *WMQ*, 3d ser., XXXIII (1976), 586–614.

she explained, "has repeatedly beat me and abused me in the most cruel manner he cou'd," forcing her to take shelter in other people's houses. Finally, she "swore the peace of him and was determined not to live with him again." A last-minute reconciliation, the day before their court appearance, kept them together for a while, since he "used all his act to make up with me promising before the Gentleman and Lady of the house where she was staying said that he wou'd never strike me again." Three weeks later, when she refused to sign a paper claiming that she had taken a false oath against him, "he fell to beating me and swore he wou'd never quit me till he had the last drop of Blood in my body," and "he abuses me in the vilest manner calling me every Name that is bad, and denies that he is married to me." Tucker got in touch with the man in Hampton, Virginia, who was protecting Elizabeth and agreed to supply her with between £150 and 200 a year "necessary for her support or to enable her to obtain a separation from her husband should she choose it." He advised Elizabeth to try to get a separation from "the Doctor," and offered her enough money to return to her parents' home in Bermuda.[128]

There was little sense of neighborhood or community supervision of marital quarrels in the eighteenth-century Chesapeake. Close friends and kin, especially the latter, tried to intercede quietly when disputes grew intolerable for one or both spouses. The flight of Mrs. Richard Lloyd of Talbot County, Maryland, illustrates the important but tentative way in which friends intervened in marital conflict. James Hollyday and his brother Henry, close friends of the Lloyds, discovered in July of 1785 that "there was a Difference between his wife and him which had proceeded to such a Length that they did not lodge in the same Room." Captain Lloyd's drinking problem ("he was seldom sober at home or abroad and in Public," James Hollyday noted) and his threatened violence against his wife had produced a serious rift in their marriage.[129]

[128]Elizabeth Cottert to St. George Tucker, Oct. 15, 1779; St. George Tucker to Captain Hunter, Oct. 20, 1779, TCP.
[129]James Hollyday to Henry Hollyday, July 5, 1785, HFP.

This situation deeply worried the Hollydays, who feared that the marital estrangement might prompt Captain Lloyd to "do an Act of desperation to himself." Henry Hollyday at first felt compelled to go immediately to see Lloyd and try to "bring him to a calmer Temper," but he reconsidered and decided to wait until he received further information about the problem from his brother James. He wanted to be "clearly convinced that some essential advantage would probably be derived from" his intervention.[130] A few days later, Mrs. Lloyd fled to her brother-in-law's house and "claimed his protection from the cruel insults of her Husband, with a determination never to put herself in his power again." Upon learning of this development, and that Mrs. Lloyd "was apprehensive of her very life," Henry was finally certain of "the immediate necessity of the interposition of their friends." After a flurry of letters between Captain Lloyd and his brother (in which he threatened to sue for his wife's return), Henry requested a statement of Mrs. Lloyd's case. Acting as the arbiter of the dispute, Hollyday decided that "both may be faulty," but he had heard from several people of the "very gross immoralities and sour Temper of the Husband," and suspected that "the poor Lady has infinite cause of complaint." Eventually, Mrs. Lloyd received a permanent separation, though property disputes and lawsuits continued during the following year.[131] It was Hollydays' position as close friends of the Lloyds and as relatively objective observers of the conflict, at least compared with members of the Lloyd family, that allowed them to assume an effective role in settling the dispute.

A fundamental ambivalence characterized husband-wife relationships in the eighteenth-century Chesapeake. Men and women courted and married out of a sense of personal autonomy and a rising belief in the importance of romance and intimacy. Parental influence in the marital decisions of their children fell significantly during the latter half of the eighteenth century.

[130]Henry Hollyday to James Hollyday, July 10, 1785, HFP.
[131]Same to same, July 14, 1785; Eliza Mayadier to Catherine Belt, Aug. 9, 1786, HFP.

Patterns of domination and inequality, however, were also apparent in planter marriages. Despite an increasingly sentimental view of marital life, husbands continued to control their wives, insisting on obedience and a pleasing disposition. Moreover, both the law and the inclination of most husbands conspired to limit the economic freedom of wives severely. Given the tension between the ideal of romantic attachment and the understanding of the proper roles of spouses on the one hand and the realities of a man's almost absolute power in the family on the other, it is not surprising that in more than a few households, the well-ordered family remained largely an ideal.

Chapter Five

Kin, Friends, and Neighbors
The Social World beyond the Family

"The circle of our nearest connections is the only one in which a faithful and lasting affection can be found, one which will adhere to us under all changes and chances."[1] When Thomas Jefferson wrote his daughter Mary Jefferson Eppes in 1799 about the "ineffable pleasures" of his family relationships, he was articulating what many well-to-do planters had come to expect of family life and kinship by the late eighteenth century: a deep commitment of parents and children—and perhaps a few particularly close relatives—to continuity and harmony in a small, intimate "family society." Members of the gentry did not preside over a large, elaborate web of kin networks; rather, the letters and diaries of middling and wealthy planters suggest that close kin relationships rarely extended beyond the immediate nuclear family. Indeed, by the latter half of the eighteenth century, families tended to value privacy and intimacy over open, inclusive households made up of dependent relatives.[2]

[1] Thomas Jefferson to Mary Jefferson Eppes, Jan. 1, 1799, in Sarah N. Randolph, ed., *The Domestic Life of Thomas Jefferson* (New York, 1939), 255.
[2] That large family dynasties, constructed out of a web of kin ties and dependent relationships, characterized southern planters, especially in the antebellum period, is suggested in an article by Bertram Wyatt-Brown, "The Ideal Typology and Antebellum Southern History: A Testing of a New Approach," *Societas*, v (1975), 1–30.

A Growing Cousinry and Kin Network

The warm, protective kin environment that inspired Jefferson was a new social phenomenon that developed most fully in families of his generation. High mortality in the seventeenth and early eighteenth centuries produced chaotic, truncated family structures in a society heavily populated with orphans and stepparents. Those children who survived usually went through several sets of parents and surrogate parents before reaching maturity. A typical household in Virginia or Maryland in 1680, for example, might have contained orphans, half- and stepbrothers and sisters of all ages growing up under the care of an uncle, brother, or friend as a father figure. The natural mother of these children might be present, but before some of them reached their majorities—eighteen for girls and twenty-one for boys—they were likely to have instead an aunt, elder sister, or stepmother as a surrogate mother. The short life expectancies severely limited parent or pseudo-parent contact with children. And in the largely immigrant population of the early Chesapeake, only a few scattered kin were present for care and support.[3]

As Chesapeake society evolved from a high-mortality, immigrant population in the seventeenth century to one dominated by longer-lived natives in the eighteenth century, families became more permanent. Improved life expectancies allowed for longer marriages, thus lengthening the period of fertility for women. As a result, families grew larger. Seven or eight children were born into the typical Chesapeake family by the mid-eighteenth century, making them almost twice the size of most seventeenth-century families. With the gradual decline in infant and childhood deaths, an average of four or five children survived to

---

[3]Darrett B. and Anita H. Rutman, "'Now-Wives and Sons-in-Law': Parental Death in a Seventeenth-Century Virginia County," in Thad W. Tate and David Ammerman, eds., *The Chesapeake in the Seventeenth Century: Essays on Anglo-American Society and Politics* (Chapel Hill, N.C., 1979), 153–82; Daniel Blake Smith, "Mortality and Family in the Colonial Chesapeake," *Journal of Interdisciplinary History*, VIII (1978), 403–47; Lorena S. Walsh and Russell R. Menard, "Death in the Chesapeake: Two Life Tables for Men in Early Colonial Maryland," *MHM*, LXIX (1974), 211–27.

adulthood—again, almost double the average number from the previous century. Of critical importance was the growing longevity of parents, most of whom now lived into their mid-fifties. As increasing numbers of parents lived to see their children to maturity, the household became more clearly focused around a recognizably nuclear family arrangement, with children growing up under the watchful eyes of their natural father and mother. Kin attachments became exceedingly important, but the central change lay in the stabilization of the conjugal unit.[4]

This rising longevity introduced for the first time on a large scale a three-generational dimension to Chesapeake family life. Grandparenthood, a rarity in the seventeenth century, became a central experience for many families by the mid-eighteenth century. The growing household size and lengthening life spans of all its members also meant that an expanding body of surviving kin grew up alongside each family. An elaborate cousinry developed, which offered important marital, economic, and—at least among the elite—political opportunities.[5]

Moreover, in the Tidewater region, population density increased, tripling between 1700 and 1790; by the late eighteenth century, the Piedmont and western sections of the Chesapeake had begun to fill up as well. Both the influx of a large slave labor force and the growing size of white families created by 1750 many relatively close-knit planter neighborhoods of black kin groups and white ones. This formation of neighborhood communities structured in part around kin groups increased the possibilities of kin marriage. Indeed, in one Maryland county the percentage of

[4]For a discussion of changing mortality rates in eighteenth-century Maryland, see Allan Kulikoff, "Tobacco and Slaves: Population, Economy, and Society in Eighteenth-Century Prince George's County, Maryland" (unpub. Ph.D. diss., Brandeis University, 1975), 439; Lorena S. Walsh, " 'Till Death Us Do Part': Marriage and Family in Seventeenth-Century Maryland," Tate and Ammerman.
[5]Kulikoff, "Tobacco and Slaves," 377–80. For the growing intermarriage of planters in local and provincial politics in the eighteenth-century Chesapeake, see Charles S. Sydnor, *Gentlemen Freeholders: Political Practices in Washington's Virginia* (Chapel Hill, N.C., 1952); and Jack P. Greene, "Foundations of Political Power in the Virginia House of Burgesses, 1720–1776," *WMQ*, 3d ser., xvi (1959), 485–507.

marriages between cousins and other blood relatives almost tripled from the first third of the eighteenth century to the last third.[6] Lengthening life expectancies, rising population density, and a growing pattern of endogamous marriage helped create more complex family and kin relationships by mid-century. But these expanding kin ties, though substantial compared with those of the seventeenth century, remained in modern terms surprisingly narrow.

"The Strongest Ties of Nature": The Bonds of Kinship

What was the quality of the kin relationships that emerged most fully during the latter half of the eighteenth century? Sibling bonds were clearly the strongest kin ties, aside from parent-child relationships. In many agrarian societies the scarcity of land often produced tension and rivalry between brothers seeking economic security in the portion they inherited from their father's estate.[7] The relatively easy access to land and the common pattern of partible inheritance, however, allowed brothers in Chesapeake families to view each other as equal members of the household rather than as rivals for family land.[8] The personal documents of brothers and sisters reveal warm, cooperative sibling relationships in many middle- and upper-class planter families.

Young women seem to have developed especially close attachments to their brothers and often depended on them for advice. Molly Tilghman lamented the departure of her brother Dick, who was going to sea as an officer in the Royal Navy in 1788. "Before the Time came, I did not think it wou'd sit so heavy on me but to part with a Brother for ever is indeed a hard thing."

[6]Kulikoff, "Tobacco and Slaves," 6–23, 323, 365–68.

[7]W. M. Williams, *A West Country Village: Ashworthy* (London, 1963), 172.

[8]See C. Ray Keim, "Primogeniture and Entail in Colonial Virginia," *WMQ*, 3d ser., xxv (1968), 545–86; and Robert E. and Katherine B. Brown, *Virginia, 1705–1786: Democracy or Aristocracy?* (East Lansing, Mich., 1964). Inheritance patterns will be discussed in Chapter 6.

Courtenay Norton was deeply fond of her younger brother and wore a locket containing his portrait. After marriage, women frequently tried to maintain close ties with their brothers through regular correspondence and, when possible, visits. This had a practical as well as an emotional dimension, for married women, deprived of most of their economic freedom, might turn to their brothers for independent financial aid.[9]

Some parents believed that brotherly affection was an important reflection of virtuous conduct and intimate family life. St. George Tucker encouraged his stepsons to deepen their fraternal attachments while studying together at Princeton in 1787.

Since you are sequestered from the rest of your friends the ties of affection & friendship I hope will every day be more closely knit between you and all... Let me not be disappointed in the hope of seeing you grow up together with the strongest attachments to each other. —I have often been unhappy in observing people of the same Family appear perfect strangers to each other—nay more, to observe a perfect animosity prevailing between Children of the same parents. There can not be a stronger symptom of human depravity, nor should I be surprised if the person who is daily at variance with his Brother, should beat his father, or suffer his mother to pine in indigence. Believe me, my dear Boys, the moral virtues are all nearly allied to each other—they must all be cherished, or they will all be impaired. —Let me then again enjoin you to live in mutual harmony with each other, to check the first impulses of wrath, and to consider that mutual good offices will endear you to each other & secure a friendship more valuable than any other, and of equal duration with your Lives. [St. George Tucker to his stepsons, June 12, 1787]

A few months later Richard Randolph, Tucker's stepson, wrote of the strong emotional bonds between himself and his brothers. "I have not experienced from My Brothers any thing but the most

[9]Molly Tilghman to Polly Tilghman, Jan. 17, 1788, Spring? 1785, "Molly and Hetty Tilghman Letters," *MHM*, xxi (1926), 225, 128. See also Catesby Cocke to Elizabeth Jones, Feb. 17, 1724, Oct. 25, 1726, JFP; Courtenay Norton to John Hatley Norton, Jan. 7, 1791, in Frances Norton Mason, ed., *John Norton and Sons, Merchants of London and Virginia (Being the Papers from their Counting House for the Years 1750 to 1795)* (Richmond, 1937), 500; and Frances Tucker to St. George Tucker, Nov. 26, 1779, TCP. For a discussion of female dependence on brothers for economic help, see Chapter 4.

Tender affection—& I cannot express my happiness Sufficiently on this account. We shall I see grow up in this attachment and be useful to each other."[10]

Few young men lived out Tucker's ideal of virtuous brotherhood, but we know that in the absence of their father, elder brothers, for example, often helped to finance their younger brothers' schooling and got them independently settled. Brothers who lived near each other frequently maintained durable friendships and patterns of mutual economic and medical aid. Henry and James Hollyday of Maryland illustrate how brothers depended on each other for a variety of daily economic and personal matters. They regularly borrowed and exchanged slaves and supplies, like butter, linen, sugar, salt, and various drugs, and helped sell each other's wheat and flour. In addition, the two shared and discussed family news, illnesses and deaths in the neighborhood, and information on medicine and crops.[11]

Brothers also confided in each other about more personal matters like problems in child-rearing or family quarrels. The education and upbringing of their nephews often bound brothers more closely together. In politically ambitious families, fraternal influence was often used to help advance a young man's political career. This strong fraternal affection emerged most clearly when brothers were separated by long distances. George F. Norton of London claimed that he was bound to his brother John H. Norton, a factor in Virginia, "by the strongest ties of Nature to love & respect." From Surry County, Virginia, Charles Smith corresponded with his brother Nathan Mallory of Orange County

[10]St. George Tucker to his stepsons, June 12, 1787, Richard Randolph to Frances Tucker, Sept. 10, 1787, TCP.

[11]On fraternal aid in education see John Preston to Francis Preston, Dec. 26, 1786, "Some Letters of John Preston," *WMQ*, 2d. ser., I (1921), 43; Joseph Watson to David Watson, Sept. 7, 1796, Feb. 9, 1799, "Letters of William and Mary College, 1798–1801," *VMHB*, XXIX (1921), 131, 139; and "The Autobiography of the Reverend Devereux Jarratt, 1732–1793," *WMQ*, 3d ser., IX (1952), 363–64. For mutual economic aid among brothers, see Henry Hollyday to James Hollyday, Oct. 9, Aug. 25, March 3, 1780, March 8, 26, June 25, Sept. 2, 1781, HFP; FTD, Feb. 2, 27, March 5, April 10, July 26, Sept. 27, Oct. 1, 6, 1786, July 3, 1788, Nov. 12, Dec. 11, 1794, Jan. 22, 1795; Thomas Jones to William Jones, Sept. 10, 1757, JFP; and William Walter Hoest, "The Plantation in a Regional Economy: Pocket Plantation, 1762–1785" (unpub. M.A. thesis, University of Virginia, 1977), 4–5.

about his health and economic condition. Smith lamented the considerable distance that kept them apart: "if I Could But see you all onse more But the distanse is so g[rea]te that I am douteful wee should never all se[e] one another in this life."[12]
Because of these close sibling ties, a person's most important kin relationships outside the nuclear family were with his uncles and aunts. Uncles frequently assumed paternal authority— sometimes at a father's encouragement—in guiding their nephews' and nieces' moral conduct and education. Richard Henry Lee, for example, sent his sons to England for their schooling and depended on his brother William "for the care and protection of my dear Boys." He hoped, Lee told William, that "their gratitude and virtue will prevent your having much trouble with them." The boys' other uncle, Arthur Lee, was asked to write the "little Boys," "advising a close attention to the business that carried them to England."[13]
Theodorick Bland closely supervised his nephews' education, often counseling his son-in-law, St. George Tucker, on the proper tutor and everything "that concern their future welfare." Indeed, Bland asked to have almost complete control of the boys' schooling, for he feared that Tucker's approach would leave them "over-tutored." Bland's warm relationship with his nephews combined the virtues of a father and a schoolmaster, the two central socializing agents for a young man. Bland demanded that the boys merit his approval by showing improvement in their letter-writing, as "marks of your esteem and duty to me." He insisted that he played no favorites with his three nephews. "I love you all equally," he said, and "if there is a difference in the marks of approbation which I show it is you who make it not

[12]George F. Norton to John Hatley Norton, Nov. 10, 1769, Mason, ed., *John Norton and Sons*, 111; Charles and Ann Smith to Nathan Mallory, Sept. 17, 1791, MFP. See also "Steven Diary," *VMHB*, XXIX (1921), 387–88; William Jones to Thomas Jones, Sept. 9, 1751, Frederick Jones to same, June 12, 1721, JFP; George Hume to John Hume, Aug. 22, 1754, "A Colonial Scottish Jacobite Family," *VMHB*, XXXVIII (1930), 231; and John Preston to Francis Preston, Dec. 26, 1786, "Some Letters of John Preston," 48.
[13]Richard Henry Lee to William Lee, Sept. 5, 1775, Richard Henry Lee to Arthur Lee, June 26, 1774, James Ballagh, ed., *The Letters of Richard Henry Lee* (2 vols., New York, 1970), I, 118, 149.

me—your own application of Idleness is the cause not my want of love for you." The instructor role of an uncle appealed to Bland, and he wanted the Tucker children to understand what he was trying to do for them as a close relative and a concerned friend. The boys' letters, he told them, "show that the time and money spent and the pains taken with your education to make you clever fellows is not thrown away and when I am old I flatter myself I shall have some reason to be proud in having had a hand in raising up three fine young fellows—who will not only do themselves honor but do Service to their Country." Bland expressed here the character of many uncle-nephew relationships in gentry families: uncles could demand a stronger moral discipline and a greater educational achievement than doting fathers, yet remain on cordial terms with their nephews and nieces.[14]

Occasionally an aunt also could exert a significant shaping influence in a boy's life. John H. Norton's aunt, Sue Turner, for example, constantly stressed to John the important paternal values she saw in John's father and her brother. Believing that the "honour of the Nortons" was "inseparable from my own," she explained her intention "to instill good Morals into your Mind, which is the sure foundation for all worthy actions to flow from." The deep affection between aunt and nephew was evident in Charles Carroll of Carrolton's disconsolate response to his aunt's death in 1760. He grieved having "lossed one who loved me & was dear to me." Martha Jacquelin acted as a surrogate mother for her nephews Neddy and Johnny Ambler who were studying in England in the late 1740s. Like the boys' parents, Martha encouraged achievement and progress in their schoolwork. She

[14]Theodorick Bland, Jr., to St. George Tucker, May 11, 1781, ibid. to Frances Tucker, April 2, 1781, ibid. to boys, Jan. 26, 1781, TCP. Bland apparently received from the Randolph boys the same deferential treatment they displayed toward their stepfather. See Richard Randolph to Theodorick Bland, Jr., Oct. 20, 1782, BP. For other examples of this didactic, moralistic quality in uncle-nephew ties, see William Fitzhugh to Benjamin Grymes, March 20, 1796, William Fitzhugh Papers, University of Virginia; Marion Anderson to James Hollyday, Feb. 9, 1766, HFP; and FTD, May 8, 1798. After a father's death, uncles often stepped in to care for their nephews. See Robert C. Nicholas to John Norton, Nov. 12, 1771, Sept. 14, 1772, Oct. 15, 1773, Mason, ed., *John Norton and Sons*, 205, 272, 355–59.

sent them money each year when they showed "a good Account" of themselves. Above all, Martha recognized her kin obligation to nurture important parental values in the children: "My Dear boys make it your studdy to give your Parents the Sattisfaction of hearing of your good behaviour, and Dilligence in learning and too all your friends the Pleasure of thinking you may one Day be a credit to your country."[15]

Uncles and aunts often performed their socializing roles in a very direct, personal fashion. Rather than formally apprentice their children through the courts, planters usually arranged for their sons, while in their early teens, to live with an uncle and aunt to learn a trade, to receive a more disciplined upbringing, or, for older boys, to find a wife. Sometimes these long visits with relatives were merely social. One young man was pleased with his stay at his uncle's in North Carolina in 1756 and wrote home to his mother and siblings that he was being treated and entertained "more like a Son and Brother, than as a distant Relative." It was not uncommon for brothers to take in each other's sons for a few years, believing that an uncle could effectively introduce a boy to his wider kin network and inculcate principles of hard work and sober conduct. George and James Hume, for example, exchanged sons in the 1740s for each to learn a trade and to get a few years of schooling. George Hume of Virginia sent his son John to live with the boy's uncle James in Scotland. John was first put in school and later became a seaman in James' ship. Hume reported back to his brother on the boy's progress, which was none too impressive. John, he complained, "takes to nothing neither his books nor of being a seaman." Consequently, James feared that "he never will be fitt for anything but to drive hoggs in the

[15]Sue Turner to John Hatley Norton, June 28, 1772, Oct. 13, 1783, March 22, 1768, ibid., 247–48, 455–56, 40–41; Charles Carroll of C to Charles Carroll of A, April 10, 1760, CARP; Martha Jacquelin to boys, April 28, 1748, in Lucille Griffith, "English Education for Virginia Youth: Some Eighteenth-Century Ambler Family Letters," *VMHB*, LXIX (1961), 14. See also Stephen Bordley to Elizabeth Bordley, Jan. 4, 1728/9, SBL; Courtenay Norton to John Hatley Norton, Aug. 30, 1775, Mason, ed., *John Norton and Sons*, 374; Peter Pelham to William Pelham, March 30, 1785, "Pelham Letters," *WMQ*, 2d ser., VIII (1928), 44.

woods." A few years later George returned the favor and took in James' son Ninian as an apprentice.[16]

For many uncles, educating or disciplining a nephew was both a serious kin obligation and an important personal matter. That an uncle acted as an affectionate relative and a principled caretaker in raising a nephew is suggested in the experience of Henry Callister. When Callister's brother Ewan, who lived on the Isle of Man, sent his son Billy to stay with his Uncle Henry and Aunt Sarah in the fall of 1761, Sarah considered it a gesture of Ewan's "brotherly love." But despite Billy's "sufficiently tractable & good natured" disposition, Henry Callister soon reported to his brother that the boy's inexperience in trade and the business world "mortifies me." Moreover, Billy appeared apathetic, which Callister insisted could not be due to a "want of genius" since genius was "so conspicuous in a numerous family" like the Callisters. Within a year, Henry returned Billy to his father in England and explained to Ewan that he was "extremely disappointed" that Billy "could be so little acquainted with business." An uncle's firm authority had failed to overcome the idle habits of his nephew. "In vain I have tried persuasion & reproach; it was too late to make any impression on him," Callister explained.[17]

Three years later Ewan sent another son, Frank, to live with Henry and Sarah Callister. Like Billy, Frank was expected to become acquainted with mercantile affairs. Frank's behavior, however, caused a major uproar in the Callister household. Frank, according to Callister, was often found "slothing whole days together by the fireside." In addition, Frank had refused to tutor his young cousins in arithmetic, as he had promised to do. When Callister's children had to work in the fields after some of the slaves ran away, Frank refused to help out. While Callister did not expect his nephew "to do any thing that my better bred

[16]Frederick Jones to Elizabeth Jones, Dec. 10, 1756, JFP; Henry Hollyday to James Hollyday, May 4, 1780, HFP; James Hume to George Hume, Aug. 13, 1747, George Hume to James Hume, Feb. 11, 1748, Mrs. Isabell Hume to George Hume, Feb. 23, 1753, "A Colonial Scottish Jacobite Family," 206–7, 214.

[17]Sarah Callister to Ewan Callister, Oct. 20, 1761, Henry Callister to same, Oct. 18, 1761, Sept. 20, 1762, CALP.

children were about," he considered it "insolent" for Frank to avoid these work responsibilities. But it was the boy's sexual contact with Molly, the Callister's house servant, that led to an emotional reprimand from his uncle. Callister was astonished that Frank had "the villainy to Debauch Molly out of the house, to protect her from your uncle and Aunt." This was the final act of disrespect that forced Henry and Sarah, after "a whole night's Deliberation," to throw their nephew out of the house. Callister found Frank's conduct disgusting, but as a concerned uncle he stopped short of disowning him: "In short when you can reflect you will find it is not cruelty but indulgence and particularly that of your Aunt that has render'd you and Molly two ungratefull and abusive wretches to your own ruin and the great disturbance of my family. This is the account my Duty obliges me to give your father; I wish he may be able to support himself in reading it, for I am not able to tell it without sorrow & confusion. I wish you first some remorse for this abominable conduct, and then I can wish you success in the world."[18] Family apprenticeships such as this one obviously involved moral as well as educational responsibil- ities—unlike most formal arrangements through the courts—and the Callisters' reluctant but firm decision to sent their nephew back to his father suggests the ambivalent position of close rela- tives in caring for kin.

A young girl's relationship to her parents' brothers and sisters was more openly affectionate and less deferential. Men showed more serious interest in nephews than nieces, but both uncles and aunts appeared to develop close emotional attachments to their nieces. Some young men with nieces relatively close to them in age often discussed their personal feelings and future plans and advised them on matters such as marriage and proper con- duct.[19] A man like Richard Henry Lee could offer little advice to his young nieces, but he enjoyed their company and their affec- tion for him. Lee treasured his niece's picture and told her father that she was "very pretty and very chatty, & loves her Uncle

[18]Henry Callister to Frank Callister, April 23, 1765, ibid.
[19]Richard Terrell to Patsy Minor, Dec. 17, July 3, 1791, CTFP.

mightily."[20] Gift-giving, an important reflection of close kin ties, anthropologists suggest, was common between uncles and nieces. Edward Pratt took great delight in his nieces, "my two Dear Babes," and frequently sent them gifts—a silk coat, shoes, stockings, and caps. And many girls as they matured developed intimate relationships with their aunts, with whom they discussed news of family and kin—especially births and weddings—and visited whenever possible.[21]

Uncles and aunts clearly represented the central kin ties beyond the immediate family for most people in Chesapeake households. But the expansion of a lateral kin network in the eighteenth century increased the contact between cousins as well. That cousin relationships grew in importance is reflected in the rising number of first-cousin marriages in the eighteenth-century Chesapeake.[22] As young people, cousins were especially significant for companionship and practical cooperation.[23] Many cousins attended school together where they often became close friends and helped each other with their school work.[24] And men and women, especially in their early years, when their contact with uncles and aunts was greatest, frequently asked about their "little Cozens."[25]

Cousins often forged useful economic ties. James Taylor and Captain Garland Burnley, for example, held a "plant patch," a

[20]Richard Henry Lee to Thomas Lee Shippen, Jan. 17, 1785, Ballagh, ed., *Letters of Richard Henry Lee*, 322.
[21]William Pratt to Elizabeth Pratt, Feb. 23, 1724, JFP. See also M. Catesby to Elizabeth Catesby Pratt, June 22, 1722, ibid.; Sarah Anderson to James Hollyday, March 20, 1759, HFP; Frances Norton to John Hatley Norton, Aug. 6, 1774, *Tyler's Historical Quarterly*, IV (1922), 68; Rebecca Nicholson to Margaret Parker, Feb. 28, 1773, PFP; and Jane Swann to Thomas Jones, March 8, 1756, Oct. 19, 1743, JFP.
[22]Kulikoff, "Tobacco and Slaves," 377–80. For evidence of growing intermarriage among cousins and other relatives in eighteenth-century New England, see Peter Dobkin Hall, "Marital Selection and Business in Massachusetts Merchant Families, 1700–1900," in Rose Laub Coser, ed., *The Family, Its Structure and Functions* (New York, 1974), 226–40.
[23]Williams, *Ashworthy*, 157, 173.
[24]See Martha Jacquelin to Neddy and Johnny Ambler, July 31, 1749, John Smith to Neddy Ambler, June 2, 1751, "Ambler Family Letters," 18–20; and John Preston to Francis Preston, Dec. 26, 1786, "Some Letters of John Preston," 48–49.
[25]Stephen Bordley to Elizabeth Bordley, Feb. 25, 1730, SBL. See also Jane Swann to Thomas Jones, Oct. 19, 1743, JFP.

vegetable garden, in partnership in Orange County, Virginia, during the 1790s. Some men perceived financial aid to cousins as a part of their reciprocal kin responsibilities. When Reuben and Samuel Terrell helped their cousin, Walter Overton, sell his land in November of 1794, they expected that Overton would be under "lasting obligations" for their efforts; but they also saw this economic cooperation with their cousin in the broader context of service to family and kin. As Samuel told his brother after the land was sold: "The prosperity of the family I have much at heart, as am assured you have."[26] Close contact, however, rarely extended beyond one's first cousin. Second and third cousins, like great-uncles and -aunts, were often termed "kinsmen" or simply "relations." This use of more generic kin terminology suggests that a person's effective kin ties were limited to the immediate families of his parents' siblings.[27]

It is perhaps not surprising that in a society in which most family wealth was transferred to blood relatives by inheritance (except for occasional gifts to nieces- and nephews-in-law), affinal kin—those related only through marriage—occupied only a peripheral area of an individual's kin universe.[28] To be sure, in-laws were warmly welcomed into a new kin network at marriage. The family of St. George Tucker, for example, affectionately greeted his new bride, Frances Bland Randolph, in 1779. Eliza Tucker received her new sister-in-law with "the tender Regard, and cordial warmth of a Sister and Friend" and asked that she write often, for it was important to Eliza to hear from "the Wife of a Brother I so tenderly Love." Henry Tucker, St. George's brother, claimed he would forego addressing Frances with the customary

[26]Francis Taylor Diary, May 17, 1790; Samuel Terrell to Richard Terrell, Nov. 10, 1794, CTFP.
[27]Such a narrow range of kinship, with close contact extending only to first cousins, may have changed little in English society since the seventeenth century. See Alan Macfarlane, *The Family Life of Ralph Josselin: A Seventeenth-Century Clergyman* (Cambridge, 1970), 139; Raymond Firth, Jane Hubert, and Anthony Forge, *Families and Their Relatives: Kinship in a Middle-Class Sector of London* (London, 1969), 171, 197.
[28]Chapter 6 discusses the tendency to concentrate most family wealth within the nuclear family.

"distant respect," but instead would treat her with "the same affectionate freedom I do my other Sisters." Above all, Henry wanted to "divert myself of Ceremony & to chat with you as the lov'd partner of a Brother." He was so taken with his new sister-in-law that he made her the godmother of his son. And Henry believed that he spoke for all the Tucker family when he asked St. George to "tell her we receive her with open Arms into a Family, which is remarkable for nothing so much as for their fond & disinterested attachment to each other."[29]

Such intimacy did not apply to most of Frances's family. While the Tuckers grew quite close to Frances after her marriage to St. George, Frances's family, with the exception of her brother Theodorick, saw little of her or St. George. When St. George dined with Frances's "Sister Counsellor," he considered it "good fortune to be so far recollected by her that she could address me by name." And despite her efforts, Frances maintained little contact with her father whom she wanted "to come & partake of our dwelling."[30]

But it was a man's in-laws in particular who rarely established strong ties in the kin network. An inherent tension frequently existed between a man and his father-in-law over questions of property and the payment of his wife's portion. The patrilineal character of inheritance often left affinal kin as distinct outsiders. In 1783 Archibald McCall was embroiled in a vicious dispute with his father-in-law, Dr. Nicholas Flood, over "some Pecuniary Transactions" regarding the ownership of some land. Dr. Flood was so antagonized by McCall's financial arrangements that he refused to help care for and educate his grandchildren while McCall, a widower, was in England. As a result, McCall was

[29]Eliza Tucker to Frances Tucker, Nov. 24, 1779; Henry Tucker, Jr., to Frances Tucker, Nov. 29, 1779; Henry Tucker, Jr., to St. George Tucker, Feb. 18, April 13, 1780; St. George Tucker to Frances Tucker, June 28, 1781; TCP. For other instances of affectionate in-law contact at marriage see Robert C. Nicholas to John Norton, April 7, 1772; George Norton to John Hatley Norton, May 4, 1772, Aug. 4, 1773; Courtenay Norton to same, May 5, 1772; Sue Turner to same, June 28, 1772; Mason, ed., *John Norton and Sons*, 231–34, 248, 348; *Carter Diary*, II, 1059–60; and William Pratt to Elizabeth Jones, June 1727, JFP.

[30]St. George Tucker to Frances Tucker, April 6, 1787; Frances Tucker to St. George Tucker, June 4, 1781, TCP.

forced to send his daughters to Scotland "where his own Relations resided" as "the most proper place" for their upbringing.[31] Financial aid seems to have been only reluctantly given—if given at all—to a man's needy in-laws. When Jonathan Boucher's sister and brother-in-law asked him for financial help, Boucher found it hard to acquiesce. For one thing, he disliked his sister's husband, whom he called "a bad Man, a bad Husband, & indeed I doubt everything that is bad." Boucher was bothered by his sister, too, "a poor, helpless, complaining Creature" whose marriage to such a man was "but too good a Proof of her Indiscretion." "Yet," he concluded, "She is my sister, & I cannot fear that shou'd want, whilst I, at least, *seem* to live in Plenty." Sibling obligations required him to help. "I cant, I must not, desert Her." Helping her husband, however, was another matter: "it goes sorely against my Grain to be saddled also with the Maintenance of a sorry fellow, of no use or Significance that I know of, but for bringing more Beggars into the World."[32] The tension, potential or real, between affinal kin over economic matters—especially between a man and his wife's family or that of his sister—precluded the development of close relationships based on mutual aid and kin cooperation. As a result, in-laws were usually seen more as "connections" than as "relatives" to whom kin felt they owed a moral obligation.[33]

Living Arrangements and the Structure of Planter Households

Gentry families expanded and contracted not only with the births, marriages, departures, and deaths of various children, but

[31]Petition of Archibald McCall, Dec. 5, 1783, in Joseph S. Ewing, ed., "The Correspondence of Archibald McCall and George McCall, 1777–1783," *VMHB*, LXXIII (1965), 449, 451. See also "The Journal of James Gordon of Lancaster County, Virginia," *WMQ*, 1st ser., XI (1903), 107–8, 196.

[32]Jonathan Boucher to Rev. Jones, April 28, 1776, June 13, 1776, Feb. 25, 1777, "Letters of Jonathan Boucher," *MHM*, IX (1914), 55–56, 60, 327.

[33]This same kind of tension between a husband and his father and his father-in-law was often evident in gentry families of eighteenth-century England. See Randolph E. Trumbach, "The Aristocratic Family in England, 1690–1780: Studies in Childhood and Kinship" (unpub. Ph.D. diss., The Johns Hopkins University, 1972), 213. See also Firth et al., 94–96, 173–74; and Macfarlane, 140–43.

with the arrival of an assortment of relatives and friends who were brought into the household from time to time. The inclusive nature of Chesapeake households is reflected in the relative openness with which needy kin were accepted as temporary members of the family. It was not uncommon, for example, for a single man to live with his father or a married brother until he had the wherewithal to marry and set up an independent household.[34] In a society where marriage was the normative condition for domestic life, single people felt obliged to attach themselves to some part of their family for emotional stability and economic support. In 1750 Stephen Bordley of Maryland, for example, was living with two brothers, William ("a Gentleman farmer"), John ("a trader"), and two half-brothers, Mathias (with "a Gentile and Beneficial place under our Government") and Beale. "We are all Single; a Strange family! perhaps you'l say."[35]

Death, orphanhood, and economic dislocation sometimes placed demands on the wider kin network as uncles and aunts took in orphaned nephews and nieces for a short while until the surviving parent remarried and widows found shelter in their brothers' or sisters' families.[36] Moreover, wives often stayed with sisters or their parents when their husbands were absent from the plantation.[37] William Byrd welcomed a variety of people into his home at Westover, including his ailing uncle and the young daughter of a local minister who came, Byrd noted, "to live with my wife." Byrd had sued the girl's mother, the widow of Rev. Jacob Ware, for unpaid debts; thus the daughter's agreement to live at Westover might have involved housekeeping chores as repayment of the family debt. Eleven days after Mrs. Ware's daughter arrived at Westover, however, she left in the middle of the night, "without any cause in the world."[38]

Families with few or no children of their own could more easily

---

[34]Francis Taylor lived with his father all of his life. See FTD. See also R. Rutherford to St. George Tucker, March 17, 1788, TCP.

[35]Stephen Bordley to Flowerdewe and Norton, Nov. 20, 1750, SBL.

[36]Robert Nicholas to John Norton, Sept. 19, 1772, Mason, ed., *John Norton and Sons*, 272; Henry Hollyday to James Hollyday, Sept. 18, 1777, HFP.

[37]See James Parker to Margaret Parker, Nov. 8, 1776, Feb. 19, 1777, PFP.

[38]*Byrd Diary, 1709–12*, 141, 126, 130.

afford—and occasionally needed—the addition of a few relatives and some friends around the house. Colonel James Gordon and his wife, who had only one child at home in the 1760s, took in a number of short-term boarders. Besides Gordon and his wife and son, their household contained six other people: Gordon's overseer Billy and his wife Betty, Gordon's cousins Robert and Molly Hening, and a teacher, Mr. Criswell, and his new wife Molly. Most of these people stayed in the Gordon home only a short while. Gordon's cousin Robert Hening, for example, was taken in after his wife's death "till he was better provided." Criswell and his wife boarded with the Gordons only during the first two months after their marriage.[39] While no systematic data are available on kin residential patterns, the scattered qualitative evidence suggests that at least among the gentry, households were sometimes large and open affairs offering temporary economic and emotional support, drawing in kin and occasionally friends.[40]

An extended-family arrangement—that is, a married couple living in the same home with the parents of one of the spouses—remained rare, however, even among the wealthy. While aging parents longed for and occasionally demanded that their grown children live nearby to provide "Enjoyment & Comfort," the impulse toward self-sufficiency and economic independence, ingrained since childhood, and the generally wide availability of land militated against the widespread growth of three-generational living arrangements, except in temporary circumstances.[41] Moreover, as we shall note later, sons received their portions of the paternal estate relatively early and thus had the opportunity to marry and establish themselves in a separate household.

One rather well-known and instructive exception to this segmental, nuclear-family living arrangement was the Landon Carter household of Sabine Hall. The Carter's eldest son and heir of

[39]"The Journal of James Gordon of Lancaster County, Virginia," *WMQ*, 1st ser., XI (1903), 219, 111; XII (1904), 7.

[40]Devereux Jarratt took special note of the fact that his family consisted "only" of his wife, her cousin and himself. "The Autobiography of Devereux Jarratt," 357.

[41]See Jane Swann to Elizabeth Jones, Sept. 7, 1757, JFP. See also Chapter 3.

the home plantation, Robert Wormeley Carter, along with his wife Winifred and their children, lived in the upstairs portion of Sabine Hall from the late 1750s until Carter's death in 1778. The almost constant intergenerational tension in the Carter household suggests that such extended-family living arrangements were often incompatible with the strongly developed sense of personal autonomy a young man expected from his parents.

Conflicts over personal lifestyle and household authority poisoned the domestic atmosphere at Sabine Hall. Landon Carter was convinced that his son Robert Wormeley's gambling habits and arrogant assertiveness were destroying family life and filial respect. To Carter, "Wild Bob" had degenerated into a mere "man of Pleasure" with his addiction to gaming and idle behavior. The "married gamester," Carter protested in March 1776, "keeps his family in the Perpetual fear of starving." Carter constantly lamented that his sons, John and Robert, behaved irresponsibly toward their families. Both had "wives very big with large gangs of children and yet they play away and play it all away."[42]

What made matters worse, Carter complained, was that this sort of parental neglect and licentiousness destroyed discipline in the household and encouraged the same idleness and disrespect in Robert Wormeley's children. Indeed Carter worried incessantly about "my insufferable grandson," Landon Carter, Jr., whose permissive parents had created in him "the most outrageous scoundrel that ever appeared in human shape." It was particularly disturbing to Carter to see such "a fine Genius ruined by a bad example at home." Young Landon's "impudent behavior" became the focal point in the contest for authority in the Carter household. In fact, Carter grew so defensive about his relationships with his son and grandson that he came to believe that Robert Wormeley was openly permissive in raising his son not out of a "tenderness as a father or master" but "because he is fond of torturing his father."[43]

The "devilish influence" behind this disintegrating structure of authority in the family, as Carter perceived it, was Robert Wor-

[42]*Carter Diary*, I, 505, II, 1000–01, 830.
[43]Ibid., II, 702, 765, 903.

meley's wife, Winifred Travers Beale. Deeply suspicious of women in general (most women, Carter felt, had "nothing in the general in view, but the breeding contests at home"), Carter reserved his most vehement criticisms for his daughter-in-law, "Madame Audacity." Her insistence on raising her children in her own way and the ill-concealed contempt she felt toward an imperious, irascible father-in-law led to many "domestic gusts" in Sabine Hall. One such quarrel bears examination, for it suggests how a three-generational family blurred lines of authority and sharpened the antagonism between affinal kin.[44] On the morning of June 27, 1766, Landon Carter decided it was time to impose some discipline on his grandson that the boy's parents had apparently failed to do. The result was a dramatic confrontation that confirmed Carter's worst suspicions about the filial disobedience that surrounded him in Sabine Hall.

> We had this day a domestic gust. My daughters, Lucy and Judy, mentioned a piece of impudent behaviour of little Landon [his grandson] to his mother; telling her when she said she would whip him, that he did not care if she did. His father heard this unmoved. The child denied it. I bid him come and tell me what he did say for I could not bear a child should be sawsy to his Mother. He would not come and I got up and took him by the arm. He would not speak. I then shook him but his outrageous father says I struck him. At Breakfast the Young Gent. would not come in though twice called by his father and once Sent for by him and twice by me. I then got up, and gave him one cut over the left arm with the lash of my whip and the other over the banister by him. Madame then rose like a bedlamite that her child should be struck with a whip and up came her Knight Errant to his father with some heavy God damning's, but he prudently did not touch me. Otherwise my whip handle should have settled him if I could. Madam pretended to rave like a Mad-woman. I shewed the child's arm was but commonly red with the stroke; but all would not do.... As this child is thus encouraged to insult me, I have been at great expence hitherto in maintaining him but I will be at no more. And so I shall give notice. [*The Diary of Colonel Landon Carter of Sabine Hall, 1752–1776*, vol. I, 310][45]

[44]Ibid., 762–63, 1123.
[45]Ibid., I, 310. In a similar account of this episode at Sabine Hall, Philip Greven interprets Carter's rage as evidence of the southern planter's proclivity toward violence and the physical punishment of children. See *The Protestant Tempera-*

The intergenerational tensions and power struggles that plagued the Carter household at Sabine Hall are evidence of the almost inevitable conflict between fathers, adult sons, and affinal kin living in close quarters. It is not surprising that so few multigenerational family units seem to have existed among the eighteenth-century gentry—except as a temporary measure—because of the importance placed on personal independence and self-reliance both within and outside the kin network.

The Rituals of Kinship

Kin gatherings were a way for relatives to strengthen and reaffirm their kin ties. Christenings and baptisms, weddings, funerals, and various holidays brought kin and close friends together. These occasions provided relatives with emotional support and a sense of continuity as part of a larger kin group.[46] In the eighteenth-century Chesapeake, kin contact increased with each childbirth, as female relatives were drawn in to help in the delivery and recovery processes. One woman was confident that her sister's lying-in would be well attended, "as she will have an excellent nurse and the family will be extremely large at that time."[47] Christenings were an especially important kin gathering, for parents tried to justify to themselves and others their assumption of the responsibility for child-rearing. Groups of a dozen or so kin and occasionally a few close friends attended. These celebrations of parenthood were usually held at home a few weeks after birth. The child's godparents, who were supposed to be and often became the spiritual guardians of the child, were chosen at this time. Usually the parents selected a brother or sister; less frequently, a close family friend. Despite the religious symbolism attached to christenings and baptisms, for the most

---

ment, 279–80. But the fragmentary evidence I have seen on this question suggests that whippings were not at all common in most planter families, especially in the latter half of the century. See Chapter 3.

[46]Firth et al., 238.

[47]Molly Tilghman to Polly Tilghman, Feb. 18, 1787, "Letters of Molly and Hetty Tilghman."

part these occasions were perceived as festive, joyous affairs with plenty of drinking and dancing.[48] Weddings probably consolidated kin groups more effectively than any other kin gathering. By uniting two families, marriage increased the potential size of kin groups, and in cases of cousin marriages, it drew various branches of the family closer together. The presence of the parents and their siblings, as well as numerous other relatives, offered support to the newlyweds' independent life together, while emphasizing the social continuity of family and kinship.[49]

Because of the relatively high mortality in the early Chesapeake, funerals and burial ceremonies provided frequent occasions for kin contact. As with christenings, funerals for very young children were an immediate family affair, but thirty or more kin and a few unrelated neighbors usually attended services for adults. Like all kin gatherings, funerals, which were sometimes held weeks after the death and burial, were followed by celebrations. Burial services, on the other hand, were smaller and carried a more sober, religious tone. In addition to strengthening the bonds of kinship, funeral and burial ceremonies had the cathartic value of helping families understand and accept death in the family.[50]

[48]See RRD, Oct. 8, 1749; *Byrd Diary, 1709–12,* 2, 249; FTD, Nov. 9, 1790, Nov. 2, 1796, June 19, 1799; Don Jackson, ed., *The Diaries of George Washington* (Charlottesville, Va., 1976), II, 154, 158; *Carter Diary,* I, 376–77; "Journal of James Gordon," 9, 232; and Hunter Dickinson Farish, ed., *Journal and Letters of Philip Vickers Fithian, 1773–1774* (Williamsburg, 1943), 47.

[49]The kin-oriented nature of gentry marriages in the eighteenth-century Chesapeake is reflected in one relatively well-documented Maryland wedding. See Allan Kulikoff, "Throwing the Stocking: A Gentry Marriage in Provincial Maryland," *MHM,* LXXI (1976) 516–21.

[50]See RRD, Nov. 12–13, 1748; and FTD, Aug. 10, 1788, May 6, 1789, Jan. 15, 1790, June 7, 1794, April 1, 1798. Natalie Davis has recently suggested that in preindustrial Catholic countries a more ritualistic observance of death distanced the living from the dead. In Protestant areas, however, the strict prohibitions against ostentatious funerals and burial services or against communication with the dead ironically left surviving family members with strong memories and unresolved tensions about dead loved ones. Deprived of a ritual mourning process, Protestant families, she maintains, were "more vulnerable to the prick of the past, more open to the family's future." Natalie Zemon Davis, "Ghosts, Kin and Progeny: Some Features of Family Life in Early Modern France," *Daedalus,* 106 (1977), 92–96. Chapter 7 contains an extensive discussion of a family and kin attitudes toward death.

Larger, more inclusive celebrations and gatherings renewed kin and friend contact. Many families organized Christmas and Twelfth Day parties each year and invited neighbors and close friends, as well as relatives, to these affairs. On Christmas Day in 1788 and 1789 several members of the Taylor family dined together. The following day, Robert Taylor invited some twenty-five guests to his home for dinner, only one-third of whom were kin. The rest were close friends of the Taylor family. Similar combinations of intimate family celebrations and large parties occurred on January 6 for the Twelfth Day celebration. James Taylor's wife sent a cake to Francis Taylor and his father. A party with over twenty friends and kin was held that evening at Reuben Taylor's home. Likewise, Landon Carter organized a three-day festival in January 1771, celebrating the new year and Twelfth Day, with over sixty guests. Many of Carter's nephews attended "and all my neighborhood except Colo. Brockenbrough who did not come although invited." And on Christmas Day in 1709, William Byrd noted that "we were merry with nonsense and so were my servants." Other festivities, besides regular balls and barbecues, such as the annual birth-night ball in November and special family gatherings drew relatives and friends together throughout the year.[51]

While these various special occasions provided important opportunities for relatives and neighbors to gather and reaffirm ties of kinship and friendship, it was the daily, less conspicuous rounds of visiting and mutual aid that most clearly shaped one's kin universe. Although Chesapeake society grew more densely populated during the eighteenth century, many planters had to travel several miles by horse or boat to see relatives and friends in their neighborhoods. Visiting, then, was almost an essential activity for families that sought to maintain close ties of kinship and friendship.[52]

[51]FTD, Dec. 26, 1789, Dec. 26, 1788, Jan. 6, 1789, Jan. 6, 1791, Jan. 6, 1792; *Carter Diary* I, 533; *Byrd Diary, 1709–12,* 122; Thomas Jones to Elizabeth Jones, Nov. 10, 1736, JFP; Jane Carson, *Colonial Virginians at Play* (Williamsburg, 1965), 252–56.

[52]According to Nicholas Cresswell, planters in the late eighteenth-century Chesapeake were unusually hospitable to travelers. See Samuel Thornley, ed., *Journal of Nicholas Cresswell, 1774–1777* (New York, 1924), 270.

Visitors filled many planter households for dinner and conversation, especially on Sundays after church. These were often large affairs, with a dozen or more kin and friends invited. According to Philip Fithian, Robert Carter and his eldest son Ben dined once with a Mr. Turberville, whose guest list included "besides his usual Family Thirteen Persons" not to mention the "Waiting Men With the Carriages"—about twenty people in all. But, Fithian noted, "it did not in any thing exceed what is every day at Mr. Carters Table."[53] John Page kept a rather complex and busy dining schedule with several friends. He once had to turn down a breakfast invitation of St. George Tucker because he was "engaged to dine With Col. Goode with a Gent who had before engaged me & several Friends to dine with him; ... We were invited last Sunday to Mr. L. Burwell's but being preengaged to Col. Harvey did not go—Burwell since has politely pressed us to dine with him tomorrow but Goode had a previous claim on Burwell, which he has insisted on."[54]

Extended visits of several days to several weeks or more were common in many gentry households. In late September 1757 Ralph Wormeley visited his uncle, Landon Carter, for five days. Molly Tilghman expected that with the arrival of about a dozen assorted relatives, in-laws and friends in the summer of 1785, "every Cranny of our house will be filled," making "a pretty complete squeeze." Molly's uncle and aunt came to visit later that year for a week and took her sister back with them. And Molly frequently stayed ten days or longer in the home of her cousins. Frances Tucker complained in June 1781 that she found it difficult "to steal every Moment from company—the house is allways full." The boredom of isolated plantation life, especially in the more scattered settlements, probably encouraged long visits to relatives and friends rarely seen.[55]

[53]Farish, ed., *Journal and Letters of Fithian*, 63–64.
[54]John Page to St. George Tucker, Nov. 22, 1788, TCP. See also FTD, Jan. 25, 1797; and Louis Morton, "Robert W. Carter of Sabine Hall: Notes on the Life of a Virginia Planter," *Journal of Southern History*, XII (1946), 354.
[55]Molly Tilghman to Polly Tilghman, 1785?, Aug. 5, 1785?, "Letters of Molly and Hetty Tilghman," 30–31, 124; Frances Tucker to St. George Tucker, June 4, 1781, TCP. After he went out on his own as a young lawyer, Beverley Tucker often made extended trips of a month or so to the "cheerful fire" of the Tucker house-

The Planter's Kin Universe: Four Case Studies

This evidence of relatively open households with frequent visits from relatives and friends is suggestive for understanding kinship in a planter society, but a more systematic examination of kin contact is necessary. Unfortunately, sources for an in-depth study of kinship are exceedingly scarce. Family papers and genealogies by their nature focus on activities or events within the family and tell us little about the daily interaction of related families and close friends. Diaries, especially those that were regularly kept and that contain the names of people seen and places visited, provide the most useful type of evidence for an intensive, quantitative assessment of kin patterns. Chesapeake planters, unlike New England Puritans, were not particularly introspective and thus not disposed toward diary-keeping. As a result, few diaries from the seventeenth and eighteenth centuries have survived, except for an occasional agricultural journal or daybook.[56]

There are four extant diaries of eighteenth-century Virginia planters, however, that do allow us to ask more probing questions about kinship than the more impressionistic evidence from travelers' accounts and letters can suggest. The following analysis will examine the diaries of Colonel William Byrd II of Westover, Landon Carter of Sabine Hall, James Gordon of Lancaster County, and Francis Taylor of Orange County, to explore a number of related questions concerning the social world of the provincial aristocracy. For example, how much daily contact did kin actually have with one another, in terms of visits and mutual medical and economic aid? What was the approximate size of a

---

hold. See Robert J. Brugger, "Heart over Head: The Antebellum Persuasion of Nathaniel Beverley Tucker" (unpub. Ph.D. diss., The Johns Hopkins University, 1974), 59. See also "Diary of M. Ambler, 1770," *VMHB*, xlv (1937), 161; John Wormley to Col. George Baylor, Aug. 16, 1782, BFP; and Victor Golladay, "The Nicholas Family in Virginia" (unpub. Ph.D. diss., University of Virginia, 1973), 195–96.

[56] See Greven, *The Protestant Temperament*, 299–303, for an excellent discussion of these "unexamined selves" in the South.

man's circle of kin and friends? And perhaps most important, were friends drawn from existing kin groups or selected from unrelated neighbors and fellow planters?

Although these four diarists shared a similar social and economic status, some important differences between them should caution us against easy generalizations. To begin with, three of the men came from the Tidewater region, but Taylor lived in a Piedmont county. All but Byrd kept their diaries during the latter half of the eighteenth century. Byrd, Carter, and Gordon clearly belonged to the economic elite of their regions, while Taylor possessed modest, middling wealth. Finally, and perhaps most important in this survey of distinctive characteristics, the four planters were at differing stages of the life cycle: Byrd and Gordon were middle-aged husbands, Carter, an elderly widower, and Francis Taylor, a middle-aged bachelor. Moreover, as we shall see, each of the diaries contains its own methodological strengths and weaknesses; consequently, each diary will be analyzed separately. Despite these important differences, the diaries can yield some useful general observations about kinship among the gentry.

A close look at the diary of William Byrd confirms some of the impressions suggested earlier, especially the open nature of many planter households. On numerous occasions Byrd was welcomed into the homes of strangers and visited his kin and friends unannounced. In November 1709, for example, bad weather forced Byrd, his wife, and his sister and brother-in-law to stop off in Elizabeth City County at the home of James Wallace. Wallace was not there when the Byrds arrived, but his wife asked them to stay for supper. Wallace came in later and poured cider and provided them with six horses. Byrd was impressed with Wallace's hospitality. "He lives very neatly and is very kind to all that come to his house." On another occasion, Byrd, his close friend Colonel Hill, and Captain Burbage rode to Major Harrison's, but finding neither Harrison nor his wife there, they went in and ate some of their food. Byrd, his friends and business acquaintances frequently dropped in on one another and sometimes stayed overnight or for several days.[57]

As Table 1 shows, Byrd was busy visiting throughout most of the year. He was either receiving guests at Westover or venturing out himself nearly four of every five days. Most of his visiting occurred in the summer and fall months. Weather conditions rarely impeded travel in these months and only late summer agues and fevers slowed down the pace of visiting.[58]

Table 1. Seasonality in visiting: William Byrd II, Oct. 1, 1710–Sept. 30, 1712

Season	No. days with friends or kin	Percentage
Fall (Sept.–Nov.)	174	91.6
Winter (Dec.–Feb.)	138	76.7
Spring (March–May)	154	81.5
Summer (June–Aug.)	167	90.7
Total	633	86.7

Byrd remained at home more frequently during the winter (December through February), largely, it seems, because of the cold weather. This seasonal pattern of visiting may have been peculiar to wealthy planters like Byrd, for the rhythms of crop cultivation and harvest would suggest an opposite trend: winter would provide more free time for travel and visiting, while the summer and fall would be the busiest months on the plantation. Indeed this latter trend may have been more common with lesser planters who had fewer slaves and overseers to carry on the work. Tied down to the plantation routine of planting, tending, and harvesting the crops during the spring, summer, and fall, it may be that most planters were free to make extensive visits only

[57]*Byrd Diary, 1709–12*, 110–11, 200, 288, 467, 469, 506, 508.
[58]In the summer of 1711 when Byrd was suffering from a severe fever and ague, he was confined at home almost 40 percent of the summer; by comparison, during the following summer, Byrd was either receiving visitors or venturing out himself to visit virtually every day.

in the winter when the crops were in and before the next year's planting had begun.[59]

The most striking kinship pattern that emerges from the Byrd diary is the unusually small circle of recognized kin. In the forty-four months the diary spans—February 1709 through September 1712—Byrd mentions only fifteen persons as relatives. Indeed, less than one-fifth (17.5 percent) of the visits Byrd made or received involved blood or affinal kin. Only six of these fifteen kin were Byrd's blood relatives—a sister, a niece and nephew, a cousin, an uncle, and Byrd's deceased father, William Byrd I. The other nine kin, those he often called "cousin" or "uncle" or "aunt," were actually cousins of his wife, several times removed. One might compare this small kin network with that of one New England diarist in the late seventeenth century who noted some forty-eight cousins alone.[60]

The narrow range of kin surrounding Byrd stemmed in part from demographic accident and the mobility of his family. Byrd came from a relatively small family. He had no brothers and three sisters, one of whom died after the birth of her first child. Moreover, most of Byrd's family, like many planter families in the seventeenth and early eighteenth centuries, remained in England. That he had so few close relatives living in Tidewater Virginia may help explain why he appeared to adopt his wife's cousins and uncles and aunts as his own.

But Byrd was close to only a few of these fifteen kin and pseudo-kin. Several of these relatives were mentioned only a few times in the nearly four years covered in the diary. Byrd's "cousin Guy," for example, appeared in the diary during just one period in January 1711 when he visited Westover for twelve days. Byrd did not have much contact with his uncle Thomas Byrd of Henrico County, either. In fact, his first mention of his uncle came after he heard on May 9, 1709, that Thomas was "dangerously

[59]For a similar conclusion, see Kulikoff, "Tobacco and Slaves," 358.

[60]See Edmund Morgan's comment on the kin network of Samuel Sewall in *The Puritan Family: Religion and Domestic Relations in Seventeenth-Century New England* (New York, 1966), 150.

sick." Two days later Byrd asked his friend Dr. Cocke to see to his uncle. When Cocke refused ("on pretence of much business"), Byrd traveled to his uncle's place, which was near one of Byrd's plantations. "I gave him the best advice I could and then went to view my plantation," Byrd noted. Nothing more was said of Thomas Byrd until February 1710 when he visited Westover and appeared close to death. Byrd offered to take in his uncle, but Thomas returned home and a month later died. Byrd's only response was to send an overseer to the estate auction.[61]

The relatives closest to Byrd were his "cousin" Elizabeth Harrison, wife of Benjamin Harrison and distant cousin of Byrd's wife; "sister" Frances and "brother" John Custis, the sister of Byrd's wife Lucy Parke and her husband John Custis; and "uncle" Philip Ludwell, another distant relative of Lucy Byrd. Elizabeth Harrison of Berkeley was a neighbor of Byrd and lived within walking distance of Westover. According to the diary, Byrd saw her an average of at least once a week throughout the period 1709–1712. He became particularly close to her after her husband's death in April 1711. In fact, on the day Harrison died, Byrd spoke to the widow and assured her he would "be always ready to do her all manner of service." Byrd and his wife made frequent visits to comfort their "disconsolate cousin Harrison." Byrd almost routinely walked over to Mrs. Harrison's house to tell her news, eat dinner or help her with business matters. Likewise, she was a regular visitor in the Byrd household, usually for diversion and companionship, but often to help nurse Lucy Byrd through pregnancies, miscarriages, and illnesses. His sister-in-law and her husband, John and Frances Custis, lived a two-hour ride from Westover and Byrd had considerably less contact with them, but he did see them about once a month. Frances made few visits alone to Westover, but when Byrd had an especially difficult time with his ague and fever in the summer of 1711, she joined Mrs. Harrison in taking care of him. Byrd and "brother Custis" visited occasionally, exchanged news about business matters, and sometimes shared slaves. Byrd maintained a similar relationship with

[61] *Byrd Diary, 1709–12,* 283–88, 33–34, 140–41, 152–54, 180, 196.

his "uncle" Colonel Philip Ludwell whom he also saw about once a month.[62] Despite these important quasi-kin ties with distant relatives of his wife, Byrd's most intimate and frequent companions were a small group of friends and neighbors unrelated to him or his wife. It was men such as Colonel Edward Hill, Dr. William Cocke, and the Reverend Charles Anderson who shared most of the business and personal dimensions of Byrd's life. These men exchanged information about plantation management and slave health and belonged to the same militia company. Byrd and his friends turned to each other in times of sickness and shared important events in the life cycle—births, marriages, and deaths—just as intimately as members of a kin group.

Byrd's closest friend was Colonel Hill, whom he saw more frequently than anyone else, kin or non-kin. Although he rarely disclosed in his diary the nature of his feelings toward friends and relatives, Byrd did occasionally comment on the virtues of Hill. After a typical evening of dinner and pleasant conversation with Colonel Hill at Westover—the two "were merry with nonsence," he noted—Byrd appraised his friend: "The Colonel is a man of good sense and good principles notwithstanding what has been said of him."[63] The almost constant need for medical attention on the Byrd plantations made Dr. William Cocke an extremely valuable man to Byrd. But Cocke became an important personal friend as well and often donated his medical services to Byrd as a gesture of friendship. During Byrd's battle with a summer fever, Dr. Cocke checked his condition almost daily. One evening, however, he came "out of pure friendship and not as a doctor." Like Dr. Cocke, Charles Anderson was both a close friend and a prominent man in the community. Byrd liked his sermons and frequently invited Anderson and his wife to Westover after church for dinner. He christened Byrd's son and Byrd attended the christening of Anderson's boy. They gave medical help to each other during family

[62]Ibid., 166, 173, 179, 181, 63–64, 221–22, 226, 254, 386, 404.
[63]Ibid., 465.

illness and provided comfort when death struck in their households.[64]

In the diary, William Byrd mentioned at least ninety-six people he knew or visited. Some of these were business acquaintances—overseers, artisans, tenant farmers, and debtors who were dependent on Byrd for their economic security. Byrd's political and economic authority made Westover an important center for everyone from visiting ship captains to political leaders. And with Byrd's considerable learning and legal training, friends and kin often asked him to intervene to solve family problems. For example, when Major Lewis Burwell became sick and was thought near death, he requested that Byrd solve any disagreement that might develop between his sons over their inheritance.[65]

The sheer size of Byrd's circle of friends and acquaintances suggests that he was not guided by any kind of familial or kinship interests in making alliances and close friendships. The fact that he had six to seven times more friends than kin and seems to have maintained closer emotional bonds with neighbors and other non-kin than with any of his blood and most of his affinal kin underscores the relatively expansive and open nature of Byrd's social world beyond the family. That he devoted so much of his time in relentless visitation, often ignoring his wife and children, indicates that he viewed his family in a remarkably diffuse, heterogeneous way. For Byrd, family was not the private, intimate circle of close kin gathered in affection around hearth and home; rather, he understood family life in a much broader, looser fashion, as an essentially public phenomenon, a kind of constant sociability and companionship with like-minded people with whom he shared important work and leisure moments in the plantation community.[66] Figure 1 graphically displays the relative importance of kin and friends to Byrd.

[64]Ibid., 371–72, 577.

[65]Ibid., 87, 179, 577, 187.

[66]Michael Zuckerman has recently developed a similar analysis of Byrd's family and kin experience which emphasizes Byrd's indifference to the intimacy of the conjugal family. See his "William Byrd's Family," *Perspectives in American History,* XII (1979), 255–311.

Figure 1. The kin and friend universe of William Byrd II, 1709–1712*

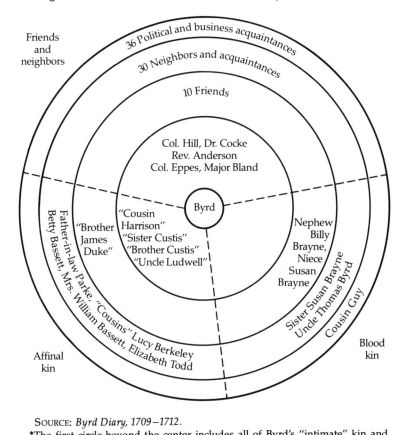

SOURCE: *Byrd Diary, 1709–1712*.
*The first circle beyond the center includes all of Byrd's "intimate" kin and friends—those he saw frequently, at least once every six weeks, for mutual aid in sickness and economic concerns. The next circle is "effective" kin and friends—those with whom he had less personal contact, between six weeks and three months, and provided little, if any aid. "Noneffective" kin and friends comprise the third circle. Here there was infrequent contact, between three and six months, some knowledge of their activities, but no mutual aid. The last circle of "unfamiliar" or "peripheral" kin and friends were those about whom Byrd knew only their names and residences—no visits or mutual aid. For these kin classifications, see Elizabeth Bott, *Family and Social Network* (London, 1957), 120–21; Raymond Firth, ed., *Two Studies of Kinship in London* (London, 1956), 45; William M. Williams, *A West Country Village: Ashworthy* (London, 1963), 168.

205

An analysis of Landon Carter's kin network involves more difficulties than did our assessment of William Byrd and his family. The Carter diary covers twenty-two years, from 1756 to 1778, but only a few of these years contained enough entries to suggest some sort of consistent pattern. Indeed, only in 1770 did Carter make entries as often as every other day in all twelve months. Most of the following analysis, then, is confined to the calendar year 1770, and adjustments will be made for the incomplete recording in the diary.[67] It should also be noted that Carter's diary was much more of an agricultural and personal journal than was Byrd's systematic, often mundane record of the day's events and people and places seen or visited. Carter often devoted several pages to a discussion of farming techniques or personal gripes, especially concerning the filial ingratitude of his son, Robert Wormeley Carter. Consequently, one suspects that the intensity of kin contact is somewhat underestimated in the diary, allowing one only to sketch the basic outline of kin activity in the Carter family.[68]

Clearly the most notable aspect of Carter's visitation pattern compared with Byrd's is the considerably larger body of kin revealed in the diary. Some sixty-eight relatives—both blood and affinal kin—were named during the twenty-two-year period. Many of these people appear to have maintained only very slight contact with Carter, as they were simply mentioned a few times between 1756 and 1778. Nonetheless, the size of Carter's recognized kin network, as reflected in the diary, was more than four times that of William Byrd. Roughly 40 percent of the visits to Sabine Hall and those outside the Carter household involved kin,

[67]During 1770, Carter made 184 entries in his diary, or 15.3 per month. Thus a crude correctional multiplier of two has been applied to the number of contacts Carter had with each of his kin and friends. It is possible, of course, that Carter—like any diarist—neglected to make entries on days when he saw no one or did not leave home. If this were true, then our adjustment may overcompensate for the underrecording in the diary. This problem simply underscores the tentativeness of these figures.

[68]For a perceptive discussion of the Carter diary and his gentry life style, see Jack P. Greene's introductory essay to the diary, now published separately as *Landon Carter: An Inquiry into the Personal Values and Social Imperatives of the Eighteenth-Century Virginia Gentry* (Charlottesville, Va., 1965).

compared with less than 20 percent for Byrd. Improving mortality rates by the mid-eighteenth century doubtless aided in the expansion of kin networks. Moreover, except for the western regions of the Chesapeake, Virginia and Maryland by the 1760s and 1770s was a settled society populated by numerous third- and even fourth-generation families with increasingly complex kin ties.[69]

The Carter family was prototypical of the growing number of these large, multi-generational families surrounded by elaborate kin networks. The son of Robert "King" Carter, an exceptionally wealthy second-generation Virginia planter, Landon Carter grew up with four brothers and five sisters. The sisters married into the Burwell, Harrison, Page, Braxton, and Fitzhugh families and Carter's eldest two brothers intermarried with the Hills and Churchills. In his three marriages, Carter produced three sons and four daughters, who married by their mid-twenties and provided him with numerous grandchildren, many of whom he saw before his death in 1778. And almost all of this growing body of kin remained in Tidewater Virginia throughout Carter's life, thereby giving his family a permanence unknown to most families of the early Chesapeake.[70]

In 1770, the year chosen to examine in detail, Landon Carter was sixty years old and a widower for the third time. As we have noted, Carter's eldest son Robert, daughter-in-law Frances, and their children lived with him at Sabine Hall, a three-generational

---

[69]One indication of the established nature of gentry society by the mid-eighteenth century was the increasing resistance it faced from newer, more iconoclastic elements from the lower orders. See the following essays by Rhys Isaac: "Evangelical Revolt: The Nature of the Baptists' Challenge to the Traditional Order in Virginia, 1765–1775," *WMQ*, 3d ser., xxxi (1974), 345–68; and "Preachers and Patriots: Popular Culture and the Revolution in Virginia," in Alfred F. Young, ed., *The American Revolution: Explorations in the History of American Radicalism* (Dekalb, Ill., 1976), 125–58.

[70]For an analysis of the evanescent family and political life in seventeenth-century Virginia, see Irene W. D. Hecht, "The Virginia Muster of 1624/5 as a Source for Demographic History," *WMQ*, 3d ser., xxx (1973), 65–92; Edmund S. Morgan, *American Slavery, American Freedom: The Ordeal of Colonial Virginia* (New York, 1975), 158–79; and Bernard Bailyn, "Politics and Social Structure in Virginia," in James Morton Smith, ed., *Seventeenth-Century America* (Chapel Hill, N.C., 1959), 90–115.

living arrangement that was unique in the eighteenth century. Besides his son and daughter-in-law, Carter's circle of close kin included five others: his son, John Carter, his daughter and son-in-law, Maria and Robert Beverley, and two nephews, Charles Carter of Corotoman and Charles Carter, Jr., of Nanzatico. Perhaps because of his advancing age, Carter did relatively little traveling. Thus his contact with kin and friends often depended on their visiting Sabine Hall. Even these close kin, then, saw Carter little more than once a month. More distant relatives—nieces and nephews and affinal kin—made up Carter's effective and noneffective kin, those he saw less than once every six weeks.

Despite a large number of recognized kin, Carter, like Byrd, seemed to spend much more time with friends than with relatives. His circle of intimate friends was as large as his group of close kin, and they appear more frequently in his diary than do his intimate relatives. In 1770 Carter mentioned the names of fifty-eight non-kin, seven of whom were close friends (intimate or effective friends). Figure 2 suggests the predominance of non-kin in Carter's circle of companions.

Carter seems to have selected his friends more out of a concern for specific personality traits than simply mutual economic interest, kin ties, or geographic proximity. Reverend Isaac Giberne was Carter's most frequent companion; he was seen or mentioned almost every two weeks. Giberne was an avid card player—Carter would have said an addict—but despite this flaw, Carter respected him and quite deliberately chose him as a friend. Reason and virtue were the principal qualities for good friendship, according to Carter. Giberne possessed these qualities, but, Carter lamented, he was not always consistent in them. After visiting Giberne one day, Carter commented on the excesses of Giberne's friendly nature. "A worthy good man but a little too unfortunately attached to some oddities that will injure him. His friendships are extremely strong but not always fixt upon proper objects and I think he is so blinded to them as often to forget evident facts and sacrifices his own reason." In main-

Figure 2. The kin and friend universe of Landon Carter, 1770*

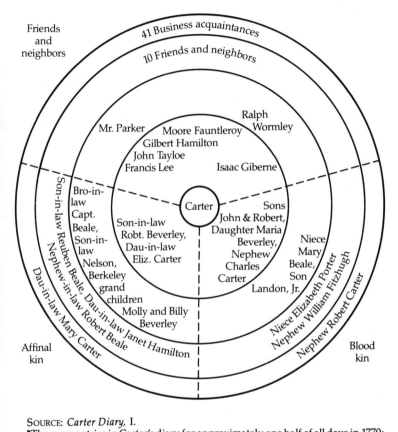

Source: *Carter Diary,* I.
*There are entries in Carter's diary for approximately one half of all days in 1770; thus the number of contacts with each person has been multiplied by a factor of two.

taining close ties to kin and friends, Carter emphasized the importance of a "*steady* turn of mind," which he found, for example, in his son-in-law William Colston.[71]

Carter's apparent preference for non-kin as friends suggests that like Byrd he viewed kin primarily in terms of a moral obligation, to serve in times of emergency, rather than as constant companions. His particular stage in the life cycle also influenced his kin activities. Without a wife, Carter may have lacked important motivation to visit relatives. Planters' wives spent much of their time making the visiting rounds, strengthening ties with kin on both sides of the family. As an aging widower, Carter seemed to have turned inward as he tended to the domestic affairs of Sabine Hall. And he occasionally became impatient with the banality of small talk that accompanied visiting. "Company," he lamented, was diverting only to those men "who can relax from the true modes of thinking and reasoning properly."[72] In short, Carter carefully selected those individuals who merited close friendship and in most cases these friends were not drawn from his wide circle of kin.

The diary of Colonel James Gordon of Lancaster County presents some of the same problems as the Landon Carter diary. Gordon began his diary in December of 1758 and continued it through the end of 1763, but like Carter, he made entries about every other day. He maintained this pace fairly consistently throughout these five years; thus the entire period covered in the diary, excluding some fragmentary entries for December of 1758, can be analyzed for our purposes.[73] Again, however, we must assume some underestimation of kin contact and visitation, even

[71]*Carter Diary*, I, 368, II, 1059–60. That geographic proximity was not a sufficient condition for friendship or even frequent contact with Carter is suggested in his reaction to the illness and death of a neighbor, "Old Starky Gower," a Richmond County farmer. Carter had frequently ministered to Gower's family in sickness in previous years, but he apparently had not seen Gower for a long time. When he heard of his death in April 1772, Carter remarked that he did not even know he had been ill, "though I lived so near him." Ibid., II, 668.
[72]Ibid., I, 372.
[73]Between 1759 and 1763, Gordon made 788 entries in his diary, a mean of 13.1 entries per month. "The Journal of James Gordon of Lancaster County, Virginia," *WMQ*, 1st ser., XI (1903), 98–112, 217–36, XII (1904), 1–12.

after adjusting for the roughly two and one half years of unrecorded activity. Fortunately for our analysis, Gordon's diary reveals more social detail than Carter's; that is, there is much more attention to names, places, and significant daily events. In sum, the Gordon diary contains both the irregularities of the Carter diary with the concern for social and personal activities evident in Byrd's secret diaries.

In 1738, at the age of twenty-three, James Gordon came to Virginia with his younger brother John from Newry, Ireland. By the 1750s Gordon had become a wealthy merchant-planter operating out of Merry Point in Lancaster County, while his brother had established himself in Urbanna, Middlesex County. Gordon acquired over 1000 acres of land and at his death owned 58 slaves and over £5000 in goods in several stores. Since he was an immigrant, Gordon's kin ties in Virginia developed largely out of the existing network of relatives he and his brother entered through their marriages. Twice married, into the prominent Conway and Harrison families of Lancaster and Surry counties, and the father of four children by 1760, James Gordon quickly enlarged his circle of kin and friends. Between 1759 and 1763 he recognized some twenty-one kin (both blood and affinal kin) and he saw most of these relatives at least once or twice during these years.[74]

An ardent Presbyterian, Gordon frequently spent time visiting with his neighbors, friends, and kin after church each week. His diary often mentions the "full house" or "large company" of ten or more guests who stayed at his home, sometimes for several days. One spring day in 1759 Gordon saw no company, *"which is surprising,"* he noted. Neighborhood visiting, as well as longer trips to see friends and kin, was an essential part of the daily social and religious life of Gordon and his family.[75]

A strong sense of community influenced the friendships and kin ties he maintained in Lancaster County. Gordon developed

[74]Lancaster County Deed Book 13, 312, 329; Book 14, 1, 118, 156, 215–16, 243, 264, 295; Book 16, 51, 121; Book 17, 6; Book 18, 4, 105, 108–9; Lancaster Will Book 15, 155, 192, 282–83, 295, microfilm, Virginia State Library, Richmond.
[75]"Journal of James Gordon," 102, 199, 218–19, 220.

close attachments to many of his neighbors and often invited "a large company of the neighbors" to his home for dinner, as on one occasion, to share a big catch of fish. Special occasions, such as Christmas, became in part neighborhood gatherings. On Christmas Day in 1760, Gordon invited six of his neighbors and friends to dinner. The next day he sent for his close friends, Colonel William Taylor, Dale and Thomas Carter, and "many of the girls of the neighborhood," to dine with the Gordon family. Gordon and his wife regularly visited friends and kin in ill health and worried about their "sick neighborhood." After visiting some of his friends in November of 1761, he observed that "the neighborhood continues very sickly."[76]

Gordon's Presbyterian faith with its principles of spiritual brotherhood and social egalitarianism doubtless contributed to his strong sense of communal life and shared purpose in the neighborhood. In an important way, his Lancaster County neighborhood was both a religious and a social community. Almost all of the church's ten elders selected in 1763, for example, were neighbors and close friends of Gordon. And in important church matters the entire neighborhood was asked to participate. When Gordon and the other elders were searching for a new minister in 1760, Gordon called on some of the local community for a broader opinion. The elders, he believed, chose not only for themselves, but for "our families & our neighbors who depended upon us."[77]

In this close-knit planter community, personal disagreements were often mediated by kin and friends. When a "difference" arose between Richard Chichester and Captain Robert Armistead, Chichester sent for Gordon, his father-in-law, to settle the quarrel. Gordon later recorded in his diary that "We got it made up, & they agreed to live in friendship." Likewise Gordon, Chichester, the Reverend Waddell, and their friends Thomas Carter and Colonel Selden, helped to settle a family dispute

[76]Ibid., 199, 196, 226.
[77]Ibid., 2, 222. The culture and social values of members of a dissenter faith in eighteenth-century Virginia are brilliantly analyzed in Issac, "Preachers and Patriots."

between a newlywed husband and wife. "After much debate," Gordon observed, "they agreed to be friends. I think Mr. C [Criswell, the husband] has very much exposed himself." Gordon's intense religious feeling also led him and Waddell, his son-in-law, to supervise neighborhood morality, intervening in matters of premarital sexual behavior, excessive drinking, and irreligious family conduct.[78]

It was in the context of a strong dissenter faith and a close neighborhood community that Gordon formed his important kin and friendship ties. Over all, 41.1 percent of Gordon's visits were with relatives, a large proportion considering the relatively modest size of his available pool of kin. Members of Gordon's nuclear family were those with whom he remained on the closest terms. His brother John, daughter Nancy Chichester, and son-in-law Richard Chichester made up his circle of intimate kin between 1759 and 1763. John Gordon lived almost a day's boat ride from James, but they saw each other at least every six weeks, and James kept in touch with his brother's financial dealings and health concerns. Considerably closer to Gordon were his daughter and son-in-law, Nancy and Richard Chichester. The Chichesters lived near the Gordons and saw them frequently. Gordon and his wife took care of Richard when he was ill and nursed their daughter through her lying-in at the birth of her first child. The Gordons even helped the Chichesters decide where to build the kitchen for the new house they were constructing in 1759.[79] As a young married couple, the Chichesters probably needed more kin support than they did in later years. But clearly the embarrassment and emotional detachment affinal kin sometimes experience did not impair the relationship between the Gordons and their son-in-law.[80]

[78]"Journal of James Gordon," 228, 6, 2, 205.
[79]Ibid., 227, 230, 108, 197–201, 235, 201, 229.
[80]The importance of understanding the changing function and significance of kin at various points in the life cycle is emphasized in Tamara K. Hareven, "Family Time and Industrial Time," *Journal of Urban History*, I, (1975), 355–89. In preindustrial, agrarian societies like the eighteenth-century Chesapeake, however, one suspects that kinship was a more constant presence throughout life than it was in industrialized, urban areas.

Gordon remained somewhat more distant from his father-in-law and mother-in-law, Colonel Edwin and Mrs. Conway. Colonel Conway was a wealthy and politically prominent Anglican planter in Lancaster County and he openly disapproved of Gordon's religious enthusiasm. Gordon marketed Conway's tobacco and visited the Conways frequently, but the diary does not reveal their having stopped by the Gordon household during the entire five years. The tension between Conway and his son-in-law burst into serious conflict in the summer of 1759, when Conway sent Gordon a note criticizing his religious beliefs. "Col. Conway seems so great a bigot that people who are religiously inclined despise his advice," Gordon concluded. Despite Conway's intolerance of religious enthusiasm, Gordon attempted to reconcile matters one day, perhaps because he felt morally obliged to have harmonious relations with his kin. After a long talk, Gordon reported, they came to a temporary truce, "but with much difficulty. The old gentleman was in a great rage at first." Within a few months, the two were fighting again, as Conway began to demand a much higher price for his tobacco than Gordon had been giving him for twenty years. Gordon exclaimed, "As I can't be of his way of thinking in religion, he seems to take opportunity to hurt my interest."[81]

Gordon maintained ties with a dozen more relatives, but not on a regular basis. His sister lived in Richmond and the distance prevented frequent contact. Nevertheless, he took pleasure in hearing of her children and visited her once when her husband deserted her. Gordon saw his cousins Samuel, David, and Robert Hening occasionally and took Robert into his home for several months after his wife's death, "till he was better provided." Nephews, nieces, and an array of in-laws composed the noneffective and peripheral kin whom he mentioned but rarely saw or depended on for any sort of aid.[82]

Like Byrd and Carter, Colonel James Gordon surrounded himself with a group of close friends, who, except for two or three

[81]"Journal of James Gordon," 101, 107, 196.
[82]Ibid., 233–34, 2, 117.

intimate kin, became his principal companions. None of his planter friends saw him as regularly as his brother, daughter, and son-in-law, but there were about six men, all prominent, wealthy, and mostly Presbyterian, with whom the Gordons frequently dined, worshiped and visited in sickness. Some of these men, such as Colonel Richard Selden and Colonel William Taylor, were, like Gordon, elders in the newly established Presbyterian church in Lancaster County and represented powerful families. A successful planter-merchant and a key figure in his religious community, Gordon recorded another sixty-eight business contacts and church friends whom he visited occasionally during these five years. In sum, Gordon's circle of close companions, both intimate and effective ties, was almost equally divided between kin and non-kin. (See Figure 3 below). The close-knit nature of the neighborhood community, the communal implications of his religious faith, and his commitment to the members of his nuclear family defined the shape and character of James Gordon's ties of kinship and friendship.

In Francis Taylor of Orange County, Virginia, we encounter a rather different pattern of kin activity. The social, economic, and family context of Taylor's life varied considerably from that of William Byrd, Landon Carter, or James Gordon. Unlike these wealthy, Tidewater gentry, Taylor was a middling planter—he owned less than ten slaves and about five hundred acres of land—in a relatively newly settled piedmont county. And perhaps most important in terms of kinship, he remained a bachelor throughout his life.

The diary of Francis Taylor, which runs from 1786 until weeks before his death in 1799, is an exceedingly illuminating document for social and family history in the late eighteenth-century Chesapeake. While the diary is short on personal reflections, there is a great deal of detail about family life, kin contact, patterns of indebtedness, and local society in Orange County. No serious gaps appear in the diary throughout the fourteen years, and Taylor made entries about twenty-five days out of each month. Perhaps only the Byrd secret diaries were more consist-

Figure 3. The kin and friend universe of James Gordon, 1759–1763*

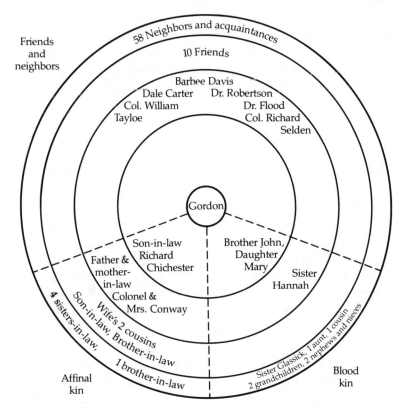

SOURCE: "The Journal of James Gordon," *WMQ*, 1st. ser., XI (1903), 98–112, 217–36; XII (1904), 1–12.

*Because of the underrecording in the Gordon diary—about 50 percent of the days have entries—the number of contacts with each person has been multiplied by two.

ently kept and provide as much detailed information about the dynamics of family and kinship. Taylor's diary, however, spans more years, and because of his middling social and economic status, it may be less idiosyncratic than the Byrd material. What is distinctive about Taylor for our purposes is that he never married. This clearly had a significant impact on his kin activities. Although being single deprived him of a substantially larger network of affinal kin through a wife's family, his bachelor status probably drew him much closer to his own relatives than most married men were to their kin.[83] Unlike married planters with families and large plantations to care for, Taylor, and perhaps most single men, had fewer responsibilities, more leisure time, and a stronger urge to escape the loneliness and routine of plantation life—all of which may have encouraged him to move about more frequently to visit relatives and friends.

Taylor's diary unmistakably reveals the daily importance of kinship in his life. Almost two-thirds (62.0 percent) of the days recorded in his diary mention contact with at least one relative, and frequently with several. As Table 2 indicates, the winter and

Table 2. Seasonality in visiting: Francis Taylor, 1787*

Season	No. days with friends or kin	Percentage
Fall (Sept.–Nov.)	54	59.3
Winter (Dec.–Feb.)	68	74.7
Spring (March–May)	59	64.1
Summer (June–Aug.)	57	61.9
Total	238	65.2

SOURCE: Francis Taylor Diary, 1787.
*The percentages shown here are based on the actual number of days in contact with friends or kin divided by 365. But since there are entries in 1787 for only two-thirds of all days (238), the proportion of time Taylor spent in the company of others is clearly underestimated in these figures.

[83]Lee N. Robins and Miroda Tomanec, "Closeness to Blood Relatives outside the Immediate Family," in Bernard Farber, ed., *Kinship and Family Organization* (New York, 1966), 134–41.

spring months seem to have been Taylor's most active period of traveling, while he remained at home more often in the fall and especially the summer months. This seasonal variation suggests that Taylor's mobility was more noticeably constrained by the special rhythms of plantation life than was that of a wealthy planter like Byrd. Taylor's increased contact with kin and friends during the winter months coincided with the relatively slack period that followed the harvest.

If his record of visits is a useful guide, Francis Taylor was involved in a daily pattern of sociability, almost constantly surrounded by friends and relatives in his Orange County neighborhood. He stayed at home no more than once a week (13.6 percent of the time) and then under duress—such as bad weather or illness. Cold and inclement weather confined him at home one winter day in 1796, which he noted: "I did not go from home & saw no white person." A number of social events brought Taylor and others—largely males—together: dining, church, muster, court days, horse races, card games, hunts, and balls.[84] As we have suggested before, the most regular gathering of friends and relatives occurred at mealtime, which was often followed by hours of card games, especially whist. Dinner invitations were not particularly formal—often a slave messenger would simply ride over and ask his master's friend or kin to drop by to eat.[85] In the Taylor family these were rarely small affairs. Once when he dined with his brother Charles Taylor, Francis took note of the unusually small company present—"none but his own family there." A company of a dozen or more friends and relatives was not uncommon and sometimes the group became even larger as others dropped by. Except for special family events such as christenings, weddings, and an occasional family dinner, most gatherings Taylor attended attracted as many of his friends as his kin.[86]

[84]FTD, Jan. 6, 1796; see also Dec. 27, 1787.

[85]FTD, March 22, 1788, Aug. 26, June 18, Dec. 29, 1792.

[86]FTD, Jan. 25, 1797, Dec. 16, 1787, March 22, March 13, 1788, Feb. 18, 1786, Sept. 27–28, 1787, Aug. 11, 1788, Dec. 29, 1792, Nov. 9, 1790, March 13, 1788. Attending Christmas dinner in 1786 were according to Taylor, almost all "family." An approximately equal number of friends and kin attended the Taylor's Twelfth Night celebration, Jan. 6, 1791.

Francis Taylor mentions some twenty-seven relatives in his diary, but he was intimately associated with a significantly larger group of kin than any of the three men we have thus far examined. Nine relatives—his father, five brothers, an uncle, and two cousins—made up an especially close circle of kin with whom Taylor shared almost all aspects of his life. During the years 1786–1788 Taylor saw most of these intimate kin at least once every week to ten days, especially his brothers James and Charles, maternal uncle Erasmus Taylor, and cousin John Taylor. Except for his contact with his uncle and cousin, Taylor, like Carter and Gordon, devoted most of his time to members of his own immediate family. Female relatives, however close genealogically, appear only occasionally in Taylor's diary (except for two sisters-in-law), providing another example, perhaps, of the emotional distance that separated men and women in the eighteenth-century Chesapeake.[87] While he had only infrequent contact with his noneffective and peripheral kin, Taylor did receive letters and regular reports from relatives and friends about the health, marital status, and financial condition of these more distant kin. On November 14, 1786, for example, Taylor noted that he "hears" that his Aunt Battaile was "dangerously ill," but he made no further mention of her condition or his response to her situation. Several members of the Taylor family moved to Kentucky in the 1780s and 1790s, and he followed some of their activities and traded family news every few months through correspondence, simply to see if all "generally were well."[88]

The circle of kin closest to Taylor was determined in part by geographic proximity, for he lived within walking distance of brothers, James and Charles, Uncle Erasmus, and his Aunt Thomas.[89] The informal and frequently unannounced visits of

[87]In 1788 Taylor mentioned some thirty-nine women, at least twelve of whom were either blood or affinal kin—just under one-third of all his recognized kin. But Taylor's contact with these twelve women represented only 14.1 percent of his total visits with kin duirng the year. The emotional segregation of men and women in Chesapeake society is discussed in Chapter 2.

[88]FTD, Nov. 1, 1786, June 13, 1796, Sept. 8, 1788, Aug. 22, 1794, April 7, June 12, Oct. 14, Dec. 21, 1796; June 14, Sept. 2, 1797; April 7, June 27, 1798; Nov. 5, 1796.

[89]FTD, March 25–26, 1787; Jan. 14, Sept. 27, Feb. 2, 1786, Aug. 11, 1788.

other relatives suggest that Taylor lived no more than a short ride from several other kin.[90] And when he was not visiting one or more of his brothers, cousins, or uncles, Taylor often kept up with who was ill, who was dining with whom, where relatives were spending the night, and other daily concerns.[91]

Fraternal bonds were especially significant for Francis Taylor. He constantly visited his five Orange County brothers and wrote two other brothers who lived in Caroline County and Kentucky. Indeed, almost two-thirds (62.1 percent) of his kin contact between 1786 and 1788 involved one or more of his brothers. Any tension between the Taylor brothers was a source of concern to Francis. After a two-month estrangement between James and Charles, the two got together for dinner and apparently reached some sort of reconciliation. "It gives me pleasure to hope that a friendly intercourse will ensue and for the future continue," Francis noted in one of his rare personal statements.[92]

More than sociability was involved in these strong sibling ties, for Taylor and his brothers depended on each other for household supplies, labor, medical care, and financial aid. Charles Taylor was a doctor and he cared for the entire Taylor family and many of their friends in times of sickness. The Taylor brothers either exchanged labor or paid one another for services performed by their slaves. Francis frequently lent his slave "Davy," "the cobbler," to his brother James to make shoes, and in return James sent two field slaves to Francis's plantation. When James needed extra help to cut his wheat in the summer of 1788, Francis sent him two slaves. And the women in the Taylor family made and repaired clothes for many of the brothers and their families.[93]

Throughout the diary there are references to mutual economic aid among members of the family. Francis, for example, lent his brother Reuben £9.15.0 in 1786 to repay a debt Reuben owed a friend. Taylor's uncle, Erasmus, was given a £14.2.0 certificate,

[90]FTD, Feb. 6–7, 18–19, 1786.
[91]Ibid., Jan. 1, 4, 5, 12, June 20, Nov. 12, 1786, Aug. 29, Sept. 2, 1787, March 29, 1788.
[92]FTD, Sept. 8, 1788, Aug. 23, Oct. 1, 1786.
[93]FTD, July 3, 1788, Feb. 2, April 10, 1786, Nov. 12, Dec. 11, 1794, Dec. 24–25, 1795, June 7, 1787.

Kin, Friends, and Neighbors

one-third of which he was to repay "when it suits him." James
Taylor, Jr., Francis's nephew, borrowed £20 from his uncle for a
trip to see family and friends in Kentucky in 1796. Taylor was
particularly attached to his father and sought to provide as much
financial assistance for him as he could. In 1786 Francis organized
the construction of his father's new home, supplying laborers,
building materials, and supervising much of the work. Colonel
James Taylor, near seventy-five at the time, gave his son £20 to
pay for the hired workers, and one of Francis's brothers, George,
furnished shingles and plank.[94]

Between 1786 and 1790—except for 1787—Francis Taylor kept
an account book for all his income and expenses. The pattern of
indebtedness indicates the economic interdependence of his kin.
According to these accounts, Taylor lent and owed money to his
uncle and all five brothers in Orange County, especially to James
and George. These family debts amounted to over half (52.1
percent) of the total amount he owed during the four years.

Although, as we have seen, Taylor's social world was heavily
influenced by his kinship ties, friends played an important role as
well, at least in terms of sociability. As Figure 4 shows, an equal
number of friends and neighbors belonged to his circle of closest
companions—both intimate and effective ties—and he recognized in his diary about the same number of friends as relatives.
Like James Gordon, Taylor belonged to an active, close-knit
neighborhood community. In 1788 Taylor and his neighbors
pooled their resources to build a schoolhouse and to establish a
"singing school." They organized numerous barbecues, fishing
parties, and dances throughout the year, usually held at the
courthouse, the social center of Orange County.[95]

In some respects the kinship patterns revealed in the diaries of
these four men are distinctive and resist generalization. As we
have noted, two of the men, Carter and Gordon, kept their

[94]FTD, April 12, 30, Oct. 21–22, 1794, June 26, 1787, Feb. 26, March 23, April 24,
May 14–18, 21, June 27, 1786, March 12–13, 1787.
[95]FTD, Feb. 4, 9, March 17, June 28, 30, July 11, Sept. 12, 13, 26, 1788, June 20,
1789, Sept. 4, 1790, April 27–28, 1791, July 10–11, 31, Sept. 17, 1795, Nov. 10,
1796, July 5, 1799.

221

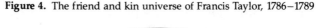

Figure 4. The friend and kin universe of Francis Taylor, 1786–1789

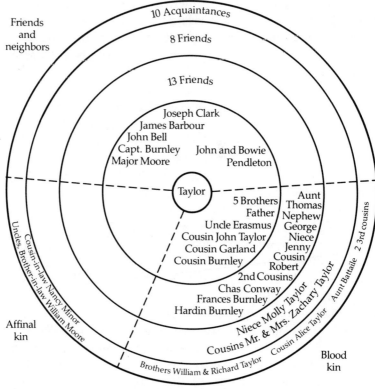

SOURCE: Francis Taylor Diary, 1786–1789.

diaries much less systematically than Byrd and Taylor, and despite the adjustments made in these cases, an unknown amount of underrecording of kin activity is inevitable. Moreover, we have drawn from only one year of the Carter diary—because of the extremely irregular pattern of entries in the other years of his journal—compared with the three- and four-year periods of analysis for the other three diarists. Perhaps most important, some of these men kept their diaries at different stages in the life cycle and in the context of varied family structures. Byrd, for example, was typical of many of the early Chesapeake families with close relatives living on both sides of the Atlantic. That Landon Carter was an elderly widower, with a son and daughter-in-law sharing his home at Sabine Hall, probably restricted his kin activities and mobility. James Gordon, the only immigrant of the four diarists, came to Virginia with but a few blood relatives and thus developed kin ties primarily through marriage. Finally, the bachelor status of Francis Taylor, who was the only diarist who did not belong to the gentry, oriented him more strongly toward his immediate family and kin than most married men who raised families of their own.

Seen in a larger, comparative perspective, however, the social world of these four men reveals striking similarities and suggests more important distinctive qualities of family and kinship in the eighteenth-century Chesapeake. Presented in Table 3 are the kin universes of a range of sample families from the seventeenth century to the modern world, as calculated by historians and sociologists.

Two central patterns emerge from these comparative data. First, the kinship universe among the gentry in the eighteenth-century Chesapeake, as reflected in these diaries, remained remarkably small. Virtually all the other families represented here recognized a much larger number of kin than any of the four Virginia diarists, from a low of 48 for the seventeenth-century English clergyman, Ralph Josselin (who named from two to three times as many kin as three of the four men under study) to a high of 139 for the Newbolt family in modern London (whose kin universe was apparently seven times the size of the eighteenth-century planters). Studies of kinship in modern America also suggest that 150 or more relatives formed the kin universe of many middle-class families.[96] Table 3 also indicates that the circle of close kin—intimate and effective kin—surrounding these Virginia planters was much smaller than that of most modern families. Even Ralph Josselin's relatively restricted network of close kin included significantly more relatives than any of the diarists except Francis Taylor.

These figures are meant only as tentative estimates, for there are problems in comparing kin universes calculated from references in diaries over a span of time, as with the four planters and Josselin, with those constructed from sociological interviews of families at a single point in time—as in the two modern examples.[97] Nevertheless, the narrow range and shallow genealogical depth of most planter kin relationships more closely resembled mobile, modern family ties, albeit on a much smaller scale, than any sort of extended family or complex kin group arrangement sometimes associated with preindustrial agrarian societies.[98]

[96]Elaine Cumming and David M. Schneider, "Sibling Solidarity: A Property of American Kinship," in Farber, ed., *Kinship and Family Organization*, 143.

[97]All of the diarists doubtless knew other distant kin, even though they were not mentioned in the diaries. Hence the number of unfamiliar kin is clearly underestimated in Table 3. But the circles extending to noneffective kin are probably complete. It should also be noted that the kin activities of the Newbolts and Daniels—both modern London families—concerned the recognition of kin by both the husband and wife—and the wife's kin connections may have been more important and wider than her husbands's. As result, the difference between the size of the modern kin universe and that of these Chesapeake planters may be exaggerated.

One important factor, however, may partially compensate for these methodological discrepancies. The analysis of the diaries covers several years and allows us to investigate kinship through a larger portion of the life cycle than does the interviewing technique of sociologists who see their subjects at one point in time. Thus, unlike the broader survey of kin activity which several years' study of a diary affords, a "picture" of a man's living intimate kin taken on a given day in his life might miss relatives who a few years earlier were important, as well as those who would become significant in the future. Studying kinship through diary references can create underestimates of kin contact and recognition as compared with interviews with both spouses, but the difference between the two approaches, especially concerning the circle of close relatives, is probably not as great as it may appear.

[98]See Philip Greven's analysis of kin networks in colonial Andover, *Four Generations: Population, Land, and Family in Colonial Andover, Massachusetts*

Table 3. Recognition of kin in premodern and modern families*

Kin	Josselin		Byrd		Carter		Gordon		Taylor		Newbolts		Daniels	
	N	%	N	%	N	%	N	%	N	%	N	%	N	%
Intimate	13	27	4	27	7	35	3	14	9	33	40	29	3	3
Effective	4	8	3	20	6	30	3	14	7	26	29	21	18	20
Non-effective	29	61	7	47	5	25	4	18	3	11	63	45	51	57
Unfamiliar	2	4	1	7	2	10	12	55	8	30	7	5	18	20
Total	48		15		20		22		27		139		90	

*For a description of the classification used here, see note on page 205.

SOURCES: Macfarlane, *The Family Life of Ralph Josselin*, 158; Bott, *Family and Social Network*, 120, contains the data on the Newbolt and Daniel families. The figures on Byrd, Carter, Gordon, and Taylor come from the diaries described in the text.

Our evidence, to be sure, concerns only a few well-to-do men in the eighteenth-century Chesapeake. Planters of lesser means may have maintained more extensive kin ties for economic and emotional security. The Taylor family's reliance on one another for companionship, labor supplies, and mutual economic and medical aid is perhaps suggestive of how families of the middling sort organized themselves. On the other hand, it is reasonable to assume that if one does not find great concentrations of kin and close contact between relatives in gentry families—where economic and geographic stability remained relatively strong—then the middle and lower orders, which were often subject to more economic dislocations, probably developed an even weaker

(Ithaca, N.Y., 1970), 98–99, 171–72, 257. Few historians have systematically analyzed kinship in the preindustrial South, but the impression remains that gentry families developed elaborate kin groupings that supported and perpetuated blood lines and planter dominance. See Gerald W. Mullin, *Flight and Rebellion: Slave Resistance in Eighteenth-Century Virginia* (New York, 1972), 19–33; Eugene Genovese, *Roll, Jordan, Roll: The World the Slaves Made* (New York, 1974), 92; and Wyatt-Brown, "The Ideal Typology and Antebellum Southern History." For a discussion of kin groups in eighteenth-century Prince George's County, Maryland, see Kulikoff, "Tobacco and Slaves," chapters 6 and 7. Kulikoff's work represents the first systematic study of kinship patterns in the colonial South.

sense of connectedness with their kin. We simply do not have sufficient systematic evidence on the daily social life of poorer families to know.

If the experience of these diarists was at all representative of Chesapeake planters, most young men from gentry families grew up in a world of kin that extended vertically no further than their grandparents and laterally to their first cousins. Then as now, however, the effective, working kin relationships were usually confined to the immediate family and perhaps an aunt and uncle or, later in life, a son- or daughter-in-law. With the possible exception of Francis Taylor's experience, friends and neighbors seem to have been more important than relatives in the daily lives of these eighteenth-century Virginians. There were few exclusively family functions, and most of these men depended as much on friends as relatives for aid and companionship.

Kin ties of course could be quite important at certain stages of the life cycle. Uncles and aunts, for example, were sometimes instrumental in guiding the education or apprenticeships of young boys, and occasionally girls, in their adolescence. In general, however, the diaries suggest that, especially for married men, kinship was not a controlling force in the social world of these planters. In fact, it appears that members of the Virginia gentry chose their companions more for compatible personalities and similar life styles than out of a concern for maintaining family solidarity.

For women a different pattern seems to have emerged in the late eighteenth century. Indeed the extent to which Chesapeake families did develop strong family and kin ties was probably owing to the women in the family who increasingly became guardians of the kin network during the latter half of the century. Mothers, grandmothers, and aunts often assumed the role of "kin specialist" in the family, the one who was most knowledgeable about kin activities and who tried to maintain frequent contact with relatives. The kin obligations adult women assumed grew in part out of the child-bearing experience and the sharp sex-related division of parental roles. With little mobility or significant economic authority in the household, mothers increasingly focused their attention on their children and the expanding body of kin, especially female relatives, who surrounded the family.[99]

Demographic and economic conditions also contributed to the growth of female kin networks. With the improvement in longevity by the mid-eighteenth century came the prospect of an "empty nest" stage in the parental life cycle. Thus women often lived to see their children marry and establish independent households. Moreover, the growing interest in the western lands of Kentucky and Tennessee in the 1780s and 1790s drew many young men and women away from their parental homes in the Chesapeake. As a result, the dispersal of kin by migration prompted aging mothers and grandmothers to maintain some sort of contact with their kin through correspondence and occasional visits.

The life of Martha Jefferson Carr illustrates the growing importance of a matrifocal kin network. During the 1790s, after most of her children had married, moved away, and begun families of their own, she corresponded regularly with her married daughter Lucy Terrell, providing her with all the family news—health problems, marriage announcements, and information about various aunts, uncles, nieces, and cousins. In one letter Mrs. Carr discussed some thirteen relatives. While this correspondence occasionally referred to the neighborhood and friends, most of it focused on matters of kinship. Despite the obvious pleasure she received from exchanging letters with her kin, Mrs. Carr deeply lamented the scattering of her family. In October 1794 she wrote her son-in-law, Richard Terrell: "Oh how are my children disperst over the face of the earth—I am quite out of spirits. May you never meet with any of those circumstances to disturb you but see your offspring happly settl'd round you." Increasingly in the late

---

[99]For a discussion of women as kin guardians in the family, see Elizabeth Bott, *Family and Social Network* (London, 1957), 137; and Robins and Tomanec, "Closeness to Blood Relatives outside the Immediate Family," 140. Chapter 2 above analyzes female bonds and identity formation.

eighteenth and early nineteenth centuries, kinship ties were forged primarily by women such as Martha Jefferson Carr, who sought to extend their maternal protection and concern to the wider kin network.[100]

Despite this rising female concern for stronger family and kin ties, for most men, neighbors and friends figured as prominently as relatives in the social world beyond the household. In contrast, kin ties were growing increasingly important for families in other settled areas of eighteenth-century America, especially New England. Third- and fourth-generation Puritans, Edmund Morgan has shown, became tribalistic in their faith, turning their spiritual energies inward on their families and kin during the eighteenth century. Family connections began to replace merit in political life as well. And increasingly friendships were formed within an expanding body of kin.[101]

Family connections expanded in the eighteenth-century Chesapeake too, but largely within the confines of the immediate family. For example, sons frequently followed fathers on the county courts as justices of the peace, especially during the first three-quarters of the eighteenth century.[102] The relatively limited face-to-face contact between kin outside the nuclear family, however, reflected the increasingly private nature of the planter fam-

---

[100]Martha Jefferson Carr to Lucy Terrell, Aug. 9, 1794, March 15, Aug. 25, 1795, March 28, 1796; same to Richard Terrell, Oct. 17, 1794, CTFP. Frances Baylor gave explicit expression to her maternal love for the Baylor kin. She wrote her married daughter that she wanted to keep all her grown children "under my wing with the rest of my dearest offspring," for Mrs. Baylor was determined "to protect those dearest to me on this earth." Frances Baylor to Louisa Henrietta Upshaw, July 18, 1813, BFP. See also the following letters of female kin guardians: Frances Tucker to St. George Tucker, Oct. 9, 1788, Anne Tucker to St. George Tucker, Feb. 18, 1780, same to Frances Tucker, April 14, 1780, TCP; Mrs. Maria Byrd to Colonel William Byrd III, Aug. 15, 1760, in "Letters of the Byrd Family," *VMHB*, xxxviii (1930), 156; Elizabeth Dulaney to Catherine Belt, Aug. 1, 1797, Nov. 9, 1798, Dec. 20, 1799; and Mary Dulaney to Walter Dulaney, Aug. 7, 1783, DP.

[101]See Morgan, *The Puritan Family*, 161–86; and Linda Auwers, "Thy Brother's Keeper: Lineal and Lateral Family Ties in Preindustrial America" (unpub. paper, Shelby Cullom Davis Center Seminar, 1976).

[102]See Daniel B. Smith, "Changing Patterns of Local Political Leadership: Justices of the Peace in Albemarle County, Virginia, 1760–1920," *Essays in History* University of Virginia, xviii (1973–74), 52–85; and Sydnor, chapter 6.

ily during the latter half of the century. As parents focused their energies on an increasingly intimate, sentimental family society, the wider kin network of uncles, aunts, cousins, and more distant relatives moved to the periphery of the individual's affectional world. These kin were called on at certain times for specific tasks, but it was neighbors and unrelated friends who, along with members of the conjugal family, formed the circle of intimate companions for most planters.

At the heart of this circumscribed range of kin relationships lay the stabilization of the child-centered conjugal family in the eighteenth century. Ironically, as individual families became more durable, longer-lived structures for socializing the young and accumulating material wealth, the idea of family and kin connectedness weakened. This is reflected in changing child-naming patterns. In the seventeenth century when early parental death and high infant and childhood mortality rates cut short the existence of many families, parents—especially fathers—sought to make at least some symbolic claim for family continuity by naming their sons after themselves. In one Virginia parish where reliable birth records have survived, almost two-thirds of all fathers (65.4 percent) named one of their sons after themselves between 1650 and 1700. In the subsequent half century, however, less than half of the fathers (44.4 percent) chose to give their own forename to their sons. Although similar parish registers are unavailable after mid-century, it is likely that the proportion of fathers naming children after themselves continued to fall throughout the eighteenth century.[103] In what were clearly

[103]Daniel Scott Smith has discovered a similar pattern in New England beginning in the late eighteenth century. Smith, "Child Naming Patterns and Family Structure Change: Hingham, Mass., 1640–1880," *Newberry Papers in Family and Community History* (1976). The Virginia data come from a larger study of family and demographic change in Charles Parish, Virginia. The Charles Parish registers are located in the Virginia State Library, Richmond. The dramatic decline after 1700 of fathers naming children after themselves may not signify a shift away from kin-oriented naming patterns, since boys were often named for uncles as well as fathers. In addition, the lengthening life expectancies of the eighteenth century and the growing body of surviving kin increased the number of available living relatives other than fathers after whom sons could be named.

child-centered families of the post-1750 period, parents were increasingly willing to recognize the individual identities of their offspring.

As Chesapeake society became a healthier environment and men found a sense of permanence in larger families, land, and personal property in the eighteenth century, parents felt less compelled to use their sons as a hold on posterity. Gradually, a segmental family arrangement emerged. Children grew up in independent households where they were taught to make autonomous choices, and above all, to become self-sufficient. Ties with parents and grandparents and perhaps an uncle were exceedingly close until marriage, and then the process began again when a new, independent household was established. Breaking away from the family of origin through economic self-sufficiency and independent marital choice, young men perceived kinship as more nearly a series of family units through which one passed from birth to death than as a continuous, growing system of mutual responsibilities and rights. Close lateral ties with a variety of extended kin rarely developed as in an interdependent family organization. Men emphasized the present condition of their own conjugal families rather than dwelling on any sort of kin ideology or some larger collectivity of kin with unique traits and a special past.[104] By the late eighteenth century the effort to nurture and protect the conjugal unit sharpened the boundaries between family, kin, and the wider community.

[104]"Segmental" and "interdependent" family organizations are analyzed in a perceptive essay by Ray L. Birdwhistell, "The American Family: Some Perspectives," *Psychiatry*, XXIX (1966), 203–12. In the modern agricultural community of Gosforth, England, W. M. Williams has discovered considerable internal solidarity of kin groups which gave each individual a strong sense of his and the community's past and his place within it. Williams, *The Sociology of an English Village: Gosforth* (London, 1956), 69–85.

Chapter Six

Providing for the Living

Inheritance and the Family

The idea of the family was most strongly affirmed in the preparation of the last will and testament. Will writing was often a kind of summing up, an important, final opportunity for an individual to come to terms with his family, kin and friends, at least in an economic sense, and to pass on his accumulated material wealth and social status to the surviving generation. In the preindustrial world when so much of each individual's and family's future depended on inheritance, wills frequently expressed "the love links and bonds between family members," especially between husbands and wives and parents and children.[1] Certain gifts, such as mourning rings and valued family objects (such as a special silver tankard or the family plate), symbolized the affection and sense of continuity between the testator and his loved ones. Moreover, in parceling out family property, directing the management of children and the maintenance of a surviving spouse, a man gave expression both to how he conceived of the family—who belonged and who did not—and to the proper balance between control and autonomy for the future of those left behind.[2]

[1]Marvin B. Sussman, Judith Cates, and David T. Smith, *The Family and Inheritance* (New York, 1970), 380.

[2]Examples of symbolic gifts of the estate can be found in the following wills: York County Wills, 1760, 1763, 1764, XXI, 20–21, 160–61, 205–6. (All citations to

Almost every man and woman who composed a will or had one drawn up for them was beset by a fundamental dilemma: the impulse to protect the family estate, to keep it intact in perpetuity, often conflicted with the affectionate desire to provide for all children, dependent kin and close friends. In short, a tension existed between the impulse to keep all the estate within the family under the control of one heir and the desire to release the property to all family members and friends. This problem of family continuity and testamentary freedom affected families differently depending on their economic status. As long as at least one male survived, the rich could afford to support numerous children, even if the practice of partible inheritance gradually fragmented the family estate over several generations. A considerably greater problem faced the poor and some families of middling means. They also sought comfort in numerous children but could ill afford many claimants for what were often very restricted resources. As a result, their options ranged from limiting the number of their children through some primitive form of contraception, to the decision to send surplus children into various trades or crafts, to the maintenance only of unmarried sons and daughters, and, ultimately, to emigration for the younger generation.[3]

Power, Authority, and Affection in Planter Wills

How did Chesapeake men and women conceive of the family estate and who shared in it? How were these problems of continuity and freedom in the family resolved among testators? As we have noted, in the seventeenth century oppressive mortality rates severely limited the growth of large kin groups who could

Virginia wills refer to the microfilm copy available from the Virginia State Library, Richmond.) A useful discussion of the meaning of wills in colonial New York is contained in David C. Narrett, "Preparation for Death and Provision for the Living: Notes on New York Wills, 1665–1760," *New York History*, LVII (1976), 417–37.

[3] See Jack Goody, "Strategies of Heirship," *Comparative Studies in Society and History*, 15 (1973), 3–20.

benefit from inheritance and could help in supporting the surviving members of the deceased's family. The narrow, circumscribed nature of the family was reflected in testation patterns in the seventeenth century. Less than 10 percent of Virginia testators in the latter half of the century bequeathed property to people outside the immediate family, and over three-fourths of Maryland testators with family made no mention of kin other than spouses and children before 1700.[4]

Throughout the eighteenth century, especially after 1750, a markedly different pattern of bequests emerged. A systematic study of two Virginia counties in the eighteenth century, York and Albemarle, shows that while male and female heads of households from the middle and lower economic ranks continued to give personal and real property almost exclusively to members of the nuclear family, testators ranked in the top 20 percent by inventoried wealth in these counties spread their estates out among a much larger body of kin and friends. Less than one-half of the testators from Albemarle County in the half century after 1750 confined their bequeathals to spouses and children. Adult siblings, cousins, nephews, uncles and aunts, other more distant "kinsmen," and unrelated friends received gifts of cash, livestock, clothes, and occasionally tracts of land.[5] (See Table 4.)

[4]Lois G. Carr and Lorena S. Walsh, "The Planter's Wife: The Experience of White Women in Seventeenth-Century Maryland," *WMQ*, 3d ser., xxxiv (1977), 542–71; James W. Deen Jr., "Patterns of Testation: Four Tidewater Counties in Colonial Virginia," *American Journal of Legal History*, xvi (1972), 155–56. A similar testamentary focus on family was evident in seventeenth-century Barnstable, where about 90 percent of all property was distributed among kin. Longer life expectancies, however, allowed for considerably more bequests to grandsons. See John J. Waters, "The Traditional World of the New England Peasants: A View from Seventeenth-Century Barnstable," *New England Historical and Genealogical Register*, cxxx (1976), 3–21.

[5]Other factors, of course, may have intervened in determining whether or not a testator made bequests outside his immediate family, including the number of minor children in a testator's family and his age at the writing of the will. Men with many small children, for example, were perhaps less likely to give family property to distant kin and friends. Older men with a strong sense of the family and kin network and several grandchildren and relatives living nearby might take a broader view of kin ties in disposing of their estate.

Table 4. Resident kin and friends of testate men and women who left minor children, 1700–1799

Date	Families N	Immediate family only N	%	Blood kin N	%	Affinal kin N	%	Friends N	%	Grand-children N	%
				York County							
1700-9	12	8	66.7	4	33.3	0	0	1	6.7	1	6.7
1720-29	42	25	59.5	15	35.7	0	0	5	11.9	7	16.7
1740-49	46	30	62.2	16	34.8	0	0	7	15.6	8	17.4
Totals	100	63	63.0	35	35.0	0	0	13	13.0	16	16.0
Upper 20 percent*											
1700-49	20	4	20.0	12	60.0	0	0	6	30.0	6	30.0
				Albemarle County							
1750-59	40	23	57.5	12	30.0	1	2.5	5	12.5	9	22.5
1760-69	30	22	73.3	6	20.0	1	3.3	1	3.3	5	16.7
1770-79	42	30	71.4	7	16.7	6	14.3	0	0	6	14.3
1780-89	47	30	63.8	11	23.4	1	2.2	3	6.4	7	14.9
1790-99	52	34	65.4	11	21.2	5	9.6	3	5.8	9	17.3
Totals	211	139	66.3	47	22.3	14	6.6	12	5.7	36	17.1
Upper 20 percent*											
1750-99	45	21	46.7	13	38.9	7	15.5	4	9.0	11	24.4

SOURCES: York and Albemarle county wills, Virginia State Library, Richmond.
*Based on top 20 percent of inventoried wealth.

Grandchildren became especially favorite legatees among testators of the gentry class: about one-fourth of these wills mentioned grandchildren in their provisions. Anxious to perpetuate property in the family as far into the future as possible and to make a concrete gesture of affection to young children, men and women often gave generously to their grandchildren. Richard Durrett, a planter in Albemarle County, divided his substantial estate in 1784 among his son, five daughters, and five grandchildren. Although he gave most of his land and slaves to his children, Durrett provided his grandson Austin Durrett with a horse, a cow and calf, two lambs, a trundle bed, £25 for some schooling, and the family prayer book. Another grandson, Richin Sanford, was given all the corn, one cow, and a yearling. A third grandson, apparently the eldest, had already received his grandfather's tools and was asked to pay 20 shillings into the estate for each year he had owned the tools. Finally, the two granddaughters shared a female slave in common and one of the girls received the title to some land her grandfather had already given her.[6]

That the wealthy rather than the poor chose to provide for a wider range of kin and friends is not surprising. Many men barely possessed enough land and personal property to maintain their wives and children. And poorer families ordinarily enjoyed less mobility and leisure time to develop strong ties of kinship and friendship beyond the neighborhood—ties that would have been reflected in legacies. The improving mortality rates of the eighteenth century also encouraged the growth of more elaborate kin networks, especially by mid-century. As a growing number of children survived to adulthood, married, and began families of their own, often in close proximity to their parents, a body of supporting kin ties developed around the family. As the eighteenth century progressed, then, the pool of available relatives with whom portions of the family estate could be shared enlarged.[7]

Friendships seemed to take on deeper, more permanent dimensions. With the growing affluence of Chesapeake planters during the eighteenth century, the opportunity to show gratitude and affection through inheritance for people outside the circle of kin grew apace. About one out of ten testators in the wealthiest

[6]Albemarle County Wills, 1784, II, 423–24. See also ibid., 1791, 1793, III, 182–85, 186–90, 1798; III, 1–3.

[7]That marriages tended to occur within a small geographic area and thus encouraged contact between blood and affinal kin is suggested by a study of early eighteenth-century Middlesex County, Virginia. Over three-fourths of all men and women in 1703–4 married people from the same county, within a mean distance of about ten miles. See Darrett B. Rutman, "The Social Web: A Prospectus for the Study of the Early American Community," in William L. O'Neill, ed., *Insights and Parallels: Problems and Issues of American Social History* (Minneapolis, 1973), 110–11. Evidence of increasing kin marriages comes from Allan Kulikoff, "Tobacco and Slaves: Population, Economy and Society in Eighteenth-Century Prince George's County, Maryland" (unpub. Ph.D. diss., Brandeis University, 1975), 6–23, 323, 365–68.

rank of Albemarle County named a friend as a legatee. (See Table 4.) Women and unmarried testators were particularly given to making generous provisions for friends, sometimes in return for medical aid during their last illness. Edward Tarpley of York County, for example, gave his friend Frances Foks £25 "in Consideration of her Care of me during my Illness."[8]

The bonds of friendship superseded the claims of kinship for Martha Hall, whose will was recorded in July 1784. She divided all of her estate among two goddaughters and several female friends, leaving nothing for her relatives. Her explanation for such filial neglect suggested that perhaps only in a last will did a woman have the complete capacity to act on her deepest feelings: "When the above [the legacies of the will] is produced to the public view this worlds Censure or Applause will neither be felt nor regarded—My relations must excuse what may seem a neglect of them in my will, which I do assure them has been dictated by what Appeared to me just & right. Those who have been my Friends in the hours of Difficulty and Distress have the last Claim to my Gratitude, Esteem, & Affection."[9]

Friends rarely received the most valuable parts of the estate— land and slaves—but their legacies could be substantial. In 1788 Thomas Walker willed all his land and slaves to his three sons and his daughter, but parceled out among six of his friends dozens of sheep, cattle, and about £1000 in cash. The importance of feelings of friendship was reflected in the will of Joseph Royle, a Williamsburg printer, who named one of his sons after his friend William Hunter. Royle stipulated in his will in 1766 that after Hunter's death a monument be erected to perpetuate the "Memory of my worthy Friend."[10]

Lengthened life expectancies, the growth of larger kin groups, and increasing personal wealth in the eighteenth century helped to enlarge an individual's family and social world. The fact re-

[8]York County Wills, 1763, XXI, 147–48. See also ibid., 1769, 1766, XXI, 458–59, 278–81.

[9]Martha Hall Will (noncupative), July 14, 1784, TCP.

[10]Albemarle County Wills, 1794, III, 232–33; York County Wills, 1766, XXI, 264–70.

mains, however, that inheritance was largely a mechanism for protecting and controlling the economic future of the testator's immediate family. Despite the gifts to kin and friends—common only among the economic elite, it should be emphasized—the central concern for most people when making their will lay in the maintenance of their surviving spouse, the education and economic security of their children, and the assurance of some kind of continuity in the family's landed estate.

The principal agents in supervising the dispensation of the estate were the executors nominated by the testator. These individuals had to take an oath and post bond equal to the estimated value of the estate in order to guarantee performance of their job as financial managers of the estate.[11] Most wills named two executors, but three or four were not uncommon among wealthier testators, while single executorships were often chosen by the poorest testators.[12] The changing pattern of executorship in the colonial Chesapeake is suggestive of the shifting composition of family and kin and the lines of authority within the household.

A wife's economic authority in the household was reflected in her husband's will, for she was usually his sole choice to manage the family estate after his death. Indeed, in the seventeenth and early eighteenth centuries from over half to two-thirds of married men named their wives as sole executors of the estate. In most families of colonial Virginia and Maryland the planter's wife was an essential part of the household and plantation economy, often working alongside her husband in the fields, as well as raising the children and tending to various chores around the house. Planter marriages in the colonial Chesapeake more closely resembled economic partnerships than romantic affairs.[13]

This pattern of strong wifely influence in the family economy changed dramatically during the latter half of the eighteenth

[11]William Waller Hening, ed., *The Statutes at Large, being a Collection of all the Laws of Virginia from the First Session of the Legislature in the Year 1619* (13 vols., Richmond, 1819–1823), I, 99–103.
[12]In his study of colonial Virginia wills, Deen found a direct correlation between rising wealth and double and triple executorships. "Patterns of Testation," 164.
[13]Carr and Walsh, "Planter's Wife."

century, especially among the wealthier classes. As sex roles became more rigidly defined and estates grew larger and more complex, men increasingly turned to other men, especially sons and friends, to supervise the estate. As Table 5 indicates, the proportion of Albemarle County men who named their wives as sole executors was far below that of men in York County during the early half of the century. The experience of families in these two counties shows a drop in female executorship from over half in early eighteenth-century York County to less than one in ten in the half century after 1750 in Albemarle County. Although wives were very rarely excluded from executorship in early eighteenth-century York County, about half of the Albemarle County men did not nominate their spouses as executors. To be sure, throughout the century a substantial proportion of wives at least shared the duties of administering the estate—about half—but the decline in female economic authority is striking. Increasingly, wives were seen more as mothers and moral guardians of the family and less as important working partners on the plantation.[14]

Husbands in the eighteenth century, nevertheless, seem to have provided for their widows as generously as men had in the early Chesapeake. The law required that a man leave his widow her "thirds," one-third of the real property (land, houses, and lots) for life and full ownership of one-third of the personal property (slaves, household goods, and livestock). In sev-

[14]A recent study of inheritance patterns in Petersburg, Virginia, during the early national period suggests a pattern of female executorship roughly similar to that of Albemarle County in the late eighteenth century, especially among the well-to-do. In Petersburg, wills indicate that as the family's economic status rose, the widow's economic authority in inheritance (i.e., executorship) declined. See Suzanne Lebsock, "Women and Economics: Petersburg, Virginia, 1784–1820" (unpub. Ph.D. diss., University of Virginia, 1977), chapter 2. Another measure of female participation in estate decisions—the witnessing of wills—reveals no significant change throughout the eighteenth century. In York County between 1700 and 1750 about 33 percent of all probated wills were witnessed by at least one woman. In terms of the total number of individuals witnessing all wills, women represented only about 14 percent. During the latter half of the eighteenth century in Albemarle County, female witnesses appeared in only a slightly smaller proportion of wills, 30 percent. Albemarle County men dominated witnessing as in early York, for they represented about 87 percent of all witnesses, 1750–1799.

Table 5. Executors named in wills of married men, 1700–1799

Date	N	Wife only executor		Wife and other		Wife excluded		Son(s) executor		Friend(s) executor		Unknown or no executor	
		N	%	N	%	N	%	N	%	N	%	N	%
					York County								
1700–09	12	6	50.0	3	25.0	1	8.3	0	0.0	2	16.7	1	8.3
1720–29	41	23	56.9	17	41.5	0	0.0	8	19.5	6	14.9	2	4.9
1740–49	45	22	48.8	15	33.3	7	15.5	11	24.4	7	15.5	2	4.4
Totals	98	51	52.0	35	35.7	8	8.1	19	19.3	15	15.3	5	5.1
					Albemarle County								
1750-59	47	5	10.6	27	57.4	14	29.8	17	36.2	23	48.9	0	0.0
1760-69	28	3	10.7	13	46.4	12	42.9	11	39.3	13	46.4	1	3.6
1770-79	40	3	7.5	16	40.0	21	52.5	23	57.5	17	42.5	0	0.0
1780-89	46	2	4.3	15	32.6	19	41.3	24	52.2	27	58.7	0	0.0
1790-99	55	3	5.4	24	43.6	28	50.9	33	60.0	32	58.2	2	3.6
Totals	216	16	7.4	95	44.0	94	43.5	108	50.0	112	51.8	3	1.4

SOURCES: York and Albemarle county wills, Virginia State Library, Richmond.

enteenth-century Maryland over three-fourths of the male testators left their wives with more than the law demanded, and when there were no children, a widow almost always received the entire estate. Very few men (about 6 percent) placed restraints on a widow's legacy, such as a provision that she could possess her portion of the estate only during widowhood or until the children came of age.[15]

Wills analyzed for Albemarle County in the latter half of the eighteenth century indicate that widows received the home plantation for life in about the same proportion as they had in seventeenth-century Maryland. (See Table 6.) Only a small percentage of testators—less than 4 percent—restricted their widows' control of land for the minority of the child. A significant change, however, was the almost fourfold increase in the proportion of wills that called for a relinquishment of the widow's claim to the home plantation upon her remarriage. Men were always wary of prospective stepparents encroaching on the family es-

[15]Carr and Walsh, "Planter's Wife."

Table 6. Bequests of husbands to wives with children, 1750–1799

Date	N	All or dwelling plantation for life N	%	All or dwelling plantation as widow N	%	All or dwelling plantation for child's minority N	%	Personal property for widowhood N	%	Dower or less or unknown N	%
1750–59	33	9	27.3	5	15.2	4	12.1	8	24.2	7	21.2
1760–69	34	15	44.1	8	23.5	0	0.0	7	20.6	3	8.8
1770–79	41	17	41.5	8	19.5	1	2.4	4	9.8	11	26.8
1780–89	39	17	43.6	12	30.8	2	5.1	4	10.3	5	12.8
1790–99	57	25	43.9	13	22.8	0	0.0	11	19.3	8	14.0
Totals	204	83	40.7	46	22.5	7	3.4	34	16.7	34	16.7

SOURCE: Albemarle county wills, Virginia State Library, Richmond.

tate, but the growing tendency to penalize a widow's remarriage suggests that husbands worried about outsiders intruding on maternal authority in the family.[16]

For many husbands the child's natural mother was the only proper focus and socializing agent of the family. Occasionally fathers gave explicit instructions that their children were to remain under their mother's influence until maturity. Henry Gill of York County, for example, declared in his will of 1720 that his son John "shall live with his mother till [he] come[s] of age to possess his estate." A woman's responsibility as a mother to small children, some men believed, superseded her right to find a new husband. This testamentary insistence on family cohesion reached an extreme in the case of Elias Love of York County. Love's will, composed in 1720, gave a portion of land and all his personal property to his wife Elizabeth, which she was to use to educate their three youngest children. To protect the estate from

[16]Looked at strictly from the widow's point of view, however, this arrangement indicates that men did nothing more than sustain their widows, while depriving them of their economic freedom. For an analysis of widowhood from this perspective, see Alexander Keyssar, "Widowhood in Eighteenth-Century Massachusetts: A Problem in the History of the Family," *Perspectives in American History*, VIII (1974), 83–119.

grasping stepparents and to ensure the performance of the educational provisions in the will, Love required his wife to endure an extended period of widowhood. "My desire is that my wife keeps her Self Single until all the Children come of age." This meant a wait of up to eighteen years for the youngest son, Elias, to reach twenty-one! If Elizabeth remarried, the estate was to be divided between her and the three youngest children, while the older brother, Justinian, twenty-four in 1720, would oversee his siblings' portions. Increasingly men sought to encourage maternal authority through provisions against early remarriage and the dispersal of the estate before the children reached adulthood.[17]

To strengthen a mother's economic authority within the household, a growing number of men allowed their widows discretionary power in distributing the personal property of the estate to deserving children. In giving his widow £200 and four slaves (plus their increase), David Anderson of Albemarle County observed in his will in 1791 that she could "dispose of the same to such of our Children and grand Children as in her opinion may be in the greatest need, and such who she may Judge as who received the least share of my estate." Other men gave their wives "liberty" to sell slaves, wood, and portions of the land and to distribute the proceeds as they wished among the children. The proportion of men who permitted their spouses this kind of discretionary authority over their children's estate doubled between the first and second half of the eighteenth century.[18]

Raising children alone could be an expensive and difficult responsibility for a widow, and husbands frequently left their spouses considerable personal property from the estate, as one

[17]York County Wills, 1720, XVI, 53, 595–96; Albemarle County Wills, 1768, 1776, II, 230–33, 337–38; 1786, 1795, III, 6–7, 240–41; York County Wills, 1760, XXI, 58.
[18]Albemarle County Wills, 1791, III, 186–90. 1752, II, 11–12; 1791, III, 186–90; York County Wills, 1760, 1768, XXI, 167–68, 476–77. Testamentary provisions for a widow's discretionary authority over personal property grew from 9 percent of all married men's wills in York County, 1700–1749, to 17.2 percent for Albemarle County men, 1750–1799. Among the upper 20 percent of Albemarle County, the proportion was even higher, 26.2 percent.

man put it, "in Consideration of bringing up my Children."[19] Younger children in particular—those under the age of thirteen or fourteen—needed to be reared and educated under their mother's direction, many men believed. Typical of these efforts to maintain strong mother-child ties was Peter Manson's request in his will written in 1720: "my loving wife should keep my Son Walter Manson and what belongs to him until he come to ye age of 14 years and give him what learning . . . she can." Educational provisions for older children, however, often involved friends or relatives serving as executors who could arrange for an apprenticeship or a more formal schooling.[20]

Despite the limitations placed on a widow's economic power over the plantation, as reflected in the declining proportion of wives named as executors, men increasingly tried to strengthen maternal influence in the socialization and education of the children. In attempting to keep the family together through testamentary provisions, husbands were also contributing to the rising importance of maternal care as the central responsibility of a planter's wife.

Providing "Independency" on the Land

In devising a will, a planter had to face the fundamental problem of how to balance this concern for maternal control and family stability against the belief in the need for his children's economic autonomy. In an agrarian society in which inheritance was so closely linked with the ability to marry and the establishment of an independent household, a father exercised powerful influence through his control of the land.[21]

[19]York County Wills, 1764, XXI, 100–02. See also Albemarle County Wills, 1753, II, 216; 1800, IV, 59.

[20]York County Wills, 1720, XVI, 100, 219–20; Albemarle County Wills, 1783, II, 409–10; 1787, 1788, 1789, 1795, III, 30–31, 57, 67–68, 240–41; 1760, II, 79–80; 1787, 1795, III, 18–19, 254–55, 265–66; York County Wills, 1726, XVI, 436.

[21]W. W. Williams has emphasized the important connections between inheritance and the independence of sons in an English village. See his *The Sociology of an English Village: Gosforth* (London, 1956), 49–51. See also W. G. Hoskins, *The Midland Peasant: The Economic and Social History of a Leicestershire Village* (London, 1957); William J. Goode, "Family Systems and Social Mobility," in Reuben Hill and Rene Konig, eds., *Families in East and West* (The Hague, 1970), 315–36.

In New England the convergence of unusually long adult life expectancies, a growing shortage of available land, and a strong sense of family and kin solidarity forced sons into prolonged dependence on their fathers. Long-lived fathers often kept their sons waiting until their late twenties or early thirties before relinquishing control of the land. This forced sons to delay marriage and, one suspects, postponed their full maturation as grown men. When paternal land was distributed at inheritance—or by deeds of gift or sale as it increasingly was during the eighteenth century—sons were usually settled near family and kin. In exchange for their portions, young men were expected to help support their aging parents. Inheritance, then, drew sons and parents into a series of mutual obligations tying the young to family, kin, and community.[22]

None of these dimensions of inheritance were foreign to Chesapeake planters and their sons in the eighteenth century, but because of a significantly different set of demographic, economic, and familial conditions in Virginia and Maryland, inheritance patterns diverged sharply from those in colonial New England. Rather than encouraging dependence on a powerful patriarch, inheritance in the Chesapeake was much more of a liberating force, releasing children relatively early in life with their portion of the patrimony to establish themselves independent of their parents.

Central to the early independence of sons in the colonial Chesapeake was the comparatively short adult life expectancy. Although mortality rates improved in the eighteenth century, so that men could expect to live into their fifties, most fathers died while all but one or two of their children were still minors (usually twenty-one for men, and eighteen for women).[23] In these cir-

---

[22]Philip J. Greven, Jr., *Four Generations: Population, Family and Land in Colonial Andover, Massachusetts* (Ithaca, N.Y., 1970), 78–99, 131–41, 227–30, 238, 256–57; John J. Waters, "Patrimony, Succession and Social Stability: Guilford, Connecticut in the 18th Century," *Perspectives in American History*, x (1976), 149–50; James Henretta, "Families and Farms: *Mentalité* in Pre-Industrial America," *WMQ*, 3d ser., xxxv (1978), 3-32; Barry Levy, "Tender Plants: Quaker Farmers and Children in the Delaware Valley, 1681–1735," *Journal of Family History*, III (1978), 116–35.

[23]Kulikoff, "Tobacco and Slaves," 439.

cumstances sons rarely grew restive under their fathers' control of the land. Deeds of gift or sale never figured prominently in the transmission of family land from one generation to the next. The inheritance many young men received as children gave them the wherewithal quite early in life to consider marriage and to assert their economic independence.[24] Moreover, the relative abundance of land in the Chesapeake allowed parents, at least among the middle and upper ranks of society, to bequeath generous portions to their sons and provide valuable labor in slaves.[25]

Given the wide availability of land and the likelihood that they would die young, it is not surprising that men tried to provide portions for all their children rather than to give the entire estate to the eldest son and leave the remaining children to fend for themselves. As C. Ray Keim has shown, primogeniture and entail were forms of testamentary control not unknown in the colonial Chesapeake, but rarely practiced.[26] Not only the plenitude of land, but the belief in rewarding deserving children and other kin and friends at inheritance militated against any predetermined disposition of the estate. Moreover, some men clearly worried that the "expectation of an estate often corrupts the morals of Youth" and thus insisted on the importance of partible inheritance—dividing the estate among all dutiful children.[27]

Evidence for a wide distribution of property among sons, though not among sons and daughters, is strong. An analysis of Albemarle County wills in the latter half of the eighteenth cen-

[24] I have argued elsewhere that the age at marriage for men was closely tied to the timing of a father's death. In colonial Charles Parish, Virginia, sons whose fathers died before they reached the mean age of marriage were married significantly earlier than sons whose fathers were still alive when they reached this age. See Smith, "Mortality and Family in the Colonial Chesapeake," *Journal of Interdisciplinary History*, VIII (1978), 424–25.

[25] On the comparative abundance of land in eighteenth-century Virginia, see Robert E. and Katherine B. Brown, *Virginia, 1705–1786: Democracy or Aristocracy?* (East Lansing, Mich., 1964).

[26] Keim, "Primogeniture and Entail in Colonial Virginia," *WMQ*, 3d ser., XXV (1968), 545–86.

[27] In 1776 Landon Carter reported the currency of this idea but rejected it claiming in his typically cynical fashion that immorality in youth occurred even without the guarantee of a substantial legacy. *Carter Diary*, II, 1069.

tury reveals that over three-fifths (62.6 percent) of all fathers who did not sell their land provided landed portions for all their sons. (See Table 7.) In less than one-fourth of the wills (22.4 percent) did a single son inherit all of the landed estate—and in some of these cases other sons had not necessarily been excluded from the family land, since they may have already received some portion by deed of gift at marriage.[28]

Table 7. Division of real property in families with two or more children, Albemarle County, 1750–1799.

Date	N	One son gets most or all* N	%	All sons receive land* N	%	Equal division sons and daughters* N	%	Land Sold and divided equally* N	%	Distri- bution unknown N	%	No land devised N	%
1750-59	30	2	7.7	17	65.4	4	15.4	3	11.5	2	6.7	2	6.7
1760-69	36	6	19.3	18	58.1	6	19.3	1	3.2	2	5.5	3	8.3
1770-79	44	8	26.7	14	46.7	5	16.7	3	10.0	4	9.1	10	22.7
1780-89	45	6	18.7	19	59.4	4	12.5	3	9.4	3	6.7	10	22.2
1790-99	57	11	23.9	20	43.5	9	19.6	6	13.0	4	7.0	7	12.3
Totals	212	33	20.0	88	53.3	28	17.0	16	9.7	15	7.1	32	15.1

SOURCE: Albemarle county wills, Virginia State Library, Richmond.
*Percentages in these columns were calculated by excluding all wills in which no land was devised or the distribution of land was unknown.

Precise figures on the size of land holdings were rarely given in Chesapeake wills, and it is therefore impossible to determine how evenly land was parceled out among various sons and daughters. In most cases, however, the eldest son inherited the home plantation and younger sons received other land, often unimproved, in outlying areas. But along with acquiring a cultivated and perhaps larger tract of land, an eldest son sometimes had to assume a caretaker role in the family, supervising the

[28]In 1772 Andrew McWilliam, for example, gave only a token remembrance of a few shillings to his married children: "They having got their share at marriage." Albemarle County Wills, 1772, II, 280–82. See also ibid., 1784, II, 423–24; York County Wills, 1760, 1763, 1767, XXI, 160–61, 54–55, 475, 727.

administration of his father's estate, providing for his mother, and overseeing younger brothers and sisters. While fathers may have occasionally given slightly larger, more valuable parcels of land to one son—usually the eldest—the central tendency was to provide for all sons as equally as possible.[29]

Daughters of course carried land outside the family when they married; consequently, they rarely inherited real property. And on the few occasions when they did receive landed portions— usually when there were no sons or grandsons—the legacy often contained a reversion clause returning the land at their death, if they died childless, to a nephew or some other male relative.[30]

To "Share and Share Alike": Distributing the Personal Estate

A wide distribution of the family estate was especially evident in the dispersal of the personal property—available cash, slaves, stock, and various household goods. Testators customarily divided personal property equally among sons and daughters. For daughters this legacy became the dower they would eventually bring to marriage. Because daughters seldom received landed estates, fathers, in an effort to give them some kind of economic security, occasionally provided daughters with more personal property than they gave to sons.[31]

[29]A recent study of Loudon County, Virginia, in the 1790s has found the same equitable distribution pattern at inheritance. See James Bradford, "Society and Government in Loudon County, Virginia, 1790–1800" (unpub. Ph.D. diss., University of Virginia, 1976), 226–7.

[30]Albemarle County Wills, 1753, 1757, II, 7–8, 204–8; III, 267.

[31]Ibid., 1783, II, 409–10; York County Wills, 1761, XXI, 60–62. Richard Henry Lee articulated the anxiety many men felt over their daughters' economic futures. With sons to provide for out of a limited, though relatively substantial estate, Lee grew "uneasy about my younger children and wish securely to provide for my poor little helpless girls." In 1770, Lee invested £100 sterling in a London bank for each of his girls to earn interest until they either married or reached their majorities. Richard Henry Lee to William Lee, July 7, 1770, in James Ballagh, ed., *The Letters of Richard Henry Lee* (New York, 1911), 50. Henry Hollyday was likewise worried over the "precarious State of their [his daughters'] fortunes" in 1780. The insecurity of it, he confessed to his brother, "preys a good deal upon the Spirits of these poor girls, particularly Marcy." Henry Hollyday to James Hollyday, 1780?, HFP.

For some men an equitable division of the estate seemed to be the overriding consideration, possibly to prevent future family quarrels over the legacies. By the late eighteenth century testators often stipulated that all personal property be valued by an executor and equally divided by lots. Those children who drew more valuable lots were to compensate the others. John Morriss of York County, for instance, asked that after his wife's death her two slaves be "appraised by men indifferently to be chosen & appointed & my sons to cast lots for the choice of the two slaves." Whoever received the male slave was to pay the other the difference in value "in order to make the division equal."[32]

Because of this concern for an even distribution of family property, one finds little evidence of family discord over inheritance. The language and provisions of only a very few wills indicate any sort of family squabbling or paternal displeasure toward sons. Occasionally, fathers did exclude sons from the estate—or threatened to do so—as a penalty for disobedient or immoral conduct. In 1764, Abraham Childress of Albemarle County reluctantly gave his second son William "all the goods he took from me when he ran off from me," one shilling, "& no more." One wealthy Albemarle County man in 1791 bequeathed 840 acres of land to his son on the condition that "he intirely declines the vicious practices of gaming and excessive drinking & applies himself closely to business."[33] These instances of paternal punishment for filial disrespect, however, were exceedingly rare (less than 5 percent), as most planters chose to use their testamentary power to express family affection and to encourage economic security among those they left behind.

A crucial implication of this essentially equitable partible inheritance system, in contrast to a single-heir system, was that many well-to-do fathers were able to place their sons on land relatively near the home plantation—usually no farther than in an adjacent county. This sharing of the paternal estate gave each

[32]York County Wills, 1746, XIX, 57–58: 1720, XVI, 483. See also, Albemarle County Wills, 1757, 1760, 1773, II, 204–8, 293.
[33]Ibid., 1764, II, 164–65; 1791, III, 116–20.

son an important link with his region of birth that may have encouraged him to stay near home and maintain at least some contact with his family of origin. In single-heir systems the younger sons, excluded from the patrimony, were almost forced into greater social and geographic mobility, as they left the homestead to look for work elsewhere as artisans, merchants, seamen, or tenant farmers.[34]

In the eighteenth-century Chesapeake, however, such forced migration and occupational mobility was probably rare, except among the lower ranks of society. Although the large landed estates became increasingly fragmented by the late eighteenth century, the home plantation was usually preserved intact and remained in the family, while children were established on more recently purchased, outlying tracts.[35] Movement to western lands often occurred in a more controlled familial context. A father might lease western tracts to other planters who subsequently improved the land so that his sons might have fresh land upon reaching maturity. Thus the son's migration westward was in part well prepared in advance by his father. Testation patterns among wealthier families, then, were both liberating and confining: sons were resettled on western lands under the aegis of the parent and within the orderly, familial conditions of the will. In this sense a father as a testator could exert some control over the movement of his family after his death.[36]

[34]H. J. Habakkuk, "Family Structure and Economic Change in Nineteenth-Century Europe," *Journal of Economic History*, xv (1955), 1–12.

[35]On the fragmentation of large landed estates in Albemarle County in the late eighteenth century, see Daniel B. Smith, "Changing Patterns in Local Political Leadership: Justices of the Peace in Albemarle County, Virginia, 1760–1820," *Essays in History*, (University of Virginia), xviii (1973–4), 65–73.

[36]More research needs to be done on migration of families of the colonial South, but one historian has speculated that paternal death signaled family movement. In *Carolina Cradle: Settlement of the Northwestern Carolina Frontier, 1747–1762* (Chapel Hill, N.C., 1964), 21–22, Robert W. Ramsey noted that the "movement of families often occurred immediately after the death of the father or family patriarch."

Chapter Seven

Bonds of Suffering

The Family in Illness and Death

"It is necessary that man should be acquainted with affliction and 'tis certainly nothing short of it to be confined a whole year in tending one's children. Mine are now never well."[1] Colonel Landon Carter of Sabine Hall recorded this thought in his diary during the winter of 1757. It was a lament shared by most planters, for disease and death were intricately woven into the fabric of family life in the eighteenth-century Chesapeake. Living in an unclean environment and constantly struggling against influenza, the debilitating effects of malaria (or the "ague and fever" as it was usually called), and the often ill effects of eighteenth-century medicine, planters in Virginia and Maryland confronted an almost daily task of attempting to slow the spread of sickness around them.

The prevalence of ill health left a distinct imprint on the inner life of the family. With the crucial responsibility of ministering to the sick, planters assumed an even more important position in the household. Moreover, the nearly constant presence of illness strengthened the bonds of kinship, knitting together a local community of suffering composed of family members and neighboring relatives and friends. Death likewise drew families together in bereavement, creating a deep sense of affection and

[1] *Carter Diary*, I, 194.

commitment between most members of the nuclear family. For the first few generations, religious and psychological explanations helped to prepare families for the inevitability and pain of death, but by the latter half of the eighteenth century, it is evident that few were inured to the loss of loved ones. Indeed, by this period families often grieved openly when death struck in their households. Sickness and death, as inescapable phenomena in Chesapeake society, provide us with important clues to the changing texture of family life and personal relationships in the eighteenth century.

Combating Disorder in the Great House: Family Sickness and the Planter-Doctor

Chesapeake plantation life was not conducive to good health. Living quarters were often dirty and crowded with children and servants, increasing the opportunity for sickness to develop and spread throughout the household.[2] The "sickly season" usually began in late summer or early fall when so many families suffered from the endemic malarial environment of colonial Virginia and Maryland.[3] "Fevers and Agues," Landon Carter declared in September of 1775, "are now a principal disorder in my family. Sometimes scarce a servant to wait on us."[4] William Byrd II described his wife's protracted struggle with a summer ague which began, according to Byrd, around August 1 and did not end until early September. During these six weeks Mrs. Byrd was plagued with recurring periods of nausea, headaches, fevers, and loss of sleep—the last exacerbated by the nightly presence of

[2]Landon Carter described the unclean condition of the schoolroom and bed chambers at Sabine Hall in this way: "Grease and dirt all over and wet with Piss and Nastyness." *Carter Diary,* II, 784. See also Julia Cherry Spruill, *Women's Life and Work in the Southern Colonies* (New York, 1972), 41–42.

[3]Darrett B. and Anita H. Rutman, "Of Agues and Fevers: Malaria in the Colonial Chesapeake," *WMQ,* 3d ser., XXXIII (1976), 31–60. See also Peter H. Wood, *Black Majority: Negroes in Colonial South Carolina from 1670 through the Stono Rebellion* (New York, 1974), 70–73.

[4]*Carter Diary,* II, 939. Carter had described August of 1757 as a "very Aguish Season" with many of his people ill and "dayly falling down with" sickness. Ibid., I, 165.

mosquitoes, which had probably given her the sickness in the first place.[5] James Gordon of Lancaster County, Virginia, complained of widespread illness among his family and friends in the fall of 1760. "Our family in great disorder with sickness," he wrote in his diary. In the space of three weeks in November of that year Gordon's son-in-law, a merchant friend, his brother, his wife, and Gordon himself had fallen into "a very low condition" and were "much disordered" from fevers, colds and toothaches.[6] In October of 1783 Robert Innes complained that "my House since latter End of July has been little better than a Hospital. My dear Betsey has not been out of her Chamber for a month."[7] That late summer and early fall was a particularly unhealthy time did not escape the notice of Henry Hollyday of Talbot County, Maryland. Henry wrote his brother James that his family suffered greatly from the "excessive heat & vast multitudes of mosquitoes" which, he lamented, "have half killed me."[8]

Sickness, however, was often a year-round phenomenon for Chesapeake families. Influenzas or "distempers" killed many people whose constitutions malaria had already weakened.[9]

[5]*Byrd Diary, 1709–12,* 565–81. Byrd's diary indicates that his wife was ill in some way about 50 percent of this forty-day period. A Maryland planter also noted the prolonged bout one of his children had with malaria. His daughter did not escape a "fit" of the ague and fever a single day for a month. Henry Hollyday to James Hollyday, Oct. 30, 1776, HFP.

[6]"The Journal of James Gordon of Lancaster Co., Virginia," *WMQ,* 1st ser., XI (1903), 205.

[7]James Innes to St. George Tucker, Oct. 9, 1783, TCP.

[8]Henry Hollyday to James Hollyday, July 13, 1780, HFP. James Gordon also noted the unhealthful nature of the fall, commenting in September of 1761 that his family was relatively healthy, "remarkable" for that season of the year, he claimed. "Journal of James Gordon," 224. See also Richard Lloyd to James Lloyd, April 4, 1779, HFP. These planters were in part responding to what demographic evidence shows more precisely—that the heaviest mortality occurred in the fall and winter months (September through March). An aggregative study of the Charles Parish, Virginia, birth and death registers from 1700 to 1760 reveals that the level of mortality (defined as the mean number of deaths per day) in the fall (Sept. 1—Nov. 30) and winter (Dec. 1—March 31) was about 30 percent higher than during the year as a whole and 80 percent higher than the mortality level of the spring and summer months. The Charles Parish registers are available in the Virginia State Library, Richmond.

[9]For a discussion of the illness and death created indirectly by malaria, see Rutman and Rutman, 50.

Planters were painfully aware of the epidemic possibilities of winter influenza attacks.[10] The winter of 1709 was especially virulent near Williamsburg; by April of that year it had "destroyed abundance of people." William Byrd fought a largely futile battle against a spreading winter "distemper" in 1710 and 1711, losing seventeen of his "people" by February. Byrd was constantly faced with sickness in his own family during the cold months of the year. According to his diary, some member of Byrd's immediate family was ill no less than three days out of every week between November 1709 and March 1710.[11]

In the face of such pervasive sickness and the scarcity of skilled medical help, planters served as amateur doctors on their estates and in the process enlarged their paternal authority in the family. To be sure, wives, especially in their husbands' absence and during their husbands' illnesses, helped in caring for sick children, and female slave "doctors" were sometimes called on to treat other slaves.[12] Still, planters generally performed the central tasks in managing illness on the plantation. Both family affection and economic self-interest urged men to assume these responsibilities. And despite the relatively heavy mortality of the eighteenth-century Chesapeake, many planters believed in the efficacy of their preventive medicine.

They remained constantly alert for cases of influenza or smallpox, watching their neighborhoods closely for the first signs of an epidemic. William Byrd received advance warning from relatives and friends of the growing influenza attack in the winter of 1709–10. Once the news reached him that "the distemper was at Captain Stith's," where ten slaves had fallen sick, Byrd bled and "gave vomits" that afternoon to six of his slaves "by way of prevention." During the next four days Byrd repeated the vomiting and blood-letting procedures several times after learning that

[10]Byrd believed that distempers occurred only in winter and left with the onset of warm temperatures. *Byrd Diary, 1709–12,* 136.

[11]Ibid., 18–89, 309, 252–322. Byrd's wife appears to have been ill on twenty-seven days during this period, or about one out of every five days.

[12]Frances Tucker to St. George Tucker, June 1781, TCP; Wyndham B. Blanton, *Medicine in Virginia in the Eighteenth Century* (Richmond, 1941), 168–69, 173–75.

the distemper had "come as far as [G-l-s] ordinary." And when his friend and neighbor Colonel Hill reported that the influenza was definitely "at his house" and that six people there were suffering from it (including Hill), Byrd immediately "gave vomits" to his house servants, Nurse and Suky.[13] A panic of greater proportion hit eastern Maryland in 1777 when a smallpox scare drove hundreds of people to receive inoculation against the dread illness. With the people of Talbot County "Universally alarmed," Henry Hollyday predicted that 1000 would be inoculated in a week's time. Hollyday had his "people" inoculated in stages over four days, and from his description of the process one gets a sense of the relative importance to Hollyday of the various people on his plantation. On the first day Hollyday had all three of his children and a visiting friend and her child inoculated. The overseers, a favorite house slave, "Old Dick," and two other skilled slaves were taken care of on the second day. During the final two days some thirty-three slaves were inoculated followed by fifteen others, "the residue of the black folks."[14]

The scarcity of qualified doctors and the distance between plantations forced planters to do most of the front-line medical work. Thomas Jones of York County and other men loaded up each year with stomach decoctions, purging powders and pills, and various other draughts to administer to their families. Medical texts (predominantly from England) and newspaper articles on medicine (such as those published in the *Virginia Gazette*) were studiously followed by some planters, who constantly sought ways to cure everything in their households from rattlesnake bites to malaria.[15]

As protectors of the family health, parents kept a watchful eye on the health of their children. Landon Carter was convinced that

---

[13]*Byrd Diary, 1709–12*, 125–28.
[14]Henry Hollyday to James Hollyday, May 2, May 17, 26, 1777, HFP.
[15]Blanton, *Medicine in Virginia*, 167–68; Physicians Bill 1747 for Thomas Jones, JFP; Robert Carter Nicholas to John Norton, Sept. 19, 1772 in Frances Norton Mason, ed., *John Norton and Sons Merchants of London and Virginia (Being the Papers from their Counting House for the Years 1750 to 1795* (Richmond, 1937), 273.

the poor eating habits of his children, encouraged by the bad example of the slave children, made them constantly sick. Carter complained that his daughter Judy, who had been "as well for many weeks as ever [a] child was," had become ill by overindulging herself in her sister's food.[16] Elizabeth Holloway cautioned her married daughter and her family against "overheating & [then] drinking quantities of cold water" in the summer and sent her ingredients for throat lozenges.[17]

For most planters the simplest, though sometimes the most inconvenient, precaution against sickness in their families was to leave unhealthy areas during the late summer and fall months — or as it was generally put, to get "a change of air." Many realized that leaving low-lying coastal regions for the interior countryside had preventive and restorative value. Dr. William Prentis, a Petersburg resident, worried about the condition of his family in the approaching fall, and he was especially concerned about his infant son John. He hoped he could "carry them into the country" for a few weeks.[18] In the midst of a particularly unhealthful fall in 1776, Henry Hollyday feared for his children's health while they were away in school in Kent County, Maryland. Kent School, Henry believed, was "a very unhealthy area at this Season of the year from the frequent thick fogs that must necessarily arise from the adjacent Marshes." Consequently he took his sons out of school for several weeks in September hoping that "exercise and change of air, and perhaps of diet" would be helpful. He preferred that his boys "lose a little time than run the risque of being lost themselves."[19]

Eighteenth-century medicine was certainly ineffective by modern standards, and it was actually counterproductive in many cases; the common practice of bleeding pregnant women is

[16]*Carter Diary*, I, 194.

[17]Elizabeth Holloway to Mrs. Thomas Jones, June 9, 1752, June 8, 1753, JFP.

[18]William Prentis to Joseph Prentis, July 6, 1800, WPC. The next summer William Prentis suggested to Joseph that he should leave Williamsburg as "a country life... would be infinitely more productive and beneficial to your family," since Williamsburg had recently become "more and more unhealthy." William Prentis to Joseph Prentis, July 28, 1801, ibid.

[19]Henry Hollyday to James Hollyday, Sept. 17, 1776, HFP. See also John Hanson to Dr. Philip Thomas, April 10, 1781, HFL.

only one illustration.[20] Nevertheless, planter-doctors often remained confident about the efficacy of their medical care. Ministering to family, slaves, and friends gave some men a sense of importance as caretakers of their "family society." Playing the role of family doctor was essential to Landon Carter. Realizing that "in such a large family of children and grandchildren ... some of them may be indisposed," Carter emphasized the need for his paternalistic counsel for good family health. He felt he had earned the right to assert his medical authority in the family because of his "constant attention to consider and relieve the care of the sick." Carter's insistence on his superior understanding of medicine disturbed some members of his household, however. When he advised his daughter Maria Beverly to give her daughter Molly a "gentle puke of Ipecacuanha," she resisted her father, claiming that Molly already had been taking too many powders and drugs. As usual, Carter remained sure of his medical expertise, remarking, "poor Mother, weak in her knowledge of such things as well as her tenderness." The community obligations of a large planter-healer were burdensome, Carter sometimes felt. In a bad "ague and fever Season" in the fall of 1771, he noted that "the whole neighborhood are almost every day sending to me. I serve them all." Believing it was the "flux" from the York and James River area, Carter gave mercury to most of the sick to rid them of worms. "Poor Women heavy with child seem to fare badly," he concluded.[21]

[20] *Byrd Diary, 1709–12,* 141–42, 344, 364.
[21] *Carter Diary,* I, 410; II, 627, 629. Jonathan Boucher succinctly stated the eighteenth-century belief in the efficacy of medicine. Chastising a friend for refusing to treat his ailment, Boucher explained that "here Resignation is so far from being a Virtue, that it really is criminal, whilst there may be suppos'd to be a Possibility of a Cure." Boucher went on to prescribe a series of cold baths for his friend. Jonathan Boucher to Rev. Tickell, Jan. 13, 1764, "Letters of Jonathan Boucher," *MHM,* VII (1912), 162. In his will of March 1767, Francis Faquier asked that if he died of any "latent diseases" unknown to the doctors, an autopsy was to be performed, rendering him "more useful to my fellow" beings in "Death than I have been in my life." York County Wills 1767, XXI, 397–98, microfilm, Virginia State Library, Richmond. Peter Gay has called this attitude of experimentation and confidence in eighteenth-century medicine "the recovery of nerve." See his *The Enlightenment: An Interpretation: The Science of Freedom* (New York, 1969), II, chap. 1.

William Byrd could be almost as confident of the power of eighteenth-century drugs and medical treatment, and he too was proud of his role as planter-physician. He believed, for example, that his wife had remained sick in February of 1710 "because I forgot to give her a glass of physic when she desired it." During the harsh winter of 1709–10 he attributed the loss of slaves by his friend Drury Stith to a "want of using remedies in time." He occasionally experimented in medical care. Because one servant voided some worms during a bout with influenza in January of 1711, Byrd began giving wormseed to all his slaves, hoping that a purge of worms could rid his plantation of the winter sickness. The incongruity of the family provider and healer becoming sick apparently bothered Byrd when he was struggling with a fever and ague one summer. He obstinately refused to accept Dr. Cocke's grim outlook on his health. The lavish care he received from his wife and friend Mrs. Dunn, who watched over him in shifts all night, seemed to annoy Byrd, for he claimed to be upset at all the "hubbub" created over his sickness.[22]

But the frequent failures of eighteenth-century medicine forced planters at times to despair of their ability to cope with sickness. This attitude of futility toward the power of disease seems to have been more common in the early years of the century. Even as Byrd labored to treat his ailing family and slaves, his confidence waned with the feeling that God's will seemed to override the best of his efforts. During the winter of 1710, Byrd grew despondent over the massive amount of sickness he saw all around him, and as the patriarch he felt partly responsible for it. "These poor people suffer for my sins. God forgive me all my offenses & restore them to their health if it be consistent with His holy will." A few days later he echoed the same feeling of in-adequacy in dealing with the persistent illness of his wife and child. "I tended them as I could but God is pleased to afflect me with his judgment for my sins." This disparity between his sense of self-efficacy as a planter-doctor and his acknowledgment of God's ultimate and often arbitrary authority over the progress of

[22]*Byrd Diary, 1709–12*, 390–91.

disease did not necessarily produce a conflict in Byrd's mind. Indeed, he could simultaneously invoke both secular and spiritual explanations when it proved convenient. He once noted in his diary, for example, that his wife had been sick with "the colic" but had recovered quickly for which he praised God, only moments later to attribute the cure to the use of "good drams of caraway water."[23] Both the power of God and proper medicine aided recovery from sickness.

The prevalence of disease enabled planters to exercise their paternal authority in the family, but, perhaps more important, illness brought families closer together. Caring for sick members of the family permitted a show of affection which otherwise might never have been so openly expressed. There is considerable evidence from family correspondence and diaries that parents and children, brothers and sisters, and to a lesser extent, more distant kin displayed a warm, protective concern for ailing family members.

When someone in the family became ill, especially a child, every effort was made to promote recovery. A sudden illness sometimes engendered considerable anxiety. The Reverend Robert Rose of Williamsburg disclosed in his diary in 1747 that his son Nat's recurring fever came on one night "with such violence that his Mother was frightened" and sat up with him all night.[24] Young Ben Carter, son of Robert Carter of Nomini Hall, "frighted" the family when he began to suffer from pains in his chest and side and started spitting blood. The family's tutor, Philip Fithian, reported that "his fond Mama discovers great anxiety." Because of Mrs. Carter's concern over Ben's illness, which she feared would lead to consumption, she asked that he leave the schoolroom and come to stay in the "great house," where his condition could be more closely watched.[25] Landon Carter recalled how illness in his family had encouraged a warm relationship between two of his sons. When Carter's son John had been

[23]Ibid., 464.
[24]RRD, July 22, 1747.
[25]Hunter Dickinson Farish, ed., *Journal and Letters of Philip Vickers Fithian, 1773–1774* (Williamsburg, 1943), 161–62, 270.

"violent ill of his disorder [the flux] in my absence at home his brother Landon acted the brotherly part and attended him through the who[le] of the disorder." Carter seemed to believe that the family's concern for its own sick was innate, a useful instinct in the often sickly households of the eighteenth-century Chesapeake. In 1770 he told a friend that "gratitude and humanity knew no such boundary as that of a partial family concern and it was often thought out of a tenderness to that virtue that man kind were providentially saved from infection."[26]

The affections parents held for children were apparent in their reaction to childhood illness. James Gordon postponed a trip to Richmond in September of 1762 because of "My dear little Betty" who appeared quite ill.[27] The usually composed William Byrd II worried incessantly about his three-year-old daughter Evelyn's illness in 1710 and called for Dr. Cocke to treat her. Although he tried to carry on his normal daily activities, Byrd skipped breakfast, as "I was so concerned for my daughter." And during the "indisposition" (due to a high fever) of his infant son Parke in May of that year, Byrd made daily reports on the boy's progress.[28] Sometimes a father was so affected by a dangerously ill son or daughter that he could not bear to treat the child. When Landon Carter's daughter "Sukey" suffered from a fever for several weeks, he lamented, "my fears will not let me practice on her as her case is of so Chronick a Kind." He later acknowledged the same problem after ministering unsuccessfully to his daughter Judy. "It is difficult for a father to practice on his child but as I cannot get the doctor I have ventured the best I can and flatter myself it has pleased God to suffer the method to be prudent and successful."[29]

The need for family medical care could also permit a closer, more affectionate attitude between a mature son and his father, thus easing what was often a rather formal relationship. Charles Carroll of Annapolis and his son Charles Carroll of Carrollton

[26]*Carter Diary*, I, 450.
[27]"Journal of James Gordon," 233.
[28]*Byrd Diary, 1709–12*, 213, 180.
[29]*Carter Diary*, I, 323.

constantly worried about each other's health, as well as the condition of the rest of the family. After Charles, Jr., returned from a visit to his father's home in the fall of 1772, he showed concern over the failing health of Charles, Sr., who reassured him that he had been feeling bad only out of worry for his sick granddaughter, "little Molly."[30] After George Taylor of Orange County, Virginia, injured himself in a fall, his son Charles "attended constantly twice a day to dress" his father's leg.[31]

Since all but a few could expect to become dependent from sickness at some point in life (and quite possibly at several points), family members, kin, and close friends learned to rely on one another for medical care. In the process of visiting and giving drugs or treatment to the sick, kinship bonds were reaffirmed and strengthened.

The experience of James Gordon and his daughter's family illustrates the intense family commitment to caring for its ailing members and close friends. In March of 1760 James Chichester, who had married Gordon's daughter Nancy, developed a painful hip infection. Gordon immediately arranged for Dr. James Robertson to see Chichester and to cut open his thigh. But Gordon soon grew "uneasy" about Robertson, whom he felt was neglecting Chichester. He sought a second opinion from another doctor. Both Mr. and Mrs. Gordon visited their son-in-law several times a week, and Gordon offered to manage temporarily the business affairs of his son-in-law. Chichester recovered four months later, but not before his wife's family had spent considerable time worrying about the best doctor and treatment for his problem. The Gordons were just as concerned for the health of their daughter, Nancy Chichester. When she became sick in December of 1762, she was brought to her father's house, where she was nursed back to health in a few weeks.[32]

In a society where sickness and death were so common, kin and friends became important insurance. The Gordons made

[30]Charles Carroll of A to Charles Carroll of C, Nov. 19, 1772, May 14, 15, 1773, CARP.
[31]FTD, Aug. 4, 8, 1790.
[32]"Journal of James Gordon," 197–201, 235.

regular visits to sick relatives and neighbors, such as "poor Mrs. Leland." And like most planter families, they called on relatives and close friends to bleed or give purges to sick members of the family.[33] Robert Rose was constantly making trips to and from the home of his mother-in-law in Stafford County, where his wife and children often stayed when ill. Brothers Henry and James Hollyday depended on each other to secure important medicine—especially bark—during the sickly months of the year; and Reuben and Francis Taylor frequently received "expert" medical aid from their brother, Dr. Charles Taylor.[34]

Death, a "Thing of Terror"

While the ordeal of illness helped to draw family and friends closer together, the experience of death in the household often sharply revealed the emotional dimension of family commitments. The various responses to death in the eighteenth-century Chesapeake allow us to glimpse at least indirectly the nature and strength of family and kin attachments.

The problem of death in Chesapeake families cannot be understood without reference to some important demographic realities. Living in what appears to have been an endemic malarial environment, residents of the early Chesapeake experienced high infant and childhood mortality rates. Probably close to one-third of all children born in late seventeenth-century Virginia and Maryland died before reaching the age of twenty.[35] Adult men (those who survived to the age of twenty) could expect to live

[33]Ibid., 226, 235. When William Byrd learned one night that neighbor and friend Col. Hill was very sick, he "rose to his assistance" and vomited him. *Byrd Diary, 1709–12*, 572. See also ibid., 26, 304–5, 497.

[34]RRD, Sept. 17, 19, 1747, Sept. 12, 1748; Henry Hollyday to James Hollyday, Oct. 30, 1776, HFP. FTD, March 29, 1788, Aug. 19, 26, 1787. See also ibid., Nov. 10–24, 1799; "The Frances Baylor Hill Diary of 'Hillsborough,' King and Queen County, Virginia (1797)," in *Early American Literature Newsletter*, II (1967), 41–42.

[35]Too little is known as yet about infant and childhood mortality rates in the Chesapeake to make any unqualified assertions. A recent study of seventeenth-century Maryland, however, suggests that almost one-half (45.6 percent) of all children died before the age of twenty. See Lorena S. Walsh and Russell R. Menard, "Death in the Chesapeake: Two Life Tables for Men in Early Colonial

only to about forty-five or fifty. The hazards of child-bearing ended the lives of women a few years earlier.[36] And because of the severities of the seasoning process, immigrants experienced considerably higher mortality rates.[37] Disease and the prospect of early death remained a central part of life in the early Chesapeake.

Given the relatively brief span of time family members had with one another, many people may have been unwilling to invest strong emotional commitments in others, even those within their own household. This understanding of the constant presence of death was often couched in the language of religious resignation. As William Fitzhugh solemnly declared to his mother in 1698, "Before I was ten years old ... I look'd upon this life here as but going to an Inn, no permanent being by God's will ... therefore am always prepared for my certain Dissolution, wch. I ca'nt be perswaded to prolong by a wish." The death of a child, for Fitzhugh, was not to be sorrowfully lamented; rather such a loss was to be "easily & cheerfully born, if natural affection be laid aside," since these unfortunate children had replaced "a troublesome & uncertain terrestrial being" with a "certain & happy Celestial habitation."[38]

Although many people perceived the transitory nature of life and tried to approach death with resignation, it was particularly men, especially during the early half of the eighteenth century, who seemed most determined to cushion the emotional pain of

---

Maryland," *MHM*, LXIX (1974), 221–22. My research on colonial Charles Parish, Virginia, indicates a lower mortality rate for infants and children—around 20 percent failing to reach maturity. "Mortality and Family in the Colonial Chesapeake," *Journal of Interdisciplinary History*, VIII (1978), 412–13. Thus the estimate of one-third of all children dying before age twenty is simply a rough compromise between these two estimates.

[36]Rutman and Rutman, 48. Life expectancy for adult men was considerably less in seventeenth-century Charles Parish, where men normally survived only to about the age of forty-one. See Smith, "Mortality and Family in the Colonial Chesapeake," 415–6.

[37]Walsh and Menard, 218, 224.

[38]William Fitzhugh to Mrs. Mary Fitzhugh, June 30, 1698, and to William Fitzhugh, Jan. 30, 1687, in Richard Beale Davis, ed., *William Fitzhugh and His Chesapeake World: The Fitzhugh Letters and Other Documents* (Chapel Hill, N.C., 1963), 358, 198.

death in this way. Women were often charged with the more passionate emotions in family life and they appear to have given freer expression to their feelings in time of death than did men.

The felt need to keep an emotional distance from important objects was succinctly put in 1735 by Thomas Jones, who lamented that "we ought not to have any immoderate concern for any thing that happens to us in this world."[39] Likewise Stephen Bordley of Maryland insisted on a calm acceptance of death; Bordley claimed that he had "lived long enough to know that nothing here is worth giving my self any moment's uneasiness abt...." In 1729 he counselled his sister not to grieve their father's death.[40] Grief was to be strictly controlled, for death was understood in the context of divine authority. Philip Ludwell II, for example, explained to his kinsman John Custis how Ludwell's sister Jane Parke had died after a violent fever and cold in the fall of 1708. Ludwell's family had sought "the best advice we could gett, but when God calls the best Physicians skill will not availe."[41]

Sickness and death maintained an almost constant presence at the William Byrd plantation and despite Byrd's medical efforts, he lost two of his sons, Parke and William. When his infant son Parke died in June of 1710, Byrd recorded in his diary the simple phrase from Proverbs, "God takes away," the same response he made to the deaths of his servants and slaves. Byrd's wife, however, could not accept her son's death with such resignation. As Byrd reported, she was "very much afflicted" and had "several fits of tears for our dear son but kept within the bounds of submission." Indeed, she remained ill and "very Melancholy" until eleven days later when she "began to be comforted." Byrd seemed proud of his religious acceptance of Parke's death and he compared it with his wife's less controlled reaction. "I submitted

[39]Thomas Jones to Elizabeth Jones, Sept. 12, 1736, JFP.

[40]Stephen Bordley to Aunt ? Nov. 16, 1734, the same to Sarah Fusby, Jan. 22, 1729, SBL.

[41]Philip Ludwell II to John Custis, Sept. 9, 1708, CP. See also Susan Cocke to Elizabeth Pratt, April 27, 1724, JFP.

to His judgment better, notwithstanding I was very sensible of my loss, but God's will be done."[42]

Maintaining a stance of indifference to death was also important to Henry Callister of Oxford, Maryland. Upon hearing of his mother's death in 1744, Callister wrote his brother, "It is quite idle to be making Tedious expressions of Grief at one's Mother's death ... I am intirely resign'd." Throughout his life Callister sought to "produce a becoming resignation" in times of death.[43]

The loss of more distant kin and friends frequently met with only a ritualized acknowledgement. "Relations" and "connections" were important to planter families, but their death created concern rather than emotional pain. The intensity of bereavement seemed almost purposely calibrated according to the genealogical proximity of the deceased. This feeling was articulated by Frederick Jones after the death of his brother in 1732: "As there is a respect due to the memory of departed relations so ought it to be expressed according to the nearness of the relationship."[44] Planters often received news—sometimes perversely inaccurate—of the death of their kinsmen in England.[45] But the distance and time of separation apparently cushioned the shock, for few showed any anxiety about their loss.[46] One finds of course more concern over the death of a relative who lived nearby. When the wife of James Gordon's cousin Robert Hening of Urbanna died in 1759, Gordon made note of the event in his diary: "Cous. Hening departed this troublesome life about eleven o'clock today." Hening lived only a short boat ride from Gordon's home in Lancaster County, but James called on a closer relative of the deceased to make the arrangements to bury her. When this plan

---

[42]*Byrd Diary, 1709–12*, 186–88, 24, 191.

[43]Henry Callister to Ewan Callister, Aug. 13, 1744; the same to Robert Greenway, March 6, 1761, CALP.

[44]Frederick Jones to Thomas Jones, July 4, 1732, JFP.

[45]Faulty communications sometimes produced unnecessary bereavement. See Susan Turner to John Hatley Norton, Oct. 13, 1783, Mason, ed., *John Norton and Sons*, 451; *Carter Diary*, I, 452; FTD, Dec. 17, 1788.

[46]Louis B. Wright, ed., *Letters of Robert Carter, 1720–1727: The Commercial Interests of a Virginia Gentleman* (San Marino, Calif., 1940), 54; "Journal of James Gordon," 201; *Byrd Diary, 1709–12*, 270.

did not work out, Gordon had her interred in "our lot."[47] Planters usually responded with even less concern at the death of a friend. Robert Carter of Corotoman accepted the loss of friends with no apparent emotional pain. At the death of "Poor John Baylor," a friend from King and Queen County, Carter was actually critical of the man, calling him "The great negro seller" and a man who made "a mighty noise while living." When his London merchant friend Richard Perry died in 1720, Carter lamented the occasion as "a great loss in the Virginia trade."[48]

Family members who were away from home were regularly informed about deaths among family and friends, but in the latter instance the notice was usually rather matter of fact. Martha Jacquelin, for instance, wrote to her nephews studying in England that a smallpox epidemic had swept through Jamestown and Yorktown in 1748 killing their "old School fellow Catsby Jones." The boys' father, Richard Ambler, later told them that their "acquaintance" Dicky Whitaker had died in October of 1748, but "he was near out of his time."[49]

Even if planters remained unaffected emotionally by the death of a friend or neighbor, they nevertheless recognized an obligation in a society where death was such a frequent event to help support the grieving survivors in the family. When William Byrd's friend and neighbor Benjamin Harrison died in April of 1710, Byrd lamented that Virginia had lost "a very useful man and [one] who was both an advantage and an ornament to it, and I have lost a good neighbour, but God's will be done." Byrd's diary reveals no further reflections on the death, but it does suggest that he and his wife went to considerable effort to console the widow. The day of Harrison's death, Mrs. Byrd visited her distraught neighbor "to comfort her and to assure her that I

[47]"Journal of James Gordon," 102. See also Charles Yates to John Yates, Nov. 1, 1782, Charles Yates Letterbook, 1773–1783, University of Virginia Library.
[48]Wright, ed., *Letters of Robert Carter*, 53–55. Carter saw the death of his slaves in exclusively economic terms. During the harsh winter of 1720, he had "great losses of my negroes in my families ... which swallows a great deal of money." Ibid., 13.
[49]Martha Jacquelin to Edward and Johnny Ambler, April 28, 1748; Richard Ambler to same, May 20, 1749, AFP.

[William Byrd] should be always ready to do her all manner of service." Byrd's wife continued to console Mrs. Harrison, while Byrd offered more practical "services" to the widow, such as seeing after Harrison's business accounts.[50]

The "Severe Shock" of Death: The Loss of Intimacy

A controlled style of bereavement—submission to God's authority with no "affectation of overflowing grief"—remained the *ideal* way to confront family death throughout the eighteenth century.[51] But changes in demographic conditions and family structure after mid-century created a different relationship between the dying person and his family. During the eighteenth century, life expectancies rose significantly; by 1750 men and women normally survived into their mid- to late fifties. As infant and childhood death rates began to decline, a growing proportion of children lived to adulthood. Thus an increasing number of parents could expect to see more of their children to maturity. Increased longevity permitted the development of larger, more complex kin networks, which included grandparents on a large scale for the first time.[52] Because of their lengthening life expect-

[50]*Byrd Diary, 1709–12*, 164, 166, 173, 179, 181, 185. Likewise James Gordon tried to reassure some of his friends who were mourning the loss of a family member. "Journal of James Gordon," 221, 109.

[51]Farish, ed., *Journal and Letters of Fithian*, 241. Even Landon Carter at least theoretically accepted the well-composed, religious approach to bereavement. He agreed that it was psychologically useful to anticipate death, since "the person constantly feeling pain must be more capable of enduring it," but he believed that psychological anticipation of loss was not enough: "No we must flye to our religion" as God "will relieve every affliction loss etc. according to his divine purpose." *Carter Diary*, II, 591–92.

[52]See Allan Kulikoff, "Tobacco and Slaves: Population, Economy and Society in Eighteenth-Century Prince George's County, Maryland" (unpub. Ph.D. diss., Brandeis University, 1975), 439. Widespread early parental loss in the seventeenth-century Chesapeake made orphanhood common. In Middlesex County about three-fourths of all children lost at least one parent before reaching twenty-one or the age of marriage. Over a third were fully orphaned at maturity. Rutman and Rutman, "'Now-Wives and Sons-in-Law': Parental Death in a Seventeenth-Century Virginia County," in Thad Tate and David Ammerman, eds., *The Chesapeake in the Seventeenth Century: Essays on Anglo-American*

ancy, family members and their circle of relatives had a more sustained opportunity to form close, enduring ties of kinship. Moreover, the rising profitability of tobacco during the eighteenth century and the large-scale importation of slaves after 1700 contributed to growing economic security for an increasing number of Chesapeake families. With more leisure time for sociability and an adequate slave labor supply, planter families turned inward, becoming increasingly sentimental, child-centered units, especially with the growing influence of maternal sentiment in the household.[53] And as religious ideology, which had explained death for most men and women in the early Chesapeake, lost much of its spiritual force during the eighteenth century, especially in Anglican communities, family members were left to face bereavement largely in the emotional context of close personal relationships and secular values.

These changes in demographic conditions and family and social life altered the general reaction to death within the family. By the mid-eighteenth century, women and men seemed less able to control their sorrow when death crossed their families. The calm, religious submission to death, toward which many still struggled, became evident only in response to the death of distant kin and acquaintances—those outside the increasingly intimate household and network of close kin and friends.[54]

Society and Politics (Chapel Hill, N.C., 1979), 153–82. In Charles Parish two-thirds of the parish children were at least half-orphaned and one out of seven became full orphans. See Smith, "Mortality and Family in the Colonial Chesapeake," 421–22. But according to Kulikoff, by the mid-eighteenth century early parental death and orphanhood were less common. Kulikoff, "Tobacco and Slaves," 34. On the growth of grandparents in the eighteenth century, see ibid., 58, and Smith, "Mortality and Family in the Colonial Chesapeake," 421.

[53]Edward Shorter traces the rise of maternal love and child-centered family life in Europe as beginning around 1750. See his *The Making of the Modern Family* (New York, 1975).

[54]According to Philippe Ariès, by the mid-eighteenth century death began to be viewed as a violent break from rational society; it was an event that produced fear and passionate sorrow—in contrast to the rather matter-of-fact response to death before the eighteenth century. He links the rising anxiety over death to growing intimacy among family members. See Ariès, *Western Attitudes toward Death from the Middle Ages to the Present*, trans. Patricia M. Ranum (Baltimore, 1974), 57–67. For a very different change in mid-eighteenth-century Puritan society, in which death, once fearfully anticipated, now became welcomed with equanimity, see David Stannard, *The Puritan Way of Death: A Study in Religion, Culture, and Social Change* (New York, 1977) 135–63.

That a philosophy of resignation toward death in the immediate family seemed somehow inadequate was recognized by a few even in the early eighteenth century. In a particularly revealing letter to a merchant friend in 1720, Robert Carter explained that he could not easily achieve the appropriate submissive style at his wife's death: "after we have preached up all the lessons of resignation we are masters of, so long as we carry flesh and blood about us nature will have its turns of victory over the best balanced minds, and all our philosophy will sometimes recoil and give ground under such severe trials. I remain a mourner to this day, and propose to myself to continue in my single state until the time comes when I must put on immortality."[55]

By the latter half of the eighteenth century, the loss of a spouse or child unleashed powerful anxiety and sorrow in the family. Death severed the strong emotional bonds between husbands and wives, and dealing with this loss was for some almost unbearable. William Prentis, for example, wrote his cousin about a friend in Petersburg, Virginia, who became so disconsolate over the death of his wife that he "shed tears, whenever the memory of the poor old Lady" was mentioned. His friend's sorrow, Prentis concluded, was so intense that it would be "some time before he will reconcile to himself to sleep in his own [house?] [a]gain."[56]

[55]Wright, ed., *Letters of Robert Carter*, 18. Over sixty years later, James Innes expressed admiration for his friend's effort to control the grief he felt for his son who had died in a swimming accident. Innes was impressed at how magnificently "he sustained so Heavy a Stroke of Adversity, how forcibly he felt the Influence of the most Heartfelt Grief, and how manfully he bore up against it. You would have admired our friend more than ever—By his redoubled attention and the dignifyed Composure which he discovered on every occasion, he [duly?] soothed and consoled his lonely wife and children whose distress far exceeded the powers of Expression—at the head of an indearing a little tribe as ever fell to the lot of one man, he went to the grave of his departed Son and after having paid the last tribute of Affection and respect his heart for one moment seemed to yield to the tumults of Grief, but instantly recollecting himself, he most tenderly embraced his two youngest Infants who were sitting on his Lap and thanked his God for his remaining [family?]." James Innes to St. George Tucker, Oct. 22, 1782, TCP. One man explicitly rejected any fatalistic approach to death. See Thomas Tudor Tucker to St. George Tucker, April 27, 1787, ibid.

[56]William Prentis to Joseph Prentis, Feb. 15, 1800, WPC. See also Thomas Jefferson's prolonged melancholy after his wife's death, Sarah N. Randolph, *The Domestic Life of Thomas Jefferson* (New York, 1939), 63.

The death of Robert Pleasants in 1772 left his wife "Susey" "almost inconsolable for her loss."[57] Mary Bland Lee struggled hard to "submit patiently" to her husband's death in 1748. But her correspondence suggests that she was engulfed in deep sorrow over the event. Her husband, she confided to brother Theodore Bland, was "one of the best and tenderest of husbands." His death was "so great an affliction to me that I han't words to express it."[58] The death of his wife in 1787 drove John Page into a severe depression. He wrote to his friend St. George Tucker: "Twenty-two Years of sweet domestic Happiness are past! Like a delightful Dream, forever to be regretted forever present to the working Mind, but never to be realized, never to be repeated even in the Delirium of Sleep!" Controlling his feelings of sorrow was a daily effort that did not always succeed: "The Conversation of Friends has often made me forget my Sorrows—Books & Business lend their Aid—but all these are insufficient; Sorrow returns with redoubled Force—How hard is the Struggle between Respect for ones Friends & Family when such Feelings are suppressed, but perhaps it is happy for the [wretched?] that the world requires this Respect; or Grief prey too much on their Minds."[59]

Children became the focal point of family affection during the eighteenth century, and their death, however common in the Chesapeake, provoked considerable sorrow in their families. In early New England a deterministic Calvinist faith created among parents a sort of "tenderness taboo" over their children.[60] Eighteenth-century Chesapeake parents, however, were largely unhindered by such religious conceptions of child-rearing, and they openly grieved over the loss of their children. William Ronald, for example, commiserated with his friend James Parker over the death of his infant son in 1769. It was very difficult for a

[57]Robert Pleasants to Samuel Pleasants, June 13, 1772, in *WMQ*, 2d ser., II (1921), 258.

[58]Mary Bland Lee to Theodore Bland, March 1, 1748, BP.

[59]John Page to St. George Tucker June 12, 1787, TCP.

[60]David E. Stannard, "Death and the Puritan Child," *American Quarterly*, XXVI (1974), 456–76.

parent to accept such a loss, Ronald noted, "when deprived of those whose infant prattle and dawning reason ... has deeply impressed their image in our Breasts."[61] John Page was similarly affected by "the Sudden Loss of my dear & promising Son Johnny" in March of 1783. "It was a severe Shock to me, my Wife & all the Family," Page explained to a friend. "I had to comfort them all."[62] Archibald McCall lost his fifteen-year-old daughter Elizabeth ("Betsey") in November of 1777 after a fever "which baffled all the Physicians & left me the most Disconsolate of Men." "This is the most severe stroke that ever befell me, & when, or if ever I get over it is more than I can say." Ordinarily planters were not quite so overcome with the death of a daughter, but as this was McCall's only child, his one hold on posterity, he attached more meaning to her life than most fathers who had much larger families and numerous sons. That "Betsey" was a central part of her father's family was evident in McCall's rhapsodic account of her character. She was, he claimed, "the most Amiable, lovely, Accomplished good child that I believe Ever existed, & an uncommon favourite of & much Beloved by all who knew her."[63]

Paternal bereavement at the death of a child, especially a grown son, sometimes centered on the suddenly disrupted network of obligations between parents and children. While mothers tended to emphasize the emotional pain resulting from the death of their children, some fathers mourned the loss primarily because it threatened the parents' psychological and possibly their financial comfort in old age. The bereavement experience of George Walker of Yorktown suggests how for a father a son's death upset the symmetry of mutual obligations and responsibilities in the family. When his twenty-two-year-old son John died in 1778, Walker confided in his sister Courtenay Norton that the "unexpected death of my Darling Son" was a

[61]William Ronald to James Parker, Oct. 14, 1769, PFP.
[62]John Page to St. George Tucker, March 24, 1783, TCP.
[63]Archibald McCall to George McCall, May 6, 1778 in Joseph Ewing, ed., "The Correspondence of Archibald McCall and George McCall," *VMHB*, LXXIII (1965), 323–24.

"great loss," particularly because of the difficult situation in which the family was now placed. "If it had been the will of the Almighty to have spared him his poor mother and myself would have been Bless'd in the decline of Life, in having as dutiful a Son, & his Brothers would have reap'd great advantage from his Advice & Instruction." Like McCall, Walker eulogized his departed child and was proud that his son had been "admired by his Relations when living & lamented by everyone who knew him." Moreover, he was known to be "virtuous learned & Brave by those he was most intimate with."[64] All the paternal training and energies invested in a young man to teach him obedience and responsibility to the family now appeared wasted. Parents such as George Walker worked out their grief largely in the context of the family.

Daughters also had a supportive role in the family; consequently, their death could be equally disruptive to paternal plans. As a three-time widower, Landon Carter intended that his daughter Sukey should remain his life-long female companion. He became deeply troubled when she was plagued with recurring, violent agues and fevers for eight months. In April of 1758 he lamented: "I dispair of her life." Carter anticipated her death with such certainty that he put her under the care of his friend Gilbert Hamilton during her last days. When she died, Hamilton gave Carter a detailed description of the progress of the disease and the manner of her death. Though he had expected her death, it stunned him. All his expectations for Sukey had suddenly vanished. "Severe stroke indeed to a Man bereft of a wife and in the decline of life because at such periods 'tis natural to look out for such connections that may be reasonably expected to be the support of Greyhairs and such an one I had promised myself in this child in particuler."[65] To fathers such as Walker and Carter, the loss of a child abruptly ended paternal expectations that their offspring would live to care for them in old age—the ultimate proof of filial duty and love.

[64]George Walker to Courtenay Walker Norton, Feb. 14, 1779, Mason, ed., *John Norton and Sons*, 418–19.
[65]*Carter Diary*, I, 217–22.

Since mothers were entrusted with the physical nurture and much of the early rearing of children, they developed a warmer, more intimate relationship with their sons and daughters. And when a child's death destroyed this affectionate maternal tie, mothers openly showed their feelings. Mrs. Sarah Hollyday, for example, became disconsolate and "reduced to a very low State" in 1780 because of "the Affliction of mind for the sickness and death" of her son.[66] Martha Jefferson Carr reported that her sister Mary Bolling was "all most worn out with grief" after the death of her youngest son in 1787.[67] Affectionate maternal sentiment for a dying daughter was poignantly evoked in the correspondence of the Gilpin family of Maryland. Mrs. Gilpin stayed in the same room with her ailing daughter Sarah throughout her three-and-one-half month illness, which ended in death in January of 1796. After Sarah's death, Mrs. Gilpin explained in a letter to her son that during the ordeal "the strong Maturnal and filial affection that always subsisted dayly Increased In sweet Union and fellowship, wherein we often Mingled our tears together, In commemoration of our Similar Confinement."[68]

The intimacy of the mother-child bond, which intensified during the latter half of the eighteenth century, becomes even more vivid in a letter from the grief-stricken Adams household of Richmond. Writing to his brother Thomas in September of 1771, Richard Adams described his wife's suffering after the recent death of their infant son Eben: "We have had the misfortune to loose our dear little Darling Eben, last month, which was a great shock to the whole family, particularly to his poor Mama, whose great Tenderness for him in a long illness had occasioned her to exert herself further than she was able to bear in tending on him, which threw her into a violent Fever, & indulging her Grief had reduced her (almost) to the point of Death, & is still lower than I ever knew her."[69]

[66]James Hollyday to Edward Lloyd, June 7, 1780, HFP.
[67]Martha Jefferson Carr to Thomas Jefferson, Dec. 3, 1787, CFP.
[68]Mrs. Gilpin to Joshua Gilpin, 1796, GL. See also Lucy Lee Orr, *Journal of a Young Lady in Virginia, 1782* (Baltimore, 1871), 19.
[69]Richard Adams to Thomas Adams, Sept. 30, 1771, "Adams Family Letters," *VMHB*, xxii (1914), 386.

Children experienced the death of parents as a profound loss. A mother had usually concentrated so much of her emotional resources in her children that when she died, the surviving children, particularly adolescent and adult sons, were shaken and at times almost disoriented by the loss. George Norton of Yorktown, for instance, was overcome with grief at the news of his mother's death in 1780. In baring his disconsolate feelings in a letter to a London friend, Norton explained that he was "shocked at the fatal loss I had just received, & the recollection of it strikes me with horror." Permanent separation from the maternal tie obviously troubled him, for he claimed he was now "bereft of one of the best Mothers & the only remaining Comfort that I had to expect in this life." He was so broken up over the death that he asked his friend to write his "relations & friends" of the "disagreeable news in as mild a manner as you possibly can."[70]

Because parents had comforted and protected their children, it was a son's obligation and inclination as a young adult to repay that concern and loving treatment. In the early death of parents, children lost their most trusted source of care and affection as well as the opportunity to fulfill their filial obligation. The Charles Carroll family of Maryland provides the most dramatic and revealing illustration of the shock young sons experienced at a parent's death—in this case, a mother's death.

Twenty-three-year-old Charles Carroll of Carrollton was studying in Europe when his father notified him of his mother's death in March of 1761. She had been ill for almost three years, and Charles, Sr., reported to his son the progress and setbacks she had experienced throughout the various stages of her long sickness. When she finally died, Charles, Sr., made a strong effort to submit quietly to the loss, undoubtedly hoping that his son would also come to accept his mother's death with the same Christian fortitude. "Religion in such cases," he advised his son, "is the only solid Comforter of the afflicted." "God who has Created us has a Right to dispose of us." Charles, Sr., emphasized the transitory nature of human existence, explaining

[70]George F. Norton to James Withers, Sept. 19, 1780, Mason ed., *John Norton and Sons*, 490–91.

"you have before us an affecting instance of Mortality, life is but as the Twinkling of the Eye to Eternity, the only serious business of life is to make that Eternity a happy one."[71]

But the young Charles could not achieve such equanimity in the face of his mother's death. Instead, he became bitter and disconsolate, especially since her death robbed him of the chance to see her again after so long an absence—nearly thirteen years. "The greatest blessing I wished for in this life was to see to enjoy my Parents after so long a separation to comfort to support them in advanced age: one is forever snatched from me!" His mother's death clearly left him emotionally unstable for a time. In a series of letters to his father following the death, Charley revealed the loneliness he felt at the loss of his mother. Pathetically dispirited, he asked if he had been on his mother's mind near the end: "did she not frequently wish to see me? did she not so much as say remember me to my dear absent son?" He then began to reflect on his childhood years with his mother, "those happy days," "in her sweet company."[72]

The death of Mrs. Carroll not only shocked and depressed her son, it also seized him with a gnawing feeling that he soon might lose his father as well. And that fear, however unfounded at the time, plunged him into severe mental anguish over his future: "If I shou'd Lose you too, which God forbid, who is there to help me? What experience have I? none: time? that depends on God. Consider how short & uncertain life is: alive today & dead tomorrow: we have before us a most affecting instance of its precariousness."[73]

Charley's lengthy separation from his parents before his mother's death doubtless made his situation unusual and certainly contributed to his strong reaction to her loss. Still the bereavement experience of Charles Carroll suggests the intensity of a son's emotional bond to his parents.[74]

[71]Charles Carroll of A to Charles of C, March 22, 1761, CARP.
[72]Charles Carroll of C to Charles Carroll of A, June 10, 1761, CARP.
[73]Ibid.
[74]John Bowlby has theorized that children, when faced with permanent separation from their parents (i.e., death), first become angry at being deserted and then try to recover psychologically the lost attachment figure. It may be that Charles

"The Great Complaint, Old Age"

Conspicuously left out of the strong family sentiment during bereavement were the aged. As Charles Carroll, Sr., had explained to his son, family members—even devoted sons—should not expect to maintain close attachments to the elderly, whose continued survival was constantly in doubt.[75] And family reactions to illness and death among the aged indicate that many people would have agreed with Carroll. If the bereavement experience is any guide to attitudes toward the aged, the eighteenth-century Chesapeake was no golden era for the elderly.[76]

Those advancing in years were keenly aware of the uncertainty of existence in old age. Upon attaining the age of thirty-six, Byrd thanked God "for granting me so many years." Thirty years later, when he was truly growing old, Byrd's birthday entry was even less hopeful, as he asked only to live out his life with his mind intact. "God preserve my head and grant I may not lose my memory and sense."[77] There was something unsettling about the age of thirty-six for Charles Carroll of Carrollton as well. When only twenty-six years old in 1764, he began to worry whether he could find a wife and raise children before his frail body gave out in ten years. "If I stay till I attain the age of 36, the chance of my living so long, are against me as I am of thin & puny habit of body."[78] Peter Fontaine also recognized that old age destroyed health. He told his brother Moses in 1749 "we must expect indispositions will creep upon such weak Constitutions as ours."[79]

Carroll, Jr., tried to reestablish union in some way with his "lost" mother (or the affection she represented) through a heightened dependence on and commitment to his father. See Bowlby, *Attachment and Loss* (2 vols., New York, 1969 and 1973), II, 247–48.

[75]Charles Carroll of A to Charles Carroll of C, Oct. 28, 1772; same to same, July 30, 1773, CARP.

[76]That the aged were venerated and relatively powerful in America until the beginning of the nineteenth century is argued by David Hackett Fisher in his *Growing Old in America: A Short History* (New York, 1977).

[77]*Byrd Diary, 1709–12*, 158; *Byrd Diary, 1739–41*, 50.

[78]Charles Carroll of C to Charles Carroll of A, May 1, 1764, CARP.

[79]Peter Fontaine to Moses Fontaine, Nov. 4, 1749, Ann Maury, ed., *Memoirs of a Hugenot Family* (New York, 1907), 33. For a similar view, see "The Autobiography of the Reverend Devereux Jarratt, 1732–1793," *WMQ*, 3d ser., IX (1952), 357.

No one understood the physical and psychological difficulties of old age better than Landon Carter. Plagued by what he considered an ungrateful, disobedient son, Carter spent his "declining" years in periodic domestic turmoil. Nevertheless, he articulated well the depression and pain of old age that many elderly planters experienced.

"The great complaint, Old Age" bothered Carter incessantly and left him resigned to the uncertainty of his health and happiness. "Life is but one continued anxiety to live," he wrote in 1771. Carter's physical pains at age sixty made him doubt the biblical injunction that man's days were three score and ten years, for he believed that "the period is now shortened . . . for I can find that even after 3 score years it is labour and sorrow." More distressing to him, however, was the neglect and indifference which most people showed the aged. Reflecting on the loneliness of his fifty-two-year-old widower friend Robert Burwell, Carter concluded that an old man had to keep his "lonely hours" occupied by reading, "for without books or a desire to read how can the aged injoy themselves, when the Young even their children seem to despise them." "It is a pity that old age which everybody covets and everybody who lives must come to should be so contemptible in the eyes of the world."[80]

It is unlikely that the aged were as neglected and despised as Carter believed. But there is considerable evidence that their illness and death stirred few emotions in their families. Pain and the almost daily prospect of death for the aged bred a feeling of calm acceptance among relatives and friends. George Gilpin of Alexandria, for example, was disappointed to learn from his brother Thomas that their "Honour'd Mother" was sick, but as George pointed out, "it is what Evry one must Expect who Arrives at ther years."[81] Theodorick Bland, Jr., advised his sister Frances Tucker in 1784 to accept with spiritual assurance the death of their aged father: "resignation to the will of Heaven is our part—if there is happiness after this life—we are sure tis his

---

[80]*Carter Diary,* II, 565, I, 487, II, 1034, 720.
[81]George Gilpin to Thomas Gilpin, Aug. 4, 1775, GL.

lot."[82] On occasion the death of an old man brought more relief than sorrow to the surviving family. When Bowler Cocke, "our Pour old uncle of Bremo," died in the summer of 1771, his nephew Richard Adams considered the death a product of "Wise Providence ... as he had lived as long as he could have any Enjoyment himself, or could contribute anything to those he left behind."[83]

Francis Taylor appeared similarly unaffected when his seventy-nine-year-old uncle Erasmus Taylor died in 1794. According to his diary, Francis had heard the day before that his uncle "was thought dying" but Taylor, who lived within walking distance from Erasmus, remained home that day. Indeed he made no further mention of his uncle until the funeral two weeks later, which was attended by "a respectable company, mostly connections & neighbours."[84] And as grief-stricken as Charles Carroll of Carrollton would shortly become over his mother's death, he advised—ironically enough—complete composure and religious submission when he heard in March of 1761 that his grandmother had died. She had been a pious and good person, Charles insisted, so her death was not an occasion to lament. Charles was distressed, however, over the effect his grandmother's death might have on his mother. He hoped she would not be too disconsolate over the loss, even though "not to be affected at the death of a Parent wou'd argue insensibility." Nevertheless, he observed, "immoderate grief is unreasonable and unbecoming."[85]

The Ritualization of Death: Bereavement and Burial

Although the expression of grief was open to neighbors and friends, death was primarily a family matter, and the mourning

[82]Theodorick Bland, Sr., to Frances Tucker, Oct. 13, 1784, TCP.
[83]Richard Adams to Thomas Adams, Aug. 8, Sept. 30, 1771, "Adams Family Letters," 380, 383–85.
[84]FTD, Dec. 18, 1794, Jan. 1, 1795.
[85]Charles Carroll of C to Charles Carroll of A, March 29, Feb. 13, 1761, CARP.

process deepened family affection. The dying, like the sick, were normally treated at home, allowing families to witness death. As a result, individuals and families were forced to come to terms with death rather than avoid it as most modern Americans do.[86] The few surviving records of death-bed scenes in the eighteenth-century Chesapeake testify to the warm yet controlled nature of family bereavement.

Maintaining one's senses near the end signified the triumph of reason at death and was a lesson to the survivors.[87] James Maury of Louisa County admired the way his mother met death because she "spent her last moments in wholesome admonitions to all about her, and in blessing us her children and all that we have." Death for her was a reward, "a most glorious end...for having so faithfully maintained" her post in life.[88] Richard Terrell's grandmother was reported to have achieved a dignified death in the spring of 1795. She experienced "Comfourt & Serenity" in the final days and remained "sencible of her approaching end perfectly resigned to death and has left behind her a respectable character."[89]

The final dialogue between the survivors and the dying family member could be a powerful emotional and religious experience for the family and friends of the deceased. Sarah Gilpin's death in 1796, her mother claimed, was "an Instructive lesson to all present to pass through the Shadow of Death." With her mother and her aunts and uncles and a few friends surrounding her bed, Sarah, according to Mrs. Gilpin, asked in her final words for God to "grant her an easy passage, and support her surviving Rela-

[86]Maris V. Vinovskis, "Angels' Heads and Weeping Willows: Death in Early America," *Proceedings of the American Antiquarian Society,* 86 (1977), 294, 297. In the U. S. in 1963, 53 percent of all deaths occurred in hospitals and others occurred in nursing homes or in accidents *away* from home, thus isolating most modern Americans from death. See Robert L. Fulton, "Death and the Self," *Journal of Religion and Health,* III (1964), 354, 367.

[87]The belief in a "calm, clear-eyed death" as a lesson and sign of grace persisted into the early nineteenth century. See Lewis O. Saum, "Death in the Popular Mind of Pre-Civil War America," *American Quarterly,* XXVI (1974), 488.

[88]James Maury to John Fontaine, Jan. 10, 1756, Maury, ed., *Memoirs of a Hugenot Family,* 397–98.

[89]Martha Jefferson Carr to Lucy Terrell, March 15, 1795, CTFP.

tives.["90] Peter Fontaine described for his brothers the poignant last moments before their sister's death in 1756. She accepted her approaching death with Christian resignation, Peter maintained, "spending her last breath in prayers for all her relations and acquaintances, and in blessing me and my little family, one by one, as we stood in tears around her."[91]

The strong emotional ties between family members in the eighteenth-century Chesapeake—especially after 1750—forced certain changes in the often perfunctory mourning process that had prevailed in the seventeenth century. Alan Macfarlane has suggested that death in seventeenth-century England was dealt with in an almost matter-of-fact fashion with no memorialization of the dead and only the immediate nuclear family participating in the funeral and burial services.[92] And in eighteenth-century English aristocratic families, the mourning ritual seemed almost completely devoid of emotion.[93] In middle- and upper-class Chesapeake families of the eighteenth century, however, parents, children, and friends often sought to make permanent statements of their affection at the loss of loved ones.

Beginning in the latter half of the century, elaborate memorials were sometimes offered to honor dead family members. In 1753, for example, Catesby Cocke composed a respectful epitaph to be inscribed on a monument honoring his father, who had died the year before.[94] When young Calista Callister died in 1759 (at about the age of ten), her mother Anna wrote a long grieving poem as a testimonial to Calista's "serene" death and to the warm bond between her and her daughter. "What was my greatest joy is now my grief," she declared at the beginning of her memorial. In the

---

[90]Mrs. Gilpin to Joshua Gilpin 1796, GL.

[91]Peter Fontaine to John and Moses Fontaine, March 2, 1756, Maury, 346. See also Joseph Fauntleroy to William Cocke, 1792, "Family Letters of the Eighteenth Century," *VMHB*, xv (1908), 436; Henry Callister to Robert Morris, Dec. 17, 1764, CALP; "Frances Baylor Hill Diary," 42–43.

[92]Alan Macfarlane, *The Family of Ralph Josselin: A Seventeenth-Century Clergyman* (Cambridge, 1970), 100–01.

[93]Randolph E. Trumbach, "The Aristocratic Family in England, 1690–1780: Studies in Childhood and Kinship" (unpub. Ph.D. diss., The Johns Hopkins University, 1972), 217–30.

[94]Catesby Cocke to Mrs. James, Sept. 7, 1753, JFP.

poem Mrs. Callister vividly described the affectionate feelings of the mother-daughter tie: "I saw her die, I saw the last breath quiver on her lips; She expired, almost without a pang, in the arms of her distracted Mother."[95]

Funeral and burial ceremonies in the eighteenth-century Chesapeake also suggest the growing primacy of family and kin sentiment. Most people in the early Chesapeake had been buried in parish church grounds. But as an expression of their increasing concern for the dead, many eighteenth-century families controlled the services on their own estates. Moreover, in many instances parishes had grown so large that it was sometimes inconvenient to transport the corpse a long distance to the church burial grounds. Thus, especially among the well-to-do, personal gardens and orchards were used "where whole families lye interred together, in a spot generally handsomly enclosed, planted with evergreens, and the graves kept decently." Families often refused to have funeral services in the church, insisting that ministers preach in the house of the deceased.[96]

Planter families in the eighteenth-century Chesapeake were ambivalent about illness and death as they approached both with resignation and anxiety. The evanescence of life and property in the seventeenth century created a feeling of resignation in the face of suffering and loss, as William Fitzhugh and others suggested.[97] But declining mortality rates and lengthening life expectancies by the mid-eighteenth century (though still grim by modern standards) allowed for a more complete emotional investment in the lives of family members.

When a member of the family became ill or died, the philosophy of resignation that earlier had "worked" proved after mid-

[95]Poem by Sarah Callister, n. d. (probably 1759), CALP. Landon Carter also wrote a poem commemorating the death of his daughter Sukey in 1758, *Carter Diary*, I, 221–22.

[96]Hugh Jones, *Present State of Virginia*, ed. by Richard L. Morton (Chapel Hill, N.C., 1956), 97.

[97]See the discussion of the instability of life in seventeenth-century Virginia in Edmund S. Morgan, *American Slavery, American Freedom: The Ordeal of Colonial Virginia* (New York, 1975), 158–79.

century less effective in controlling grief and explaining loss. At the same time, families were unwilling to give themselves completely over to grief in times of suffering as they would by the 1830s.[98] Indeed, there was a selective anxiety about illness and death among eighteenth-century planters which suggests some important things about their families.

The family's response to illness and death reflected the increasingly close emotional attachments among its members. Children grieved the loss of maternal affection and paternal direction. The anxiety and sorrow parents felt at the death of their offspring suggest the rather modern, child-centered orientation of these planter families. A symmetrical view of the life cycle—with parents and children dependent on one another at different stages in life—led parents, especially fathers, to see death in a family context, for they often revealed their distress at a child's death in terms of unfulfilled filial obligations. But the loss of others within and outside the family created much less grief and anxiety. Ties of kinship and friendship were doubtless strengthened through visitation and medical aid in illness, but then, as now, the death of elderly kin or of people outside the immediate family rarely produced an emotional bereavement.[99]

[98]Antebellum southerners were not in the least resigned to death or sickness; rather it drove them to considerable anxiety and melancholy. See Russell L. Blake, "Ties of Intimacy: Social Values and Personal Relationships of Antebellum Slaveholders" (unpub. Ph.D. diss., University of Michigan, 1978).

[99]For a modern assessment of the bereavement process, see Colin M. Parkes, *Bereavement: Studies of Grief in Adult Life* (London, 1972).

Chapter Eight

Toward a History of
Early American Family Life

Several years ago Michael Zuckerman, commenting on the growing wave of colonial New England community studies, observed
that "we have to get out of New England or we will never know
the significance of what we know."[1] Since then social historians
have launched a thorough reevaluation of colonial southern society, while a smaller number of scholars have begun a more
intensive exploration of the social history of the mid-Atlantic
region, especially Pennsylvania and New York.[2] Much more
work—both the painstaking but essential labor of demographic
reconstruction and the more broadly interpretive studies of family and social values—remains to be done. Nevertheless, after
more than fifteen years of unusually profitable and imaginative
research by colonial historians, it is now possible to sketch at least
a tentative synthesis of early American family life.[3] Indeed this

---

[1]"Reply," *WMQ*, 3d ser., xxix (1972), 468.

[2]For a critical discussion of some of the new social history of the colonial
Chesapeake, see Daniel Blake Smith, "Mortality and Family in the Colonial
Chesapeake," *Journal of Interdisciplinary History*, viii (1978), 403–27. Important
new work on community and family in Pennsylvania and New York includes
Stephanie Wolff, *Urban Village: Population, Community and Family Structure in
Germantown, Pennsylvania, 1683–1800* (Princeton, 1977), and Thomas
Archdeacon, *New York City, 1664–1710: Conquest and Change* (Ithaca, N.Y., 1975).

[3]An earlier, somewhat different version of this chapter appears as part of a
larger essay, "Perspectives in American Family History," *Working Papers* (Regional Economic History Research Center, Eleutherian Mills-Hagley Foundation),
iii (Summer 1979).

study of Chesapeake planter families, when combined with other recent accounts of early American family and kin life, allows us to glimpse the shape and some of the main lines of family experience in our preindustrial past.

Until very recently, early American family history was simply the story of colonial New England family life writ large. This is not surprising given the relative wealth of vital statistics and town and church records, as well as the large share of literary sources—from sermons to family papers—that have survived from the region. But it is becoming increasingly evident that regional variations in early American family life were often sharp and persistent, in some cases lasting into the early nineteenth century. Families in New England, the middle colonies, and the South, while undoubtedly sharing much similar cultural baggage, nevertheless organized themselves and learned values in strikingly different ways.

Concern for studying the family in colonial America can be traced to the publication in 1960 of Bernard Bailyn's *Education in the Formation of American Society,* a slim but provocative volume that argued that the extended families and strong kin structures colonists had known in the Old World disintegrated amid the opportunity and abundance of the New World experience. Mobile nuclear families emerged in early New England, Bailyn suggested, as new, innovative family forms broke free from the patriarchal household of traditional society in England and Europe. Here, then, was the inchoate form of the modernization argument, with colonial families structured according to the immediate needs and functional demands of a frontier setting rather than simply repeating traditional family patterns.[4]

Since the publication of Bailyn's work, scholars studying both sides of Anglo-American family life have dramatically revised his view of American exceptionalism concerning the family. Peter Laslett and other historical demographers from the Cambridge Group have shown that the seventeenth-century English family was far from an extended, patriarchal unit. High mortality rates

[4]New York, 1960; see especially pages 15–36.

cut deeply into patriarchalism and fertility, leaving most families in early modern England small and nuclear.[5] Moreover, the shortage of land and periodic economic depressions in the early seventeenth century promoted a good deal of short-term mobility and migration, hardly the prerequisites for well-ordered, patriarchal households.[6]

Ironically, though, it was Bailyn's own student, Philip Greven, who most effectively redirected scholarship on colonial New England family life. Sensitive to the pioneering work of historical demographers like Laslett and Louis Henry in France, Greven produced a study of demographic change and inheritance patterns in colonial Andover, Massachusetts, that essentially argued the reverse of his mentor's earlier claims: patriarchal family life, he suggested, actually received a new lease on life in seventeenth-century New England, largely because of remarkably long life spans and an enduring commitment to communal values. Long-lived fathers controlled the land, thereby delaying their sons full autonomy until relatively late in life, protecting the family estate and securing their own care in their declining years.[7] As John Waters, James Henretta, and others have more recently discovered in other religious communities in the northern colonies, an intimate reciprocity existed between fathers and sons in which agricultural production needs and parental values were closely intertwined. Fathers, while recognizing their responsibility to settle their sons independently, nevertheless controlled the family assets to ensure that their sons labored for them productively and promised to maintain them and their widows in old age. The early New England family, then, was an embracive economic farm unit in which important decisions ranging from the leasing and purchasing of land to the choosing of marriage partners were determined largely by family and kin, rather

[5]Peter Laslett, *The World We Have Lost* (New York, 1965), 81–106.
[6]Lawrence Stone, "Social Mobility in England, 1500–1700," *Past and Present*, XXXIII (1966), 16–55.
[7]*Four Generations: Population, Land, and Family in Colonial Andover, Massachusetts* (Ithaca, N.Y., 1970), 72–99.

than by independent transactions between unconstrained individuals.[8]

If the imperatives of agricultural village life governed father-son ties and marriage decisions, the influence of a strong Protestant faith molded the values and child-rearing practices of families in New England and in Quaker settlements of the middle colonies. For children growing up in the highly structured world of these early religious communities, learning one's place within the family and society loomed large in child-rearing efforts. Plymouth parents, Demos suggests, were preoccupied with stifling aggressiveness and willfulness in their offspring and themselves—both manifestations of innate childhood sinfulness. The almost obsessive attempts among parents to root out autonomy and assertiveness in their children, he claims, reflected a social and religious world that prized above all self-control and obedience to community norms and the dicates of a Calvinist God.[9]

As we have seen, though, family life took on a significantly different structure and meaning in the colonial South. "Well-ordered" families were slow to develop here, especially in the Chesapeake. In large part it was the disease-ridden, immigrant-dominated character of seventeenth-century Virginia and Maryland that loosened the ties of family and kin. These early colonial families were riddled by sickness and death, creating chaotic family structures and an abundance of stepparents and orphans. With the high incidence of early parental loss and the presence of only a fragmentary kin network, the possibility of strong patriarchal authority developing in these early generations was seriously limited. These were strangely "modern" households, at

[8]John J. Waters, "The Traditional World of the New England Peasants: A View from Seventeenth-Century Barnstable," *New England Historical and Genealogical Register,* LXXX (1976), 3–21; idem; "American Colonial Stem Families: Persisting European Patterns in the New World" (paper presented to the Newberry Library Early American History Seminar, Jan. 17, 1978); James Henretta, "Families and Farms: *Mentalité* in Pre-Industrial America," *WMQ,* 3d ser., XXXV (1978), 3–32.

[9]John Demos, *A Little Commonwealth: Family Life in Plymouth Colony* (New York, 1970), 135–39. See also, Greven, *The Protestant Temperament;* 21–43; Barry Levy, "Tender Plants: Quaker Farmers and Children in the Delaware Valley,

least in terms of the early autonomy of children and the absence of kin control in family decisions.[10]

By the early decades of the eighteenth century, however, a more permanent family and kin life was developing. As Chesapeake plantation society matured and prospered with the growth of a strong tobacco and slave economy and became for the first time a predominantly native-born population, family ties deepened and more elaborate kin networks emerged throughout the Tidewater. Internally, these early eighteenth-century households were characterized by a series of power relationships between husbands and wives and parents and children that underscored the belief in order and authority in the family. Moderation and restraint, especially regarding emotional attachments in the home, governed family conduct. A father stood as the sovereign head of the household, settling his sons in predetermined careers and expecting deference and obedience in return. Planters likewise manipulated, and often controlled, their children's marriages, largely out of an interest in family and social standing and economic security. Despite these authoritarian family relationships centering on the power of the father-husband, the web of kinship and friendship stretched relatively wide as households were often large, inclusive affairs with much visitation and contact outside the family for men and their sons.

American social and economic life began a dramatic transformation in the latter third of the eighteenth century, a period of "deep change" that profoundly affected family and kin experi-

1681–1735," *Journal of Family History,* 3 (1978), 116–35; Joseph E. Illick, "Child-Rearing in Seventeenth-Century England and America," in Lloyd deMause, ed., *The History of Childhood* (New York, 1974), 321.

[10]See Darrett B. and Anita H. Rutman, "Of Agues and Fevers: Malaria in the Early Chesapeake," *WMQ,* 3d ser., XXXIII (1976), 31–60; Rutman and Rutman, "'Now-Wives and Sons-in-Law': Parental Death in a Seventeenth-Century Virginia County," in Thad W. Tate and David Ammerman, eds., *The Chesapeake in the Seventeenth Century: Essays On Anglo-American Society And Politics* (Chapel Hill, N.C., 1979), 153–82; Lorena S. Walsh and Russell R. Menard, "Death and the Chesapeake: Two Life Tables for Men in Colonial Maryland," *MHM,* LXIX (1974), 211–27; Lorena S. Walsh, "'Till Death Us Do Part': Marriage and Family in Seventeenth-Century Maryland," in *The Chesapeake in the Seventeenth Century,* 126–52; and Smith, "Mortality and Family."

ence.[11] What some historians consider a "modernization" of American personal and family values appears to have been at work in many planter households after 1750 as well. Certainly the emotional texture of family life and the nature of authority in the household were substantially altered in much of late eighteenth-century America, particularly in the South and the mid-Atlantic region.

In the Chesapeake what is most striking in the post-1750 period is the development of a more openly affectionate, intimate family environment in which emotional attachments were deeply values, indeed cherished. These kinds of relationships were particularly evident in response to death in the family. While the loss of a spouse or child in the seventeenth and early eighteenth centuries often produced studied resignation, a death in the family after mid-century tended to unleash powerful anxiety and sorrow among the survivors. Increasingly, families were knit together by close emotional bonds that were revealed in the loss of a loved one.

The growing intimacy of family life was also demonstrated in a new perception of children. In well-to-do families, infants and small children became the centerpiece of family attention and affection, as childhood was perceived as a distinct stage of life characterized by innocence, delightful "prattling," and the growth of an individual identity. Acting on Lockean child-rearing principles, modified by the increasingly secular values of a plantation society, parents tended to raise their offspring with a large measure of indulgence and optimism about the capacities and virtues of children.

The growing presence of slave labor, both inside the "great house" and out in the fields, unquestionably accentuated the sense of freedom and affection children experienced in Chesapeake households. Slaves, after all, performed most of the difficult work on the plantation, leaving young boys to explore their world alone, and later, as young adults, to learn the "command

[11]The expression "deep change," which suggests a fundamental reorientation of social and economic values in a culture, comes from David Hackett Fischer in his forthcoming multivolume social history of America.

experience"—supervising and controlling their own servants.
Moreover, it was the master's slaves, instead of his children, who
often served as convenient objects of parental discipline and
wrath around the house, thus allowing the parent-child relationship to remain an essentially warm, positive one, untarnished by
the difficulties of discipline.[12]

Kinship likewise bore the imprint of heightened intimacy
within the conjugal family, at least in the middle and upper ranks
of society. By the end of the century, planter kin ties had become
narrow in range and shallow in genealogical depth, hardly re-
sembling the paternalistic, kin-dominated social world often associated with the preindustrial South.[13] The limited contact between kin outside the nuclear family suggests the increasingly
private nature of the planter family during the latter half of the
century. As parents turned inward on a more intimate, sentimental "family society," the wider range of kin (such as uncles, aunts,
and cousins, as well as more distant relatives) occupied a less
central place in the individual's emotional world. To be sure,
these kin could be useful in performing certain tasks (educating
nephews, taking in a son-in-law for a short while, for example),
but it was the conjugal family, along with a few select friends and
neighbors, who made up the most intimate circle of companionship for southern planters.

Elsewhere in eighteenth-century America, family patterns
similar to these, though less pronounced, emerged at roughly the
same time. According to Greven, the patriarchalism so dominant
in early Andover faded considerably during the middle decades
of the eighteenth century. The growing shortage of land forced a
good deal of geographic mobility and weakened the "modified
extended family" system. Rather than wait for their inheritance,
sons increasingly bought their portions—and hence their economic independence—from their fathers and left for available

[12]For a similar conclusion see Greven, *The Protestant Temperament*, 274–77.
[13]See Gerald Mullin, *Flight and Rebellion: Slave Resistance in Eighteenth-Century Virginia* (New York, 1972), 19–33; Eugene Genovese, *Roll, Jordan, Roll: The World the Slaves Made* (New York, 1974), 92; and Bertram Wyatt-Brown, "The Ideal Typology and Antebellum Southern History: A Testing of a New Approach," *Societas*, v (1975), 1–30.

287

land on the frontier or for new starts in other towns. While parents often aided them in this resettlement process, thereby maintaining some paternal control, the result was that sons fashioned their own economic lives while removed from day-to-day paternal supervision, something their seventeenth-century ancestors had rarely managed.[14]

If family control of sons' economic independence declined during the eighteenth century, parental supervision and manipulation of marital decisions also weakened significantly, especially during the latter third of the century. Daniel Scott Smith has shown that in postrevolutionary Massachusetts, personal autonomy carried more importance than parental desires in marriage choices.[15] Quaker families in this period also appear to have experienced a pronounced rise in marriages "out of union," as sons and daughters increasingly found mates from outside the Quaker fold.[16] Mutual love and companionship—what Lawrence Stone calls "affective individualism"—replaced concern for lineage, property, and kin control during the late eighteenth century.[17] In some instances these "participant-run" marriages may have been occasioned by premarital pregnancy—the increase in which is yet another index of autonomy from parental control in the latter half of the century. The upsurge in premarital pregnancy throughout much of eighteenth-century America developed largely out of a trend toward growing secularization and weakening community and parental authority.[18]

[14]Greven, *Four Generations*, 222–58; Robert Gross, *The Minutemen and Their World* (New York, 1976), 75–108, 207–9.

[15]See his essay, "Parental Power and Marriage Patterns: An Analysis of Historical Trends in Hingham, Massachusetts," *Journal of Marriage and the Family,* xxxv (1973), 419–28. See also Gross, *The Minutemen and Their World,* 211.

[16]J. William Frost, *The Quaker Family in Colonial America* (New York, 1973), 164–67; Barry J. Levy, "The Light in the Valley: The Chester and Welsh Tract Quakers in the Delaware River Valley, 1681–1750" (unpub. Ph.D. diss., University of Pennsylvania, 1976), 71–73.

[17]Stone, *The Family, Sex and Marriage in England, 1500–1800* (New York, 1977), 221–69. Shorter, *The Making of the Modern Family* (New York, 1975), 121–58, likewise dates the rise in romantic courtship and independent marital choice with the post-1750 period.

[18]Daniel Scott Smith and Michael S. Hindus, "Premarital Pregnancy in America, 1640–1971," *Journal of Interdisciplinary History,* v (1975), 537–70.

Families in Early America

In the middle colonies, where our knowledge of the colonial family is still incomplete, these forces for mobile, autonomous family life may have been quite strong, even from the early eighteenth century. In a recent quantitative study of eighteenth-century Germantown, Pennsylvania, Stephanie Wolff has characterized families as individualistic and free from tightly structured kin ties and obligations. Extended-family living arrangements were rare, as most families lived in small nuclear households isolated from relatives, emblematic of the "fragile and transient" nature of kin ties in this Pennsylvania settlement. Sons did not endure prolonged economic dependence on their fathers, for they received their shares of the family estate and were set out on their own at an early age. All of which suggests an associational society with a series of rational, temporary relationships rather than a kin-oriented world of internalized, unchanging obligations and customs.[19]

By the end of the eighteenth century, then, the regional variations in family life that were so pronounced in the colonial era may have diminished as more mobile, affective, and privatistic families became common throughout much of the country, especially in the South and mid-Atlantic region. Above all, the conjugal family was an increasingly child-centered, intimate unit that produced children who valued emotions and individual needs over parental or kin obligations in choosing marriage partners and careers. A "segmental" rather than an "interdependent" family organization typified most American families in the late eighteenth century. Increasingly committed to economic self-sufficiency and independent decision-making in marriage and career, young men viewed kinship more as a series of temporary alliances in life than as an unending, growing body of reciprocal rights and responsibilities. As concern for privacy rose, a smaller, more intimate family environment emerged as an emotional force independent from and increasingly antagonistic to the social world beyond the household.[20]

[19]Wolff, Urban Village, 228–313, 326.
[20]See Kirk Jeffrey, "The Family as a Utopian Retreat from the City: The Nineteenth Century," Soundings, LV (1972), 21–41.

To be sure, kin control and patriarchal authority had hardly vanished in preindustrial America, especially in New England. Third- and fourth-generation Puritans, Edmund Morgan has argued, became tribalistic in their faith, turning their spiritual energies inward on their families and kin during the eighteenth century.[21] Moreover, family connections mattered as much as merit in New England political life in the eighteenth century.[22] And the expanded work opportunities for wives and daughters outside the family in the growing number of New England textile mills did not necessarily break the bonds of family and kin, for much of what was earned outside the home was used to sustain these families in a changing New England economy.[23] Clearly, powerful community and kin demands still tugged at young men and women in this region during the late eighteenth century, but change was in the air. New England family life was in a transitional stage, poised between the patriarchal and communal values rooted deep in that region's heritage and the independent, segmental family values that would become dominant during the first half of the nineteenth century.[24]

Identifying these general shifts in early American family life is difficult itself; determining with any kind of precision the forces behind these new family values and behavior carries even graver problems and on occasion can be nothing more than informed

[21]Morgan, *The Puritan Family*, rev. ed. (New York, 1966) 161–86. In a recent article Gerald F. Moran claims that Puritan parents continued to exert strong religious influence in their own families well into the eighteenth century. See "Religious Renewal, Puritan Tribalism, and the Family in Seventeenth-Century Milford, Connecticut," *WMQ*, 3d ser., xxxvi (1979), 254.

[22]See Linda Auwers, "Thy Brother's Keeper: Lineal and Lateral Family Ties in Pre-Industrial America" (unpub. paper, Shelby Cullom Davis Center Seminar, 1976).

[23]Nancy F. Cott, *The Bonds of Womanhood: "Woman's Sphere" in New England, 1780–1835* (New Haven, 1977), 19–62; Thomas Dublin, "Women, Work and the Family: Female Operatives in the Lowell Mills, 1830–1860," *Feminist Studies*, iii (1975), 30–39; Louise A. Tilly, "Women's Work and the Family in Nineteenth-Century Europe," *Comparative Studies in Society and History*, xv (1975), 36–64.

[24]For a similar assessment, see Nancy Cott, "Eighteenth-Century Family and Social Life Revealed in Massachusetts Divorce Records," *Journal of Social History*, x (1976), 2–43; Cott, "Divorce and the Changing Status of Women in Eighteenth-Century Massachusetts," *WMQ*, 3d ser., xxxiii (1976), 586–614.

speculation. Recently, broad interpretive themes such as modernization theory have become popular ways to conceptualize American family history, but the amount and quality of historical evidence to support such an abstract, often confusing, theory is hardly compelling at this stage.[25]

It is far from clear, for example, that the movement toward more privatistic, affectionate, individualistic family forms in the second half of the eighteenth century was the consequence of a general modernization trend throughout early American society and economy. To be sure, certain modern family and personal values emerged in well-to-do families of eighteenth-century America, especially in the Chesapeake. If by modernization we mean the triumph of individualism over familialism, the decline of fatalism, the growing belief in self-advancement and autonomy of choice, the increasing strength of emotional ties in the family, and the improvement in maternal care and childrearing,[26] then many Chesapeake planter families, particularly after 1750, had come a long way toward more modern family experiences.

But even as Chesapeake families were moving toward these new family values, forces both within the household and the larger society and economy were pulling families in a different direction—toward a rather traditional experience of family and social organization. Although Virginia and Maryland underwent significant changes in some areas of political and social life in the

[25]The major interpretive statement for modernization as a conceptual tool for understanding family history is found in Tamara Hareven, "Modernization and Family History: Perspectives on Social Change," *Signs: Journal of Women in Culture and Society,* II (1976), 180–206. The "rise of capitalism" argument has also been employed to explain social change and the family. For this perspective see Christopher Lasch, *Haven in a Heartless World* (New York, 1977), and several works by Edward Shorter: *The Making of the Modern Family* 255–67, 4, 280; "Capitalism, Culture and Sexuality: Some Competing Models," *Social Science Quarterly,* LXII (1972), 338–56. The problem with the "rise of capitalism" thesis is that precisely where the accumulation of capital and economic change was the greatest—the factory and mill towns of New England—the commitment to these new attitudes toward the family was most tenuous. In contrast, the South, which possessed few traits of a capitalistic economy, nevertheless showed some of the strongest evidence of change in family life during the last half of the eighteenth century.

[26]Hareven, "Modernization and Family History."

eighteenth century, an almost exclusively agricultural economy persisted throughout the century, limiting the scope of change in the family. We can see in attitudes toward women, father-son ties, and the relationship between home and work the repetition of patterns long associated with traditional agrarian societies.

The eighteenth-century Chesapeake offers convincing evidence that men and women became "modern" at different rates. As we have suggested, women may have held more economic authority and higher social status in the seventeenth century, when their relative scarcity made them an especially valuable commodity in the marriage and labor markets. By the early decades of the eighteenth century, however, a balanced sex ratio weakened the female advantage in marriage opportunities, while the growing use of slave labor gradually eliminated much of their economic value on the plantation. As a result of these demographic and economic developments, women were increasingly confined to the home and urged to fulfill their child-bearing and child-rearing obligations. At a more fundamental level, the sex-related distinctions made concerning educational training and the development of proper character traits suggest that eighteenth-century Chesapeake society offered women little more than the opportunity to become agreeable companions for their husbands and useful mothers to their children.[27]

Sons clearly received much more parental encouragement than daughters to become independent and to develop qualities of self-confidence and self-reliance. Nonetheless, the plantation system and the relatively wide availability of land limited the extent to which sons could become independent of their father. Sons succeeded to land distributed by their father at inheritance, and although they usually received their shares comparatively early in life, this controlled settlement on family land suggested paternal designs and continuity as well as youthful economic

[27]Mary P. Ryan, *Womanhood in America* (New York, 1975), 106–9; Joan Hoff Wilson, "The Illusion of Change: Women and the American Revolution," in Alfred F. Young, ed., *The American Revolution: Explorations in the History of American Radicalism* (Dekalb, Ill., 1976), 383–445.

independence. With the relative abundance of land, most sons routinely followed their father in the management of tobacco plantations, preserving family land and personal property.

The predominantly agricultural economy of the eighteenth-century Chesapeake, then, shielded planters from one of the most dramatic changes in the family: the separation of the workplace from the household. Beginning in the late eighteenth century with the growth of textile mills and small manufacturing firms in New England and the middle states, work was transformed into an activity separate from life within the home. The transfer of production out of the household into factories encouraged a larger measure of mobility and individualism at the expense of the family's traditional role as the chief social and economic institution.[28] Planters in Virginia and Maryland, though, did not experience such polarization in work and family life. While the scale of the plantation economy had changed considerably between 1700 and 1800—it had become a more profitable, commercial agricultural economy—the fundamental rhythms of family life in a rural existence had not. The natural cycle of the year still governed the work routine, fathers and sons worked the land, and the family house, land, and livestock stood forth as evocative symbols of the collective accomplishments of a family's labor—and increasingly, that of its slaves. In this preindustrial society, then, the drive for mobility and achievement was followed in the context of the family and for the welfare of future generations on the land.

Family influence was also strongly felt in the schooling of children. Indeed, the absence of public schools and any sort of rationalized, age-graded educational system in the eighteenth-century Chesapeake left schooling completely in the hands of parents. Educating children on or near the plantation with tutors or at neighborhood schools funded privately by groups of planters allowed parents significant control in yet another part of their children's socialization process. Chesapeake parents, then, pro-

[28]See James Henretta, *The Evolution of American Society, 1700–1815: An Interdisciplinary Analysis* (Lexington, Mass., 1973), 194–96, 213–14.

foundly shaped the school experience of their offspring, unlike modern families, who have gradually lost their educational function to a compulsory public school system.[29]

All of these factors maintained parental authority despite the sweeping political and social changes ushered in during the half century after the Revolution. It is currently fashionable among historians to see conflict in the household as the familial analogy to the movement for independence from the mother country, but the evidence from both parents and children in the eighteenth-century Chesapeake indicates that patterns of deferential conduct and harmonious father-son ties persisted throughout the century. Republican ideology did not tap any kind of inchoate rebellion in the family.[30]

If modernization theory seems too rigid and simplistic to comprehend the complexities of change in eighteenth-century Chesapeake society, what then best explains the transformation in family and personal values among these planters and other families in American society after 1750? Inelegant as it may be as theory, a number of phenomena can be identified that help us understand why family life took the direction it did in the postrevolutionary era. A combination of increasing geographic mobility, especially among the lower orders; growing affluence in the middle ranks; a pronounced, though not uninterrupted, trend toward secularization; and an upturn in literacy, particularly among women—all these forces shaped family behavior in critical ways during the late eighteenth century.

At the lower end of the social and economic ladder, many sons, especially in New England, were forced by dwindling land

[29]Demos, 182–90. The absence of compulsory school laws in the South, as well as a weak Protestant faith, Kenneth Lockridge argues, explains the stagnant literacy rates among adult men and women in eighteenth-century Virginia. Lockridge, *Literacy in Colonial New England: An Enquiry into the Social Context of Literacy in the Early Modern West* (New York, 1974), 82–83, 97.

[30]For the "revolution in the family" thesis, see Gordon S. Wood, "Rhetoric and Reality in the American Revolution," *WMQ*, 3d ser., XXIII (1966), 3–32; Edwin G. Burrows and Michael Wallace, "The American Revolution: The Ideology and Psychology of National Liberation," *Perspectives in American History*, VI (1972), 169–89; and Winthrop D. Jordan, "Familial Politics: Thomas Paine and the Killing of the King, 1776," *Journal of American History*, LX (1973–74), 294–308.

supplies into leaving their family farms for new western lands and fresh starts in towns and cities. Young plowboys from the poorer ranks of northern rural society traded the declining prospects of agricultural work for more attractive opportunities as laborers and artisans in urban centers. As a result, boys got their "start in life" considerably earlier than before.[31] In the South the gradual exhaustion of soil in the tobacco plantations of the Tidewater and Piedmont during the postrevolutionary years pushed many younger sons (and sometimes entire families) into the frontier territories of the trans-Appalachian West. Such accelerated movement created in effect, if not by intention, considerable economic autonomy and more mobile households.[32]

Among the more well-to-do, a rising standard of living and greater economic opportunities by the late eighteenth century (as reflected in the rise of the professions and the emergence of a market economy) allowed a growing number of families more leisure time. Family activities during leisure hours—travel, entertainment, home education, and visitation of close kin and friends—promoted a stronger sense of family togetherness and sociability. What encouraged the spread of this sentimental "family society" in the South was the large-scale introduction of slave labor, begun in the early 1700s, which not only increased the profitability of tobacco plantations but also freed women to concentrate more fully on child-rearing. The rise of maternal influence and better child care after mid-century depended in part on economic growth and the growing use of house servants.[33]

[31]Joseph F. Kett, "Growing up in Rural New England, 1800–1840," in Tamara K. Hareven, ed., *Anonymous Americans: Explorations in Nineteenth-Century Social History* (Englewood Cliffs, N.J., 1971), 1–16; Kett, *Rites of Passage: Adolescence in America 1790 to the Present* (New York, 1977), 30–31, 60. See also note 14 above.

[32]Jackson Turner Main, "The Distribution of Property in Post-Revolutionary Virginia," *Mississippi Valley Historical Review,* XLI (1954), 241–58; Richard D. Brown, *Modernization: The Transformation of American Life, 1600–1865* (New York, 1976), 106–7.

[33]On the rising standard of living of eighteenth-century planters of all ranks, see Lois Carr and Lorena Walsh, "Personal Consumption Patterns in Southern Maryland, 1658–1776," paper presented to the 42nd meeting of the Southern Historical Association, Nov. 12, 1976, Atlanta; Aubrey C. Land, "Economic Base and Social Structure: The Northern Chesapeake in the Eighteenth Century," *Journal of Economic History,* XXV (1965), 639–54; Alice Hanson Jones, "Wealth Estimates for

With the ranks of the urban middle class expanding by the early nineteenth century, the conjugal unit drew even closer together. A strong commitment to the values of achievement and personal ambition in these families fueled geographic mobility and occupational diversity, as men removed themselves from traditional ties to community and kin. Moreover, in New England and the urban centers of the mid-Atlantic region new wage-earning work patterns associated with industrial and factory labor replaced household production. In these areas, work was increasingly taken out of the home, further segregating the sexes while enhancing the consumption-oriented nature of the household. The family as an emotional refuge from the working world would soon become a commonplace image in antebellum America.[34]

Closely linked to the higher standard of living in many eighteenth-century households was a strong secularization process. There were, of course, significant evangelical outbursts over the rising commitment to luxury and worldly matters, but for most American families by the late eighteenth century it was the growing spirit of competition and material gain that influenced their family and personal values.[35] Thus, fewer and fewer parents in New England, as well as in the more secular cultures of the South, saw innate sinfulness and untoward aggressive impulses in their offspring. In the absence of strong religious faith in the

---

the American Middle Colonies, 1774," *Economic Development and Cultural Change,* XVIII (1970), No. 4, pt. 2, 128. Edward Shorter suggests that with respect to maternal care and privacy families were "born modern" surely an exaggerated claim, but probably accurate in comparison with child-rearing patterns in early modern Europe. See Shorter, *The Making of the Modern Family,* 168–204, 242, 250.

[34]See Jeffrey, "The Family as a Utopian Retreat."

[35]For a thoughtful analysis of the growth of individualism and the competitive ethic in the late eighteenth century, see Rowland Berthoff and John M. Murrin, "Feudalism, Communalism and the Yeoman Freeholder: The American Revolution Considered as a Social Accident," in Stephen G. Kurtz and James H. Hutson, eds., *Essays on the American Revolution* (Chapel Hill, N.C., 1973), 281–88; Berthoff, "Independence and Attachment, Virtue and Interest: From Republican Citizen to Free Enterpriser, 1787–1837," in Richard Bushman, et. al., eds., *Uprooted Americans: Essays to Honor Oscar Handlin* (Boston, 1979), 117–120; Brown, *Modernization,* 106–7; Robert V. Wells, "Family History and Demographic Transition," *Journal of Social History,* IX (1975), 1–20.

home, parents raised their children under more permissive, optimistic assumptions about childhood and the world beyond the family, assumptions that were grounded in an essentially pragmatic, secular outlook and growing material wealth.[36]

Finally, the changes occurring after 1750, especially the increasing emotional content of family relationships and the growing significance attached to motherhood, may well be related to improving literacy rates, especially among women, and the emergence of a wide audience for sentimental education, romantic literature, and family advice books. It is significant that the rise of the child-centered, intimate "family society" coincided closely with the growing ability and proclivity of women to write letters and keep diaries. Deducing behavior and value changes in family life from literature and prescriptive materials is problematic. However, the widespread appeal in America after 1790 of romantic, sentimental novels like *Clarissa,* as well as the growth in child-care and conduct-of-life books, such as Maria and Richard L. Edgeworth's *Practical Education* (1798), has to be reckoned with. Sentimental educators like the Edgeworths sought not only to edify but also to encourage intimacy within the family; women, it was believed, were particularly well suited to such a controlled, family-oriented education.[37]

None of these factors alone "caused" such dramatic changes in family values. One could argue, after all, that heightened geographic mobility, for example, was a symptom rather than a cause of an emerging individualistic, privatistic ethos in American family life. Any or all of these phenomena, as well as other still unknown factors, acted with such subtlety and complexity in the

[36]Which is to say that by 1800 a significant proportion of families exhibited traits Greven has called "genteel"—self-assurance, belief in self-efficacy, security in worldly matters, and the view that religion was more a ritualistic process than an expression of inward piety. Greven finds this and other personality modes as essentially timeless in early America, but the evidence I have seen places the "genteel" mode largely in the late eighteenth century. See *The Protestant Temperament,* 265–331.

[37]See Kenneth Lockridge, *Literacy in Colonial New England,* 92–97; Joseph F. Kett, "The American Family as an Intellectual Institution, 1780–1880," paper presented to the History of Education Workshop, University of Chicago, April 1, 1978; Cott, *Bonds of Womanhood,* 102–3.

minds and life experiences of men and women that it would be presumptuous for the historian to declare, centuries later, that it was just these four sets of factors that made families begin to see themselves and the larger world so differently. When a man uprooted himself from a settled eastern community and headed for new territory to start afresh for himself and his family, this was not necessarily "rising individualism" at work, for we know that men rarely uproot themselves *entirely* from kinfolk and past tradition. Most migration was a form of chain migration in which family and kin played an important, practical role in organizing the resettlement process—brothers often aiding brothers, for example, and later joining them along the route westward. What we tend to see as sudden movement and the apparent abandonment of old, ancestral ways was sometimes nothing more than the decision to search out a new place to carry on more successfully rather traditional ways of making a living and raising a family.

Still, what the sources make undeniably clear is that by the late eighteenth century, many men and women were developing an altered view of the family and the world beyond it, a perspective that was deeply rooted in a strong moral sensibility and the belief in the need for emotional warmth within the family. This was a pattern of behavior that tended to emphasize the importance of independence of choice in life's central decisions, marriage and career, and that offered an increasingly narrow view of with whom one properly shared the private intimacies of family and kin life. The life of the family in American history, insofar as we can glimpse it through the surviving records, had taken a new direction.

That direction was not necessarily along the road to modernization or any other theorized destination. The regional differences and the wide diversity and uniqueness of much of family experience—even in this simpler "premodern" era—defy such embracive conceptualizations. Nevertheless, it remains for us to continue to inquire deeply into the long-neglected subject of the American family in past time. The accumulation of more historical research on the family from all perspectives may never produce any lawlike generalizations, but if it moves us closer to understanding what individuals and families in the past feared, hoped for, and received in their time, then we will have learned something very important.

Index

A

Adams, Richard, 271, 276
Adolescents, attitudes toward, 132. *See also* Apprenticeship; Children
Advice literature, 67, 140, 160, 297
Affinal kin, 187–189, 212–214. *See also* Kinship network
Albemarle County, (Virginia), testation patterns in, 233–234, 244–246
Ambler, Mary, 67–68
Ambler, Richard, 93, 96, 98–100, 264
Anderson, Rev. Charles, 203
Apprenticeship, 90, 184–185. *See also* Adolescents, attitudes toward
Ariès, Philippe, 266n

B

Bailyn, Bernard, 282
Beale, Winifred Travers, 193
Benedek, Therese, 86n
Birth intervals, 27
Bland, Theodorick, Jr., 117–118, 158, 181–182, 275–276
Bordley, Stephen, 61, 94, 190, 262
Boucher, Jonathan, 136, 189
Bowlby, John, 273–274n
Breastfeeding. *See* Nursing practices
"Breeching of the boy," 56–57
Burwell, Nathaniel, 92
Byrd, Lucy, 31, 163–164, 166–168
Byrd, William II, 21, 33, 49, 59, 69, 111, 136; attitude toward old age, 274; authority over daughter's marriage, 140–141; kinship network of, 199–204; living

arrangements at Westover, 190; as a planter-doctor, 250–252; quarrels with wife, 166–168; response to death, 262–265; sexual life of, 163–164

C

Callister, Billy, 184–185
Callister, Calista, 278–279
Callister, Ewan, 184
Callister, Henry, 31, 184–185, 263
Callister, Sarah, 278–279
Careers, paternal attitudes toward, 117–120
Carr, Martha Jefferson, 30, 39, 46, 228, 271
Carroll, Charles (of Annapolis), 32, 70, 99, 101–102, 113, 145–146, 258–259, 272–274
Carroll, Charles (of Carrollton), 32, 45, 70, 99, 101–102, 113, 145–146, 182, 258–259, 272–274
Carter, Ben, 109, 257
Carter, Bob, 110–111
Carter, John, 103
Carter, Landon, 122, 132, 144, 249–250, 270; attitude toward maternal nursing, 36–37; and childbirth process, 28–30; conflicts in Sabine Hall, 192–194; on disciplining children, 112; kinship network of, 205–210; on old age, 275; as planter-doctor, 253–255; on socialization of daughters, 61; on women, 70
Carter, Robert (of Nomini Hall), 109–111, 197, 257

Index

Inside the Great House

Designed by G. T. Whipple, Jr.
Composed by Partners Composition
in 10 point VIP Palatino, 3 points leaded,
with display lines in Palatino Bold.
Printed offset by Thomson/Shore, Inc.
on Warren's Number 66 Text, 50 pound basis.
Bound by John H. Dekker & Sons, Inc.
in Holliston book cloth
and stamped in All Purpose foil.

Library of Congress Cataloging in Publication Data

Smith, Daniel Blake.
   Inside the great house.

   Includes bibliographical references and index.
     1. Family — Chesapeake Bay region — History —
18th century. 2. Plantation life — Chesapeake Bay
region — History — 18th century. I. Title.
HQ555.C46S63   306.8′09755′18   80-14557
ISBN 0-8014-1313-3